AGAINST THE TIDE

Other Books in the EMS Series

ABOUT EMS
www.emsweb.org

The Evangelical Missiological Society is a professional organization with more than 400 members comprised of missiologists, mission administrators, reflective mission practitioners, teachers, pastors with strategic missiological interests, and students of missiology. EMS exists to advance the cause of world evangelization. We do this through study and evaluation of mission concepts and strategies from a biblical perspective with a view to commending sound mission theory and practice to churches, mission agencies, and schools of missionary training around the world. We hold an annual national conference and eight regional meetings in the United States and Canada.

AGAINST THE TIDE

Mission Amidst the Global Currents of Secularization

W. Jay Moon & Craig Ott, Editors

Against the Tide: Mission Amidst the Global Currents of Secularization

© 2019 by Evangelical Missiological Society
All rights reserved.

Scripture quotations marked "NASB" are from the New American Standard Bible® (NASB), Copyright © 1960, 1962, 1963, 1968, 1971, 1972, 1973, 1975, 1977, 1995 by The Lockman Foundation. Used by permission. www.Lockman.org.

Scripture quotations marked "NIV" are from the Holy Bible, NEW INTERNATIONAL VERSION®, NIV® Copyright © 1973, 1978, 1984, 2011 by Biblica, Inc.® Used by permission. All rights reserved worldwide.

Scripture quotations marked "ESV" are from The ESV® Bible (The Holy Bible, English Standard Version®), copyright © 2001 by Crossway, a publishing ministry of Good News Publishers. Used by permission. All rights reserved.

Scripture quotations marked "NLT" are taken from the *Holy Bible*, New Living Translation, copyright © 1996, 2004, 2015 by Tyndale House Foundation. Used by permission of Tyndale House Publishers, Inc., Carol Stream, Illinois 60188. All rights reserved.

Published by William Carey Publishing
10 W. Dry Creek Cir
Littleton, CO 80120 | www.missionbooks.org

William Carey Publishing is a ministry of Frontier Ventures
Pasadena, CA 91104 | www.frontierventures.org

Andrew Sloan, copyeditor
Melissa Hicks, managing editor
Mike Riester, cover design
Mike Riester and Jeanne Logue, interior design

ISBNs: 978–1-64508–176–0 (paperback),
        978–1-64508–178–4 (mobi),
        978–1-64508–179–1 (epub)

Printed in the United States of America
23 22 21 20 19   1 2 3 4 5   IN

Library of Congress Control Number: 2019945891

Contents

Introduction

Craig Ott

It can be fairly said that most societies around the world are experiencing the forces of secularization as a movement away from traditional religious ways. This does not mean that people are necessarily less religious, but that the role of religion both in personal lives and in the pubic square is changing. Even the most traditional societies are affected. How does the process of secularization impact the task of Christian mission in the modern world? The 2018 national conference of the Evangelical Missiological Society took up this question. This volume brings to readers a small selection of the many papers presented at that conference.

The term "secularization" means many things to many people. Charles Taylor (2007, 1–3) helpfully describes three ways in which secularization can be understood: (1) at the **political level**, it is the attempt to make government free from the influence of religion, usually marginalizing religion in public discourse; (2) at the **sociological level**, it is a process of decline in religious belief and/or practice, especially so in relation to formal religious authority and identity; and (3) at the **cultural level**, it creates an environment in which religious beliefs are not only one option among many, but an option that is challenged, making religious belief more difficult. How are Christians to engage society missionally where religion is marginalized in the public square, where religious practice is in decline (at least in traditional terms), and where belief in the transcendent is challenged or relegated to the level of personal opinion? What are the implications for evangelism, discipleship, congregational life, and social involvement?

To set the stage for the discussion of this volume, I begin with a broad sketch of secularization in Western[1] cultural contexts, and then contrast it with secularization in non-Western contexts. The challenge of mission in such secularizing contexts will be briefly addressed, followed by an overview of the chapters that will follow in this volume.

The Story of Secularization: How the West Was Won

Western Christians have faced the challenge of secularization with increasing intensity for centuries, though most acutely so since the mid-twentieth century. Secularization is based upon the fundamental idea that the religious can be differentiated from the secular, and thus separated from public life. Furthermore, matters of faith are viewed as being based upon an alternate epistemology to other ways of knowing. Generally speaking, such distinctions are a relatively modern development. Historically religious beliefs and practices—be they Christian or otherwise—have been part and parcel of culture and integral to society and public life. Beliefs in the natural and supernatural were not different categories of knowing, and in many cases were hardly differentiated. Secularization describes the process of challenging that view of reality and promoting an alternate approach to life.

In terms of political secularization, throughout the history of Christianity the relationship of church and state, faith and public discourse, has been complex, conflicted, and at times tumultuous. D.A. Carson writes of the first century, "...nowhere was there a state that was divorced from all gods, what we would call a secular state, with the state and religion occupying distinct, if overlapping, spheres" (2008, 56). Although the Roman Empire was generally a religiously tolerant state, the earliest Christians were a marginalized and often persecuted minority religious movement. Within a few centuries, the situation reversed and Christianity became the dominant public faith in the late Roman Empire. The wedding of church and state became what we call Christendom. This arrangement sought to place Christianity at the center of social and political life, but was fraught with power struggles between popes and kings, between priests and princes. At times principalities were even

---

1 The term "Western" will be used frequently throughout this volume with reference to socio-geographic regions heavily influenced by European cultural and intellectual traditions. We are, however, aware that the concept of "Western" is problematic due to globalization, migration, and increasing ethnic diversity in nations that were formerly populated primarily by persons of European descent, or where such persons dominated society. It must be added that despite the legacy of Enlightenment thinking, there is no single coherent "Western worldview" or philosophy.

ruled by a prince-bishop, whereby ecclesial and state powers were unified. At other times political potentates viewed religious orders as having become too powerful and "secularized" monasteries confiscating properties. Some have suggested that Martin Luther and the Reformation planted the seeds of secularization (e.g., Gregory 2017). Nevertheless, until the eighteenth century the Christian faith as such was not fundamentally questioned as foundational to civil society. Though there have always been skeptics and dissidents, belief in God and basic Christian doctrines were a given.

The legacy of the Enlightenment, technological advancements, urbanization, and scientific method were key factors that set in motion the modern forces of secularization in Western cultures in all three of Taylor's categories. The Enlightenment elevated the place of human rationality in epistemology and in effect divided knowledge into public truth, which is subject to rational examination and scrutiny apart from religious convictions, and private truth that truth, which is of a personal and subjective nature. Because religious claims were not open to empirical scrutiny, they were relegated increasingly to the private sphere. Even with the formal separation of church and state anchored in the constitution of the United States, religion continued to play a major role in public life. By the early twentieth century, most nations of Europe had formally moved away from the wedding of church and state. The Communist revolution in Russia further fueled the forces of secularization there and later in Eastern Europe. Large national churches in most of Western Europe, however, continued to receive government subsidies, receive "church taxes," and offer confessional religious instruction in public schools. The church was generally reserved a privileged (albeit shrinking) space in the public square. Broadly speaking, a Judeo-Christian worldview remained a consensus among the majority of people, though this is not to suggest for a moment that personal piety was particularly strong.

By the mid-twentieth century, the place of religion in public life, even as a kind of moral compass, was increasingly challenged and marginalized. At the personal level, whether one measured religiosity in terms of *beliefs* (e.g., in the existence of God, the afterlife, church doctrines), *behaviors* (e.g., attendance at religious services, prayer), or *belonging* (formal membership in a religious community), most indicators seemed to point to downward trends. This development birthed the classic secularization thesis claiming that as societies modernize religion will decline (e.g., Berger 1967).

Nevertheless, people have generally remained stubbornly religious, even in modern societies. Indeed, in many places religion seemed to be resurging. It's been suggested that Mark Twain's famous quip, "Rumors of my death are greatly exaggerated," might well apply to secularization theory's proclamation of the impending death of religion. Classic secularization theory was contested and revised. Peter Berger, an early proponent of the secularization thesis, proposed a *desecularization* thesis (e.g., Berger 1999). Jürgen Habermas came to speak of a post-secular society characterized by "the continued existence of religious communities in an increasingly secularized environment" (2008, 19). Some studies even claimed that attendance at religious services in the United States actually increased consistently through the period of modernization, plateauing around 1980.[2] One observer has even argued that rising religious participation may be a consequence of secularization (Philips 2004)!

The process of secularization appears in some ways schizophrenic. On the one hand, numerous studies in the United States document in recent decades an ongoing, if not accelerating, decline in church affiliation and an increase of the "nones": those who do not self-identify with any religion (e.g., Pew Research Center 2015). On the other hand, 90 percent of Americans still believe in God or some kind of higher power (Pew Research Center 2018b). Similar trends are observable in Europe, where formal church membership is plummeting. Yet the majority still hold to some form of religious belief. For example, a Pew study of religious belief in Western Europe found that "Although many non-practicing Christians say they do not believe in God 'as described in the Bible,' they do tend to believe in some other higher power or spiritual force." At the same time, "A clear majority of religiously unaffiliated adults do not believe in any type of higher power or spiritual force in the universe" (Pew Research Center 2018a).[3]

In other words, *belonging* is declining and *belief* is changing. Grace Davie (1990) famously called this "believing without belonging," but even believing is not the same. Others have called this "post-institutional spirituality," whereby religion is increasingly individualized and popular (e.g., Turner 2014; Wood 2010).

---

2 For example, Finke and Stark (1992) present data that attendance at religious services in America grew from 17 percent in 1776 to 45 percent in 1890 to 62 percent in 1980.

3 On the religious landscape in Western Europe, see also Lienemann-Perrin 2004, 132-43.

Eastern Europe presents yet another picture. Despite decades of opposition to organized religion and the promotion of atheism in Warsaw Pact nations under the influence of oppressive Communist governments, religion and religious sentiments were far from extinguished. A 2017 Pew study found that although identification with the Roman Catholic Church is declining, in Orthodox regions of post-Communist Eastern Europe identification with the church is remarkably high and widely understood as an expression of national identity. For example, in Russia 71 percent self-identify with the Orthodox Church, up from 37 percent in 1991. During the same period, the "nones" in Russia dropped from 61 percent to 18 percent. The highest rate of self-identification with the Orthodox Church is in Moldova, with 92 percent. Belief in God is also quite high, at 75 percent in Russia and 95 percent in Moldova. But in Moldova only 13 percent, and in Russia only 6 percent, claim to attend weekly religious services (Pew Research Center 2017). Here we see *belonging* and *believing* without a corresponding rate of *behaving*.[4]

Country	Belonging Self-identify as Orthodox	Believing Believe in God	Behaving Attend weekly religious services
Russia	71 percent	75 percent	6 percent
Moldova	92 percent	95 percent	13 percent

Pew Research Center 2017

All of this illustrates the complexity of attempting to describe religiosity in secular societies that are also increasingly individualistic, pluralistic, and diverse. Even in the context of Europe, secularization has different expressions. Yes, in the midst of modernization and secularization people are still religious, but they are religious *differently*.

In North America and most of Western Europe, the increase of religious pluralism and lack of any broad religious consensus further complicates the role of religion in society. In America, politicians still close speeches by saying "May God bless America," public events include generic prayers, and analysists attempt to identify religious voting blocks. But despite attempts of religious groups to engage public discourse, exercise political power, or reestablish religiously rooted cultural values, religion is largely considered

---

4 On the religious landscape in Eastern and Central Europe, see also Lienemann-Perrin 2004, 122-31.

a separate domain with a tenuous public role. This arrangement, however, is not necessarily bad for religion, and state secularism is not inherently anti-religious.[5]

By not privileging any particular religion in public life, it is frequently argued that secularism is in fact the best guarantee of religious freedom (e.g., Berlinerblau 2012). Bryan Turner states, "Political secularization was in fact the cornerstone of the liberal view of tolerance in which we are free to hold our private beliefs provided these do not impinge negatively on public life" (2010, 651).[6] Although in recent study attention has turned to the resurgence of religion and alternative spiritual ties, the forces of secularization remain a formidable challenge to religion. Ambivalence toward secularization is evident. For example, statements of the Roman Catholic Church describe on the one hand a "healthy secularism" that preserves a separation of church and state, but on the other hand the fear that Western secularism has gone too far, becoming hostile toward religion and a threat to the faith (Allen 2009). More simply put, in the words of Lesslie Newbigin, "Secularization opens up the possibilities of new freedom, and of new enslavement of men" (1966, 19).

Secularization's Long Reach: Not Only a Western Phenomenon

The story told thus far describes largely the experience in Western culture. Turner observes, "By contrast, contemporary anthropological and sociological research clearly illustrates the vitality of religion in the rest of the world especially as a result of modern pilgrimage, religious revivalism in Asia, and Pentecostal and charismatic movements in South America and Africa" (2010, 650). A recent collection of essays titled *The Secular in South, East, and Southeast Asia* responds with numerous case studies to the question of "why most of the world remains a realm of spirits and religious expression, making the Western story of secularism recounted by Taylor into the exception, rather than the rule" (Dean and van der Veer 2019a, 4).

---

5 Ten Chin Liew distinguishes between *state secularism* and *perspectival secularism*: "State secularism prohibits the state from enforcing purely religious rights and duties. All citizens are treated equally, and allowed to practice their respective religions without harm to others, or to lead lives free from religious obligations they have not voluntarily accepted. *Perspectival secularism,* as I shall call it, is opposed to religion, at least to those based upon belief in God and the afterlife. It seeks to provide an alternative outlook to the religious" (2010, 7).

6 Of course, here the word *private* in "free to hold our private beliefs" is critical, and how one defines *negatively* in "provided these do not impinge negatively on public life" is where the dividing line becomes controversial.

Nevertheless, in an age of globalization there is hardly a context in which the forces of modernization and secularization are not felt somehow impacting the practice and influence of religion—albeit in different ways than in the West. Resurgence of religious fundamentalism, such as that experienced in Iran, is just one response to globalization and secularization (Denmark 2010). Akeel Bilgrami's *Beyond the Secular West* (2016) responds to Taylor's *A Secular Age* by providing a fascinating collection of case studies describing secularization in a wide variety of contexts outside the "Latin West." Richard Madsen gives an overview of the secularization process in several Asian[7] countries using Taylor's aforementioned threefold framework. He summarizes that Taylor's categories do not necessarily apply to the experience in Asia. Despite the efforts of some secular governments, religion has not moved from public practice to private belief. But rather, "Asian religions are practiced under new cultural conditions of belief..." (2011, 266).

Another recent work, *Varieties of Secularism in Asia*, presents a collection of similar essays demonstrating that secularity comes in forms other than that proposed by Taylor—secularity, for example,

> ...in which spirits are embarrassing and can be rhetorically allocated to the realm of "belief," but in which they cannot be sloughed off as a snake sheds its skin. The spirits, rather, impinge on individuals who are not entirely and always buffered from them and they seem to exist in a social order where no easy distinction between political immanence and spiritual transcendence is possible. (Bubandt and van Beek 2012a, 3)

All of this simply underscores the view that just as there "multiple modernities" as the forces of modernization spread across the globe (Eisenstadt 2002), so too there are "multiple secularites" (Burchardt, Wohlrab-Sahr, and Middell 2015).

One critique of Western conceptualizations of secularization is that it is based upon an overly essentialized understanding of religion (e.g., Asad 2003). It argues that the Enlightenment's attempt to define religion comes via an unnatural abstraction of religion and reification of religious belief. Recent studies in sociology of religion have challenged an overly cognitive approach to understanding religion and given increased attention to religion and the body, religious habitus and embodiment, and lived religious experience (e.g.,

---

7 On secularism in Asia, see also Siam-Heng and Liew 2010; Bubandt and van Beek 2012b; van der Veer 2014; Dean and van der Veer 2019b.

Turner 2008). For many, religion is less a matter of beliefs per se and more the glue of communal identity expressed in common rituals, traditions, values, and daily practices. Religion, politics, and culture are often intertwined and hardly distinguishable. This is most visibly evidenced today in resurgent Islamic states where sharia law is the law of the land.

At the same time, some secularists have argued that forms of secularism with the concept of a separation between religion and government predate Western colonialism in Africa and India (e.g., Igwe 2014; Aiyar 2008). If they're correct, then secularization has not only been a phenomenon moving "from the West to the rest" or a fruit of the Enlightenment.

One should not underestimate the difficulty of attempting to describe secularization in regions as complex and diverse as Asia or Africa. In the words of one observer, "The secularization of Africa has been marked by contrasts and contradictions, false starts and setbacks, misconceptions and misrepresentations, dilemmas and ambiguities due to the complex interplay of religion and politics in the region" (Igwe 2014). Secular institutions in postcolonial Sub-Saharan Africa are spreading. Michael Parker summarizes the findings of a conference held in 2014 in Cairo on the subject of "Declining Religious Participation: Secularization and Discipleship in Africa" by saying that "it is clear from the evidence given at the consultation that the rise of secularization in Africa is a real phenomenon that, for all people of faith, is both significant and urgent" (2015, 66).

Some observers claim that this has had little impact on belief systems and the influence of religion in the public and private sphere (Takyi 2017). Benno van den Toren describes how secularization in Africa can play out differently than in the West—for example, in "the tendency to use highly supernatural practices to pursue secular goals" (2003, 12; see also Metego 1997). He later calls this the secularization of religion itself (2015).

India provides a telling example of the complex and controversial nature of religion in public life outside of Western cultural contexts, and a large body of literature has emerged on the topic of secularization in India. Political movements such as the Bharatiya Janata Party advocate Hinduvata, a nationalist movement seeking to make India a Hindu state, claiming that to be Indian is to be Hindu. Yet others follow Jawaharlal Nehru's policy of a secular state for postcolonial India. For example, Indian National Congress politician Mani Shankar Aiyar argues for a separation of the state from religion, whereby the state protects religious freedom and religion even thrives. Thus his vision of Indian secularism is not anti-religious or irreligious. He claims, "No other civilization has as long a record as ours of a polity based on secularism. Yet the history of India is not the story of secularism vanquishing communalism. It is more the history of a kind of dialectic between the forces of tolerance and compassion, on the one hand, and the forces of communalism, fundamentalism and fanaticism, on the other" (2008, 123). Although the vast majority of people in India remain deeply spiritual, Aiyar argues that spirituality "must remain a private and personal matter of the citizen" (ibid.). Secularism in this sense would promote religious flourishing by allowing religious freedom and abolishing the hegemony of any one religion. At the same time, religious belief would become privatized.

Examples from around the globe could be added to illustrate the complexity of the many faces of secularization. Suffice it to say, the popular conception that secularization is largely a Western phenomenon, while non-Western societies remain deeply religious and untouched by forces of secularization, is false and misleading. Yet secularization does manifest itself differently in different contexts. In Taylor's terms, there is in most of the world a growth of political secularization, but less so of sociological or cultural secularization. The true picture is, in fact, even more complex than that. For example, regarding much of Asia, Bubandt and van Beek observe, "What we find most striking is that democratic reform has appeared to stimulate rather than curb the entanglement of the spiritual with the political" (2012a, 6). Needless to say, there are many forms of secularism and the process of secularization must be examined on a case-by-case approach.

Missional Engagement with Secularization

The various manifestations of secularization present both challenges and opportunities for the progress of the gospel. As noted above, political secularization can open the way for religious freedom and Christian mission in places where religious states formerly forbade proselytization. Sociological and cultural secularization present more of a challenge. What are the implications of such developments for the mission of the church?

In the West, the rise of secular values, the decline of religious participation, and the loss of any religious consensus have created numerous challenges for evangelism, discipleship, and mission efforts. Among the general population, a Christian worldview cannot be taken for granted. Common ground for a shared discourse based upon fundamental concepts such as God, sin, heaven, and hell is no longer a given. A majority of people have redefined or rejected altogether such concepts. Moreover, conservative Christian values and beliefs are increasingly viewed as outdated, intolerant, or bigoted. Beliefs about the transcendent are relegated to the realm of opinion and private experience. Religious institutions have not only lost much of their privileged position in society, but have little respect and are viewed with suspicion. Secularization and the shift of values have thrust the church into a crisis of credibility, integrity, and moral respectability. Recent scandals involving clergy have further undermined the standing of organized religion. Add to this the daily gravitational pull of secular lifestyles untethered from biblical values. All of this makes evangelism and discipleship an uphill battle. The church is forced to reconsider its public posture and mission strategy.

Just as the face of secularization in the non-Western world is different, so too the challenges and opportunities are different. Despite the global forces of secularization, Christianity has flourished and grown in the non-Western world at an astonishing rate. That may not remain the case. Some have suggested that secularization is responsible for much of the decline in the churches of South Korea and elsewhere (e.g., Yoo and Noh 2018). In an attempt to resist the secularizing forces of globalization, some countries, such as Iran, have politically reasserted traditional religious values and limited religious freedom. This restricts typical missionary efforts and has led, in some cases, to persecution of Christians.

There is no shortage of literature on the broader topics of Christianity as public faith and Christian apologetics in a secular context.[8] More explicitly, missiological literature addressing the question of how to understand and engage secularization is less abundant. It is apparently much easier to theorize about secularization than to propose practical answers.[9]

The Roman Catholic Church has taken up the challenge of secularization with perhaps the most vigor, with numerous publications and conferences, such as a colloquium on secularism in Africa in 1972 (Església Catòlica 1973; Shorter 1997) and a 2013 conference on "Religion and Secularism in a Global Age" in Rome (Rouse 2013). An essay, "Secularization and Contemporary Catholic Mission," engages the work of Taylor and Hans Urs von Balthasar, calling the church to authenticity and inner transformation as a response to the challenge of secularization (Chau 2018).

---

8 Additionally, worth mentioning are the mostly short-lived attempts in the 1960s by various theologians to accommodate secularization, such as Rudolf Bultmann's "demythologizing" of Christianity, "death of God" theology, and popular works such as Harvey Cox's The Secular City.

9 Even articles with promising titles such as "Secularisation, the World Church and the Future of Mission" (Kirk 2005) often remain rather theoretical.

Already mentioned is the small Protestant conference held in 2014 in Cairo on the subject "Declining Religious Participation: Secularization and Discipleship in Africa." It produced a number of significant essays published in the *Cairo Journal of Theology* (vol. 2, 2015).[10] Among other concerns, the question was posed as to what Western churches can learn from African churches in addressing the challenges of secularization (Paul 2015, 71). In 2012, two missionary organizations in the Protestant Church in the Netherlands established at the University of Groningen a chair in secularization studies "in order to foster critical reflection on the church's understanding and misunderstanding of secularization" (ibid.). I'm not aware of any such academic chair sponsored by North American mission agencies!

Newbigin was one of the earliest missiologists to seriously address the challenge, starting with *Honest Religion for Secular Man* (1966), which was followed by numerous related publications. In 1998, Bert Hoedemaker authored a small book, *Secularization and Mission: A Theological Essay.* The edited volume, *Contexuality in Reformed Europe: The Mission of the Church in the Transformation of European Culture* (Lienemann-Perrin, Vroom, and Weinrich 2004), includes several chapters in a section titled "Mission, Secularization, and Pluralism," but these discussions have little to say about mission in terms of evangelism, discipleship, and church planting. Some writers have proposed a more radical rethinking of the church and mission to address the secular challenge. For example, Hong Eyoul Hwang (2003) advocated Minjung Theology in Korea as an answer, and Philip Wickeri (2010) has argued that in light of secularization and religious pluralism the *missio Dei* should no longer be the point of departure in mission theology and practice—answers not much to the liking of evangelicals.

The Lausanne Movement has, from its inception, addressed the topics of mission in the context of Christian nominalism, atheism, modernization, and Western cultures. More explicitly to our concern, a "mini-consultation on reaching secularists" was held in 1980 that produced a substantial strategy paper, "Christian Witness to Secularized People" (Lausanne Committee on World Evangelization 1980). It more recently launched a "Global Secularization Initiative" to address the increasing secularization of society around the world.[11]

---

10 Available online at http://journal.etsc.org/wp-content/uploads/2015/09/Cairo-Journal-of-Theology-2-2015-v2-Sept12.pdf.

11 See https://www.lausanne.org/networks/initiatives/lausanne-global-secularization-initiative.

Proposals for mission in the secularizing non-Western world are even harder to find. The aforementioned article by van den Toren (2003) briefly proposes constructive suggestions for Christian engagement with secularization in Africa. A few others have also attempted to address secularization and mission in Africa (e.g., Shorter and Onyancha 1997; Harries 2015; Bjork 2016). One of the more insightful, albeit brief, proposals is put forth by Abel Ngarsouledé (2015), who advocates a Trinitarian model involving also Bible translation and a reassertion of relevant theological themes.

A starting point for facing the challenge of secularization may well begin with more self-critical reflection within the church itself. In terms of materialism and the bifurcation of the natural and supernatural, Western Christians have imbibed more of the spirit of secularism than they like to admit. Former bishop of the Methodist Church in Malaysia, Hwa Yung, experienced how modern education and Western theology nearly eradicated his belief in the supernatural. He writes, "A 21st-century reformation will demand reinserting the supernatural into the heart of Christianity. This will result not only in a sounder biblical theology but also a more powerful missional church. The world will then understand what Jesus meant when he said, 'But if it is by the Spirit of God that I cast out demons, then the kingdom of God has come upon you' (Matt. 12:28, ESV)" (Yung 2010, 33).

Robert Nash notes the inability of evangelicals to effectively engage secularization, writing that "…evangelical Christians must embrace an entirely new understanding of what it means to be a Christian and to be the church in the world if the great mission of American Christianity to secular people is to be successful" (2004, 512). He continues, "Christians will never convince such people of the truth of the Christian faith without somehow ceasing to be secular people themselves" (ibid., 520).

There is no doubt also some truth to the claim that Western missionaries themselves have been agents of secularization due to their underemphasis of the supernatural and dichotomized worldview (e.g., Newbigin 1966; Miller 1973; Ayandele 1979; and sources cited by Ngarsouledé 2015, 92n13). In this regard, Christians, and especially missionaries, will need to give heed to the exhortation of Romans 12:2: "Do not conform to the pattern of this world, but be transformed by the renewing of your mind. Then you will be able to test and approve what God's will is—his good, pleasing and perfect will" (NIV).

Where This Book Will Take Readers

A modest attempt to tackle the question of secularization and mission was the aforementioned 2018 national conference of the Evangelical Missiological Society. A selection of those papers are presented in this volume.

We begin with two foundational chapters by Harold Netland and Shawn Behan. Netland delineates the concepts of modernity and secularization, providing definitions and distinctions that will help frame the following discussion. He also provides a brief examination of how secularization has played out in modern Japan, highlighting cultural differences in the secularization process. Behan moves the conversation forward with an overview of Christian responses to secularization and then offers a reassessment and consideration of opportunities that secularization can open up for Christian mission.

The remaining chapters examine secularization and mission in specific geographic settings, starting with North America, then moving to Europe, and then finally to examples in Asia and Africa.

Rafael Anzenberger's chapter, "Engaging the Secular Mind: An Urgent Call to the American Church," transitions readers to a section dealing with secularization and mission in North America. He picks up the theoretical conversation, addressing the need to rightly tell the story of secularization and to move beyond missiological theory to the confident sharing of the gospel. Readers will be intrigued by his connecting the biblical story of Jesus and Nathanael to the contemporary challenge of evangelism in a secular context.

As the United States is increasingly a secular, religiously plural and culturally diverse society, approaches to evangelism that were compelling for many generations are no longer effective. Basic concepts, terminology, and plausibility structures have shifted, and common ground is often difficult to find. Jay Moon's chapter, "Evangelism in a Secular Age: Complexities and Opportunities," elucidates this changing situation. The gospel is, however, multifaceted, with dimensions often overlooked in traditional evangelistic methods. Moon argues that a key to effective evangelism is to begin by communicating that dimension of the gospel that most readily resonates with the worldview of the recipient. He goes on to present a creative way of evangelism training that takes into account these challenges and introduces learners to the various dimensions and how to connect them with potential conversation partners.

In chapter 5, Elisabeth Seversen describes the religious landscape of American young adults. She then reports the findings of her empirical research investigating how churches are successfully engaging and assimilating emerging young adults. Her findings are enlightening and point in a hopeful direction. They will also challenge many readers to reassess their evangelistic approach to young adults.

Perhaps no country has epitomized the spirit of secularization as has France. Stephen Thrall outlines the development of *laïcité* (secularity) that is rooted today in the French constitution. Against this backdrop, Thrall elucidates the present predicament in Western Europe and then, drawing from the examples of Daniel in Babylon and Paul in Athens, describes pathways to (re)connect with people in a secular society.

Although formal religious institutions in Europe have sinking memberships and diminishing public influence, at the popular level a remnant of many Christian values remains a strong societal force. This is demonstrated in Stephen Kern's chapter, "Germany's Refugee Response: Implications for Ministry in a Secularized World." Kern rightly points out that being secular does not necessarily mean being anti-religious or irreligious. The German response to the refugee crisis demonstrates that even nonreligious people have humanitarian sentiments rooted in the *imago Dei*. Such sentiments may well provide common ground and an entry point for the gospel.

As noted above, in Eastern Europe the processes of secularization have taken dramatic twists and turns quite different from that of Western Europe and America. One might have thought that Communism was perhaps the strongest force of secularization in the twentieth century—impacting literally hundreds of millions of lives, suppressing organized religion, often persecuting religious leaders, and promoting state-sponsored atheism. Marc Canner describes the surprising reversal regarding religious affiliation and sentiments in post-Communist Russia. The Orthodox Church has become a symbol of Russian identity and nationalism. He further analyzes several American missionary efforts undertaken in post-Communist Russia and the reasons behind the difficulties they have faced. He concludes by highlighting the need for better missionary preparation and deeper understanding of the unique cultural context and history.

The concluding two chapters look at cases in the contexts of Asia and Africa. Tony Chuang provides a glimpse into secularization in China and Taiwan in his chapter, "A Chinese Modernity: What Fengshui, Ancestors, Mazu, Buddhism, and Mao Can Teach Us about a Different Kind of

Secularization." He demonstrates how categories and definitions commonly used to describe secularization in Western societies do not fit the experience of secularization in China and Taiwan, where the boundaries between tradition, religion, ethics, and belief are blurred.

Boye-Nelson Kiamu interacts with various Western theories of secularization and applies these to the modern political situation in Liberia. Christianity played a foundational role in the formation of Liberia as a nation, and there are currently political efforts to formally declare Liberia a Christian nation. This has raised a debate over the role of religion in the public square. Kiamu rejects the idea that secularization is bad for religion, but rather argues that "secularization provides an opportunity for the church to reclaim and practice its prophetic role in true humility."

This collection of essays presents the opportunities and the challenges of secularization for the mission of the church, with hopeful signs and reassurance that God is still at work in a secularizing world. These chapters will hopefully stimulate further research, reflection, and missionary engagement in the context of secularization. They are only the hors d'oeuvres, so to speak, that precede the main course. Each local church and each mission organization will need to prepare that main course by taking up the task of first understanding secularization (or the reaction to secularization) and then discerning the appropriate missional response suited to their specific context.

References

Aiyar, Mani Shankar. 2008. "Secularism, Atheism, Agnosticism." *India International Centre Quarterly* 35 (2): 122–35.

Allen, John L., Jr. 2009. "Benedict's Ongoing Battle against Secularism." *The National Catholic Reporter*, November 6. https://www.ncronline.org/blogs/all-things-catholic/benedicts-ongoing-battle-against-secularism.

Asad, Talal. 2003. *Formations of the Secular: Christianity, Islam, Modernity*. Stanford, CA: Stanford University Press.

Ayandele, E. A. 1979. "Mission in the Context of Religions and Secularization: An African Viewpoint." Chapter 11 in *African Historical Studies*, 249–80. London: Frank Cass and Company.

Berger, Peter L. 1967. *The Sacred Canopy: The Social Construction of Reality*. New York: Anchor Books.

———, ed. 1999. *The Desecularization of the World: Resurgent Religion and World Politics*. Grand Rapids: Eerdmans.

Berlinerblau, Jacques. 2012. *How to Be Secular: A Call to Arms for Religious Freedom*. Boston: Houghton Mifflin Harcourt.

Bilgrami, Akeel, ed. 2016. *Beyond the Secular West*. New York: Columbia University.

Bjork, David E. 2016. "Endangered Discipleship: Secular and Religious Resistance in Africa." *Africa Journal of Evangelical Theology* 35 (1): 49–66.

Bubandt, Nils, and Martijn van Beek, eds. 2012a. "Varieties of Secularism—in Asia and in Theory." In Varieties of *Secularism in Asia: Anthropological Explorations of Religion, Politics and the Spiritual*, edited by Nils Bubandt and Martijn van Beek, 1–27. New York: Routledge.

———, eds. 2012b. *Varieties of Secularism in Asia: Anthropological Explorations of Religion, Politics and the Spiritual*. New York: Routledge.

Burchardt, Marian, Monika Wohlrab-Sahr, and Matthias Middell, eds. 2015. *Multiple Secularities Beyond the West: Religion and Modernity in the Global Age*. Berlin: Walter de Gruyter.

Carson, D. A. 2008. *Christ and Culture Revisited*. Grand Rapids: Eerdmans.

Chau, Carolyn. 2018. "Secularization and Contemporary Catholic Mission." *Journal of Religion and Society*, Supplement Series "Religion and Secularism," edited by Patrick Murray and Ronald A. Simkins, 17: 123–32.

Davie, Grace. 20101990. "Believing without Belonging: Is This the Future of Religion in Britain?" *Social Compass* 37 (4): 455–69.

Dean, Kenneth, and Peter van der Veer. 2019a. "Introduction." In *The Secular in South, East, and Southeast Asia*, edited by Kenneth Dean and Peter van der Veer, 1–12. CITY Cham, Switzerland: Palgrave Macmillan.

———, eds. 2019b. *The Secular in South, East, and Southeast Asia*. CITY Cham, Switzerland: Palgrave Macmillan.

Denemark, Robert A. 2010. "Fundamentalism and Globalization." In *The International Studies Encyclopedia*, 2553–72. Oxford: Wiley-Blackwell.

Eisenstadt, Shmuel N., ed. 2002. *Multiple Modernities*. New York: Routledge.

Església Catòlica. 1973. *Sécularisation en Afrique? Secularisation in Africa?* Rome: Secretariatus pro Non Credentibus.

Finke, Roger, and Rodney Stark. 1992. *The Churching of America, 1776–1990*. New Brunswick, NJ: Rutgers University.

Gregory, Brad S. 2017. *Rebel in the Ranks: Martin Luther, the Reformation, and the Conflicts That Continue to Shape our World*. New York: HarperOne.

Habermas, Jürgen. 2008. "Notes on Post-Secular Society." *New Perspectives Quarterly* 25 (4): 17–29.

Harries, Jim. 2015. *Secularism and Africa*. Eugene, OR: Wipf & Stock.

Hoedemaker, Bert. 1998. *Secularization and Mission: A Theological Essay*. Harrisburg, PA: Trinity Press International.

Hwang, Hong Eyoul. 2003. "Searching for a New Paradigm of Church and Mission in a Secularized and Postmodern Context in Korea." *International Review of Mission* 92 (364): 84–97.

Igwe, Leo. 2014. "The Untold Story of Africa's Secular Tradition." *Conscience* 2014 (1). https://consciencemag.org/2014/02/19/the-untold-story-of-africas-secular-tradition/.

Kirk, J Andrew. 2005. "Secularisation, the World Church and the Future of Mission." *Transformation* 22 (3): 130–38.

Lausanne Committee on World Evangelization. 1980. "Christian Witness to Secularized People," Lausanne Occasional Paper 8. https://www.lausanne.org/content/lop/lop-8.

Lienemann-Perrin, Christine. 2004. "Emerging Contextual Missiologies in Europe: Reflections on Part II 'Mission, Secularization, and Pluralism.'" In *Contexuality in Reformed Europe: The Mission of the Church in the Transformation of European Culture*, edited by Christine Lienemann-Perrin, Hendrik M. Vroom, and Michael Weinrich, 121–46. New York: Editions Rodipi.

Lienemann-Perrin, Christine, Hendrik M. Vroom, and Michael Weinrich, eds. 2004. *Contexuality in Reformed Europe: The Mission of the Church in the Transformation of European Culture*. New York: Editions Rodipi.

Liew, Ten Chin. 2010. "Secularism and Its Limits." In *State and Secularism: Perspectives from Asia*, edited by Michael Heng Siam-Heng and Ten Chin Liew, 7–21. Singapore: World Scientific.

Madsen, Richard. 2011. "Secularism, Religious Chante Change, and Social Conflict in Asia." In *Rethinking Secularism*, edited by Craig Calhoun, Mark Juergensmeyer and Jonathan VanAntwerpen, 248–69. New York: Oxford University.

Metego, Elio Messi. 1997. *Dieu peut-il mourir en Afrique? Essai sur l'indifférence religieuse et l'incroyance en Afrique noire*. Paris/Yaoundé: Presses de l'UCAC.

Miller, Elmer S. 1973. "Christian Missionary: Agent of Secularization." *Missiology* 1 (1): 99–107.

Morelli, George. 2018. "Healing Society: Revisiting Witnessing Christ in a Secular Age." Antiochian Orthodox Christian Archdiocese of North America. http://ww1.antiochian.org/content/healing-society-revisiting-witnessing-christ-secular-age.

Nash, Robert N. 2004. "Reaching Secular People." *Review & Expositor* 101 (3): 511–21.

Newbigin, Lesslie. 1966. *Honest Religion for Secular Man*. London: SCM.

Ngarsouledé, Abel. 2015. "Sociological and Theological Perspectives on Secularization in Africa." *Cairo Journal of Theology* 2: 88–102.

Parker, Michael. 2015. "Message from the Editor: Secularization in Africa?" *Cairo Journal of Theology* 2: 65–66.

Paul, Herman. 2015. "Secularization in Africa: A Research Desideratum." *Cairo Journal of Theology* 2: 67–75.

Pew Research Center. 2015. "America's Changing Religious Landscape." Religion and Public Life. http://www.pewforum.org/2015/05/12/americas-changing-religious-landscape/.

———. 2017. "Religious Belief and National Belonging in Central and Eastern Europe." Religion and Public Life. http://www.pewforum.org/2017/05/10/religious-belief-and-national-belonging-in-central-and-eastern-europe/.

———. 2018a. "Being Christian in Western Europe." Religion and Public Life. http://www.pewforum.org/2018/05/29/being-christian-in-western-europe/.

———. 2018b. "Key Findings about Americans' Belief in God." http://www.pewresearch.org/fact-tank/2018/04/25/key-findings-about-americans-belief-in-god/.

Phillips, Rick. 2004. "Can Rising Rates of Church Participation Be a Consequence of Secularization?" *Sociology of Religion* 65 (2): 139–53.

Puniyani, Ram. 2017. "What Is Our Nationality: Indian or Hindu?" *The Milli Gazette*, February 22. http://www.milligazette.com/news/15406-what-is-our-nationality-indian-or-hindu.

Rouse, Richard. 2013. Report on "Religion and Secularism in a Global Age." Pontifical Council for Culture, March 1. http://www.cultura.va/content/cultura/en/eventi/major/secularism.html.

Shorter, Aylward. 1997. "Secularism in Africa: Introducing a Problem" *African Christian Studies*, 13, No. 1. Online at https://sedosmission.org/old/eng/shorter.htm.

Shorter, Aylward, and Edwin Onyancha. 1997. *Secularism in Africa: A Case Study: Nairobi City*. Nairobi: Paulines Publications Africa.

Siam-Heng, Michael Heng, and Ten Chin Liew, eds. 2010. *State and Secularism: Perspectives from Asia*. Singapore: World Scientific.

Takyi, Baffour K. 2017. "Secular Government in Sub-Saharan Africa." In *The Oxford Handbook of Secularism*, edited by Phil Zuckerman and John R. Shook, 201–13. New York: Oxford University.

Taylor, Charles. 2007. *A Secular Age*. Cambridge, MA: Belkamp.

Turner, Bryan S. 2008. *The Body and Society*. London: Sage.

———. 2010. "Religion in a Post-Secular Society." In *The New Blackwell Companion to the Sociology of Religion*, edited by Bryan S. Turner, 649–67. Oxford: Wiley-Blackwell.

———. 2014. "Religion and Contemporary Sociological Theories." *Current Sociology Review* 62 (6): 771–88.

van den Toren, Benno. 2003. "Secularisation in Africa: A Challenge for the Churches." *Africa Journal of Evangelical Theology* 22 (1): 3–30.

———. 2015. "African Neo-Pentecostalism in the Face of Secularization: Problems and Possibilities." *Cairo Journal of Theology* 2: 103–20.

van der Veer, Peter. 2014. *The Modern Spirit of Asia: The Spiritual and Secular in China and Asia*. Princeton, NJ: Princeton University Press.

Wickeri, Philip L. 2010. "The End of *Missio Dei*—Secularization, Religions and the Theology of Mission." In *Mission Revisited: Between Mission History and Intercultural Theology*, edited by Volker Küster, 27–43. Berlin: Lit Verlag.

Wood, Matthew. 2010. "The Sociology of Spirituality: Reflections on a Problematic Endeavor." In *The New Blackwell Companion to the Sociology of Religion*, edited by Bryan S. Turner, 267–85. Oxford: Wiley-Blackwell.

Yoo, Kisung, and Paul Sung Noh. 2018. "The Korean Cyber Monastery Movement: Overcoming the Challenges of Secularization." *Lausanne Global Analysis* 7 (5). https://www.lausanne.org/content/lga/2018–09/the-korean-cyber-monastery-movement.

Yung, Hwa. 2010. "Recover the Supernatural." *Christianity Today* 54 (9): 32–33.

Key Terms Related to Secularization

To frame the discussion in this volume, we offer the following definitions and conceptualizations of modernity, secularization, and religiosity. Because of the different and often unclear ways that this terminology is used, studies can seem confusing or contradictory.

Modernization—the ongoing process of social and intellectual transformations which developed from the emergence of science, industrialization, the market economy, and the increasing dominance of technology in all of life. Modernization began around the fifteenth century in Europe and has since spread globally.

Modernity—the ways of living and thinking that grow out of modernization and the powerful intellectual movements of the past four centuries. These inclu0de, but are not limited to, the European and American Enlightenment movements. Intellectually, modernity is characterized by critical inquiry in all domains of life.

Multiple modernities—as the forces of modernization spread globally, entering new cultural contexts, modernity takes different forms and expressions, and is thus not uniform in its manifestations.

Secular—a term describing values, lifestyles, social order, public policy, or anything that is not consciously influenced by religion and makes no reference to the transcendent, sacred, or spiritual dimensions of life; from the Latin *saeculum*, meaning "worldly" or "temporal."

Secularization—an empirically observable, historical process of social, intellectual, and cultural change usually related to modernization, such that traditional religious patterns are modified in significant ways.

Secularism—an ideology that advocates values and public policies that are free from religious influence. Secularism is not necessarily hostile to religion, but typically assigns religion to the private sphere, limits religious influence in the public sphere, and rejects preferential treatment of any particular religion.

Laïcité—a widely used French term for secularism, first used in the late nineteenth century but having roots in the ideals of the French Revolution. It advocates strict separation of church and state, but is often also associated with freedom of thought and/or anticlericalism.

Secularity—the quality of being secular. Charles Taylor describes three dimensions of secularity related to different meanings associated with the term:

- **Political**—the removal or marginalizing of religious influence in government and public life.

- **Societal**—the decline of religious beliefs and practices by increasing numbers of the population, often accompanied by a decline of identification with formal religious institutions.

- **Cultural**—a cultural climate or intellectual environment in which religious beliefs are not merely privatized, but religious beliefs are increasingly difficult to maintain. Religious belief is optional, and not the most plausible option, because meaning in life can be found without appeal to the transcendent.

Multiple secularities—just as there are multiple modernities, so too there are multiple forms of secularization. Particularly in non-Western contexts, secularization may not fit Taylor's threefold typology. Nevertheless, societal change through modernization does influence and alter the ways in which people are religious.

The secularization thesis—the theory that as a society modernizes, religious belief and practice will decline and have diminishing influence in society and in people's lives. Although popular in the 1960s and 70s, the theory is now contested and has been widely rejected or modified.

Desecularization—the process whereby a society that was increasingly secular and experiencing a decline in religious influence experiences a popular resurgence of religion.

Religiosity—religiosity is expressed in many ways. The following threefold typology has been commonly used to differentiate forms of religiosity:

- **Beliefs**—adherence to specific beliefs about God or transcendence, life after death, supernatural powers, religious doctrines or creeds, etc.

- **Behaviors**—involvement in religious activities such as attendance at religious services, prayer, performance of religious rituals, reading religious scriptures, donating time or money to religious causes, adherence to religious moral codes.

- **Belonging**—self-identification with formal religious institutions, such as a church or religious denomination, synagogue, temple, or a specific religious tradition. A person or society may not be equally religious in all three forms of religious expression.

Contesting the religious/secular divide—some scholars oppose the very concept of separating religious from secular aspects of life. They argue that religion and culture are intertwined and that it is artificial to distinguish or attempt to extricate the transcendent from the immanent in everyday life. This problematizes the entire discussion of secularization.

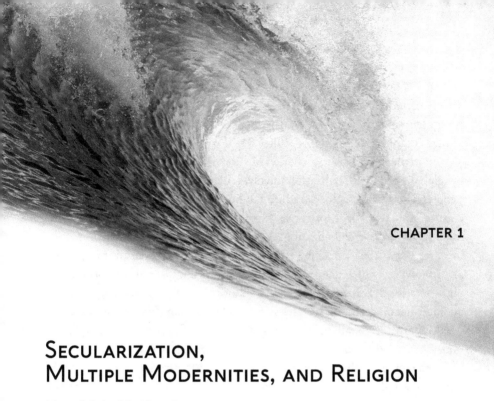

CHAPTER 1

SECULARIZATION, MULTIPLE MODERNITIES, AND RELIGION

Harold A. Netland

Let's begin by acknowledging the obvious: The world of the twenty-first century is very different from the world of the twelfth century. We have Twitter—they did not. Seriously, one way to depict the contrast between then and now is to say that the twelfth century was premodern, whereas we live in a highly modern world. Our world has been shaped by modernization and is characterized by modernity.[1] This has implications for those involved in Christian mission. If we are to be effective in making disciples of Jesus Christ today, we need to have some understanding of how modernization has affected the ways in which people think and live in particular contexts.

But what do we mean by modernization and modernity? We might think of modernization as the ongoing process of social and intellectual transformations that developed from the emergence of science, industrialization, the market economy, and the increasing dominance of technology in all of life. Modernization began around the fifteenth century in Europe and since then has spread globally. Modernity, in turn, can be thought of as the ways of living and thinking that grow out of modern-ization

---

1 I do not make a sharp distinction between modernity and postmodernity.

and the powerful intellectual movements of the past four centuries. These include, but are not limited to, the European and American Enlightenment movements. Intellectually, modernity is characterized by critical inquiry in all domains of life.

From the sixteenth century onward, modernization has been accompanied by globalization. Globalization involves increased interrelatedness among peoples worldwide, across traditional boundaries in politics, economics, culture, and religion. Most areas of the globe today are being affected by modernization and globalization. Although there are certain commonalities in the ways that societies worldwide undergo modernization, there are important differences as well. Modernization is not uniform in its manifestations. This has led many to follow Shmuel Eisenstadt in speaking of "multiple modernities" as a result of modernization (Eisenstadt 2000).

Modernization and globalization have significantly affected religion, both on the individual and the social institutional levels. One way to think about the religious changes brought about by modernization is in terms of the notion of secularization. Always controversial, the concept of secularization is often misunderstood, and since the dawn of the twenty-first century it has been regarded by many as having been refuted. In what follows I will first distinguish three concepts—secularization, secularism, and the secular. Then I will briefly contrast what we might call the classical secularization thesis with more recent understandings of the impact of modernization on religious commitments. I will then turn to the question of Asian societies and ask whether secularization can be a helpful way of thinking about transformations in religion in Asia.

Secularization, Secularism, and the Secular

It is important to keep the terms *secularization, secularism,* and *secular* somewhat distinct (see Casanova 2011). *Secularization* refers to an empirically observable, historical process of social, intellectual, and cultural change such that traditional religious patterns are modified in significant ways. There is, of course, much debate over just what these changes amount to, but for now the important point is that secularization, if it is occurring, is a process of social transformation that is in principle discernible by careful observation and collection of data. Whether secularization is happening is an empirical question to be answered by responsible investigation of the relevant evidence. One's personal feeling about this process of change—whether positive or negative—is an entirely different matter.

Secularism, on the other hand, is a way of thinking and living—an ideology or worldview. As typically used, secularism refers to a way of thinking that is opposed to religious commitments. So secularism is often understood as maintaining that this world is all that there is; there is no transcendent reality. Whether secularism as a worldview necessarily follows from secularization is a controversial and disputed question.

The term *secular* is used in multiple ways. Minimally, the secular is whatever is distinguished from the sacred or the religious. In some cases, "secular" is closely aligned with secularism, so that to be secular is to embrace secularism as a way of thinking and living. This use of "secular" clearly opposes the secular to the religious. But there are other uses of the term as well.

A key component of secularization is the idea of differentiation—resulting in, for example, a clear separation of institutions in education, health care, and government from religious legitimation and authority. Where this occurs, we say that these institutions are secular. One can acknowledge differentiation in this respect without necessarily embracing secularism. A secular education or a secular government need not be hostile to particular religious traditions. A properly secular government, for example, might be one that is impartial in its treatment of religious or nonreligious perspectives. Whether one favors a secular government or educational system, in this sense, depends in part upon one's location. Many American Christians are unhappy even with this notion of secular government or secular education, since they are convinced that Christian values and assumptions should be reflected throughout the government and educational system. Christians in Japan or India or Iran or Pakistan, by contrast, often wish for a more secular government—that is, one that is genuinely impartial and does not favor any particular religious tradition.

Secularization

Although there is no single theory about secularization, there was a dominant way of thinking about modernity and secularization in the 1960s and 70s. We might call this the classical secularization thesis. It maintains that modernization inevitably results in secularization, with secularization being understood as the observable decline of religion. It is expressed in Peter Berger's influential 1967 work, *The Sacred Canopy*. Berger argued that "secularization has resulted in a widespread collapse of the plausibility of traditional religious definitions of reality" (1967, 127).

Steve Bruce is probably the most influential current defender of the classical thesis today, and he insists that modernization does involve a measurable decline in religion in three areas: popular involvement with churches; the scope and influence of religious institutions; and the popularity and influence of religious beliefs (1996, 26). Drawing heavily upon data from Europe, and Great Britain in particular, Bruce claims that secularization is clearly occurring and that similar patterns can be expected in other modernizing societies. Significantly, according to Bruce, the end point of secularization is not atheism but religious indifference (2002, 42).

But by the 1980s and 90s the classical thesis was being subjected to trenchant criticism. Critics charged that the evidence simply does not support the widespread and inevitable decline in religion that the classical model predicts. Even Peter Berger observed that "The world today is massively religious, is *anything* but the secularized world that has been predicted (whether joyfully or despondently) by so many analysts of modernity" (1999, 9). Writing in 2002, Berger acknowledged that the older model could no longer be sustained: "It is fair to say that the majority of sociologists dealing with religion today no longer adhere to the equation of modernity and secularization" (2002, 291). Critics pointed out that advocates of the classical thesis tend to consider only developments concerning Christianity and the West, ignoring data on modernization and religions in Asia, Latin America, and Africa.

Thirty-five years ago, sociologist James Davison Hunter quipped that at the heart of secularization is the fact that "being religious is not as easy as it used to be" (1983, 4). The intervening decades have shown that lots of people in modern societies are still highly religious, so perhaps Hunter's observation needs some modification. I suggest that what the notion of secularization is trying to capture is the fact that being religious *in traditional ways* is not as easy as it used to be. Modern people are often still religious, but the ways in which they understand and express religious commitments today are different.

Many Christians enthusiastically embraced Berger's very public rejection of the classical secularization thesis, taking this as decisive refutation of secularization itself. But this, I think, is to misunderstand Berger's position. What Berger rejected was the idea that modernity necessarily brings about decline in religion and that this process works out in much the same way wherever modernization occurs. In his later writings, especially in his last book, *The Many Altars of Modernity*, Berger makes clear that there is something to the notion of secularization but that we need to rethink what it is and how it works. "I am now prepared to concede that the secularization theorists are not quite as wrong as I previously thought" (2014, xii).

Berger argues that in thinking about secularization we should give much greater prominence to the notions of pluralization and pluralism in modern societies. "Our main mistake was that we misunderstood pluralism as just one factor supporting secularization; in fact, pluralism, the co-existence of different worldviews and value systems in the same society, is *the* major change brought about by modernity for the place of religion both in the minds of individuals and in the institutional order" (ibid., ix). This, in turn, has a relativizing effect on individuals and societies.[2]

Similar themes are found in the recent work by the Canadian philosopher and historian Charles Taylor. In his massive and influential study, *A Secular Age*, Taylor draws extensively upon both intellectual and social history to tell the story of a transformation in the "social imaginary" of Western Europeans over the past five hundred years. As Taylor sees it, one way to get at the magnitude of these changes is to raise the following question: "Why was it virtually impossible not to believe in God in, say, 1500 in our Western society, while in 2000 many of us find this not only easy, but even inescapable?" (2007, 26).

Two components of Taylor's rich and complex answer to this question are especially significant.

First, Taylor provides a multifaceted account of intellectual and social changes over five centuries, resulting in a shift away from living in conscious awareness of a transcendent dimension to a "this worldly" or "immanent frame" for thinking and living. Whereas in earlier times there was a conscious awareness of the spiritual or transcendent dimension, the secular age is marked by loss of the transcendent dimension. "The crucial change here [which secularization brought about] could be described as the possibility of living within a purely immanent order, that is, the possibility of really conceiving of, of imagining, ourselves within such an order, one that could be accounted for on its own terms, which thus leaves belief in the transcendent as a kind of 'optional extra'—something it had never been before in any human society" (2011, 50–51).

---

2 "Pluralism relativizes and thereby undermines many of the certainties by which human beings used to live. Put differently, certainty becomes a scarce commodity....Modernization unleashes all the forces that make for pluralism—urbanization, mass migration (including mass tourism), general literacy and higher education for increasing numbers, and all the recent technologies of communication....[M]ost of our contemporaries are aware of the fact that there are different ways of life, different values, different worldviews" (Berger 2014, 9, 15).

Second, adapting Max Weber's concept of *Entzauberung*, Taylor provides a perceptive analysis of the disenchantment of the modern world. The premodern European world was one in which "magical" rituals, spiritual beings, and forces could affect not only nature but also human affairs. "In the enchanted world, the line between personal agency and impersonal force was not at all clearly drawn" (2007, 32). God and the spiritual realm provided the framework, the "social imaginary," within which the social order gained its legitimacy and persons found their meaning and purpose—what Taylor calls their "fullness." Taylor argues that the key difference between the world of 1500 and that of 2000 is "a shift in what I [call] 'fullness,' between a condition in which our highest spiritual and moral aspirations point us inescapably to God, one might say, make no sense without God, to one in which they can be related to a host of different sources, and frequently are referred to sources which deny God" (ibid., 26). One way to look at secularization, then, is to see it as the process whereby plausible alternatives to the "God-reference of fullness" arise. Disenchantment involves a different way of thinking and living taking over so that one finds fullness in living strictly within the immanent frame.

A disenchanted world is not necessarily a nonreligious world. But in a secular, disenchanted world, religion looks different. Taylor and Berger persuasively argue that religious commitments are different under conditions of modernization. As Taylor puts it, this change "consists, among other things, of a move from a society where belief in God is unchallenged and indeed unproblematic, to one in which it is understood to be one option among others, and frequently not the easiest to embrace....Belief in God is no longer axiomatic. There are alternatives" (ibid., 3). For both Berger and Taylor, then, modernity undermines the "taken for granted" nature of religious commitment.

Secularized Asia?

Taylor's *A Secular Age* has stimulated extensive discussion about the applicability of his thesis to societies elsewhere, especially in Asia.[3] Modernization and globalization clearly are affecting religious traditions in Asia, although there are significant differences between Asian modernities

---

3 See, for example, the essays in Warner et al. (2010) and Bilgrami (2016). Taylor himself acknowledges that his discussion was restricted to Western contexts and that it is important to explore how "multiple modernities" manifest themselves in other contexts. See Taylor (2007, 21).

and those of Europe and North America. I conclude with a few observations about secularization in Asia.

First, part of what makes secularization plausible in modern European contexts is the fact that there is a clear benchmark against which religious changes can be measured. Although not monolithic, European Christendom did provide an overarching intellectual, cultural, social, and political framework legitimatized by the church and Christian commitments. It is not difficult to map the fragmentation of this overarching framework and departures from it in Western societies from the seventeenth century onward.

In many Asian societies, however, it is not so easy to identify the premodern benchmark against which the transformations of secularization are to be measured. In premodern India, for example, there was no single overarching religious framework analogous to Christendom in Europe. A variety of religious and intellectual traditions competed for social and intellectual dominance, including the many traditions that in the nineteenth century came to be identified as Hinduism. Similarly, in China and Japan there was not just one religion that historically dominated the public space, but rather several interrelated, though often competing, religious traditions.[4]

Moreover, the idea of secularization presupposes that we can identify what is religious and distinguish it from what is not religious—what is secular. The distinction between the religious and the secular in Europe in the eighteenth and nineteenth centuries became increasingly clear. But how are we to identify what is religious and distinguish that from what is secular in Asian societies?[5] Religion in Asia has a strong social and ritual component, and it is often not clear if a ritual or practice is religious or cultural. Among Chinese and Japanese there has been a long-standing debate whether Confucianism is a religion, an ideology, or a social ethic (Van der Veer 2013; Sun 2013).

A related issue concerns the place of belief in religions in Asia. How significant are changes in beliefs in assessing the impact of modernization?

---

4 In China there was a dramatic decline in individual religious beliefs and practice, as well as in the social significance of religion, from 1949 onward. But this was not due to the effects of modernization and globalization as such, but rather to the forced policies of the Maoist regime, which tried to eradicate religion. On religion under Communism, see Yang (2012).

5 Elisabetta Porcu, for example, discusses the difficulties in distinguishing what is religious from what is cultural or social in the activities expected of residents in the Japanese *chossssnaikai*, or neighborhood associations, which typically include caring for objects from sacred shrines (Shinto) or statues for the bodhisattva Jizo (Buddhist folk religion). See Porcu (2012).

Beliefs have always been important in Christianity, and thus one marker of secularization has been significant change away from traditional or orthodox Christian beliefs. But in much of Asia religious beliefs play a more minor role than they do in the West. As Richard Madsen observes, "When Western scholars have looked for religion in Asian societies, they have often looked for it in the form of private faith. But in most Asian societies, much of religion is neither private nor faith." That is, "It is not faith in the sense of a personal belief in doctrines" (2010, 251).

And yet Madsen does note that with modernization there are significant changes on the communal or social level.

> Although religion in most Asian societies has been more a matter of communal practice than individual belief, the meanings of such communal practice have been changing. This is the result of social mobility, social differentiation, and the expansion of cognitive horizons. Social mobility happens mainly when people move from the countryside to the city, from agricultural to industrial labor or commerce. Social differentiation refers to the separation of work (which is increasingly dependent on a globalized economy) and education from family and kinship. The expansion of cognitive horizons is the result of the exposure to diverse people and ideas through exposure to modern media and to life in the metropolis. Most Asian societies have experienced all three of these processes, but the processes have unfolded in different ways along different paths. (ibid., 255)

So modernized religion in Asia can look somewhat different from what we find in Europe and North America.

As we saw, Charles Taylor highlights the loss of transcendence and the disenchantment of the world as distinctive markers of secularization in the West. Do we find similar transformations in Asian societies? This is difficult to determine, but one could argue that in many Asian societies the same reductionism does not seem to be at work. Even with high degrees of modernization, the line between what Taylor calls the transcendent and the immanent frames remains fluid and blurry; the one blends into the other. The enchanted world of spiritual beings and forces that impinges upon the physical world and human activity seems to be very much a part of many highly modernized Asian cultures.

Although Japan, for example, is one of the most modernized and technologically advanced societies in the world, many Japanese live with an awareness of supernatural realities. Themes about supernatural beings and forces, magic, and occult powers are common in popular Japanese movies (*anime*), cartoons (*manga*), and literature. Well-educated professionals flock to fortune-tellers or mediums, seeking advice on life decisions.

To take an especially tragic example, the widespread Japanese practice of *mizuko kuyo* rituals demonstrates the fluidity between this world and the other world, life and death, and the causal efficacy of actions in one world upon the other world (LaFleur 1992; Hardacre 1997). Abortion has been widely practiced in Japan since the end of World War II, and around the 1970s some Buddhist temples and priests developed and began marketing rituals for the aborted child and the mother. *Mizuko kuyo* are special rituals performed by Buddhist priests to appease the souls of the aborted and to alleviate the sense of guilt of the mothers. The rituals are embedded within, and gain their meaning from, a larger cosmological framework in which the boundaries between this world and the other world are blurred and permeable. Traditional Buddhist assumptions about the cycle of life and death operate alongside modern scientific understandings of the natural world.

An especially powerful component of this framework is belief in *tatari*—that is, the belief in revenge or retribution enacted by the spirit world, including the soul of the unborn, toward the living. In a perverse combination of the premodern and modern, the widespread fear of *tatari*, or retribution, has been skillfully marketed through the media to promote the lucrative business of *mizuko kuyo*. In some ways, then, the world of the modern Japanese is still an enchanted—or perhaps better yet, a haunted—one.

At this point we might be tempted to dismiss the notion of secularization as irrelevant to modern Asian societies. Indeed, Japan is sometimes held up as a clear counterexample to the claim that modernization results in the decline of religion (Stark 1999, 268). But the reality is more complicated. For the past several centuries Japanese society has been dominated by an eclectic mix of Shinto, Buddhist, and folk animist beliefs and practices, all of which revolve around a strong sense of national kinship rooted in ancestral practices and the imperial family.[6]

---

6 Nevertheless, the idea that there should be some separation between religion and the state is widely accepted. John Nelson states, "In contemporary Japan as in Europe and North America, secularism (*sezoku*) generally refers to an ideological position (backed by political principles) that there should be a negotiated separation of religion from the state. In Japan, the concept first gained traction during the rapid modernization of the country in the late nineteenth century. It was not until Japan's defeat in the Pacific War and the advent of a new constitution written largely by the Allied Occupation that secularism became a social and political policy of secularization, intended to curtail government patronage of select religious organizations" (2012, 40–41).

But despite this history there are strong indications that traditional religious institutions and activities are losing social significance. John Nelson states, "If we can agree that secularization in a society means the diminished capacity of religious doctrine and leaders to influence social and political institutions, and that the ensuing legal and social institutions of society gradually encode the privatization of religious belief and practice, then [statistics provided by recent surveys] are evidence that Japan has one of the world's most secular societies" (2012, 51).

Ian Reader, one of the leading scholars of religion in Japan today, has produced impressive studies showing a marked departure from older forms of religious activity.

> I contend that Japan, rather than providing comfort for the opponents of secularization theory, shows almost the exact opposite and that secularization (in terms of the idea of a "decline of religion" and a public withdrawal from engagement with the religious sphere) is a growing force to be reckoned with in Japan today. Moreover, there are clear correlations between modernisation, urbanisation and higher levels of education (factors often cited as formative forces in the secularisation process), and declining levels of religious belief and practice, whether individually or institutionally. (2012, 10–11)

In particular, Reader concludes that "organized, established Buddhism in Japan is in a serious state of decline, one that threatens the continued existence of a major religious tradition that for over a millennium has been an important element in the socio-cultural fabric of Japan" (2011, 235). The decline he speaks of concerns the institutionalized public Buddhism that deals with death, funerals, and rituals for the deceased, an area where Buddhism has for several centuries had a virtual monopoly. Given the significance of funerals and the ancestral cult for traditional Japanese religious practices, a decline in these areas is highly significant. Whereas funerals in Japan traditionally have been Buddhist, in the past several decades there has been a significant increase in nonreligious funerals, so that in 2006 26 percent of all funerals in Tokyo were nonreligious and had no Buddhist elements at all. Surveys also indicate a steady decline in Japanese households that maintain the traditional Buddhist altar (*butsudan*) or Shinto altar (*kamidana*) (ibid., 241).

Reader summarizes the results of post–World War II research as follows:

The numerous surveys and questionnaires carried out by public bodies, newspapers and scholars over the entire post-1945 period have shown a general decrease in the numbers stating that they either have religious beliefs or have specific religious adherences. In the Yomiuri newspaper surveys, which have been conducted regularly since 1952, the figures have fallen consistently—from 64.7% having religious belief in 1952 to 56% in 1965 and progressively until a low of 20.3% in 1995…and while it has risen marginally (to 22.9% in 2005) it remains far lower than in previous decades. (ibid., 239)

There are also changes in beliefs about the afterlife. In 1999, only 14.9 percent of young people reported firmly believing in the existence of life after death, with 36.0 percent saying they believe in it to some degree, down from 29.9 percent and 40.2 percent respectively in 1992 (Reader 2012, 18). Spiritual pilgrimages to sacred shrines and temples have also been a popular form of religious participation for a long time. But Reader produces data indicating a significant decline in participants in pilgrimages, so that pilgrimage sites are transforming themselves into centers of tourism to attract visitors (ibid., 23–29).

Furthermore, the public perception of religion among Japanese is highly negative. Public dissatisfaction with religion, including Buddhism, is so pervasive that new phrases have been adopted—*shukyobanare* ("estrangement from religion") and *bukkyobanare* ("estrangement from Buddhism"). Reader states, "The Japanese avoid religious organisations and declare repeatedly in surveys that they do not have faith and that religion is not important; they are turning in increasing numbers to ways of dealing with death that repudiate their Buddhist traditions and that are overtly secular and non-religious" (ibid., 34). Reader concludes that evidence from Japan shows that secularization theory should not be dismissed prematurely. "The Japanese case informs us that secularization is a force to be reckoned with in the modern world rather than an idea to be consigned to the grave" (ibid.).

Where does this leave us? First, the earlier secularization thesis that insists on a necessary decline in religion under modernization clearly is untenable. Religion, in one form or another, continues to thrive in many modernizing societies. But simply dismissing secularization as having been refuted is also unwarranted. There are clear indicators of decline in traditional religious beliefs and practices in many societies. Modernization and globalization do affect traditional religious beliefs, practices, and institutions in significant ways, in Asia as well as in Europe and North America. But we should avoid trying to impose one model or paradigm for religious change on all modernizing societies. In trying to understand current religious realities, we must look carefully at the multiple local contexts in which modernization and traditional religion intersect, noting both the unique features of particular settings as well as broader patterns that modernizing societies worldwide might share.[7]

References

Berger, Peter. 1967. *The Sacred Canopy: The Social Construction of Reality*. New York: Anchor Books.

———. 1999. "The Desecularization of the World: A Global Overview." In *The Desecularization of the World: Resurgent Religion and World Politics*, edited by Peter Berger, 1–18. Grand Rapids: Eerdmans.

———. 2002. "Secularization and De-secularization." In *Religions in the Modern World*, edited by Linda Woodhead, Paul Fletcher, Hiroko Kawanami, and David Smith, 291–98. London: Routledge.

———. 2014. *The Many Altars of Modernity: Toward a Paradigm for Religion in a Pluralist Age*. Boston: Walter de Gruyter.

Bilgrami, Akeel, ed. 2016. *Beyond the Secular West*. New York: Columbia University Press.

Bruce, Steve. 1996. *Religion in the Modern World*. Oxford: Oxford University Press.

———. 2002. *God Is Dead: Secularization in the West*. Oxford: Blackwell.

Casanova, José. 2011. "The Secular, Secularizations, Secularisms." In *Rethinking Secularism*, edited by Craig Calhoun, Mark Juergensmeyer, and Jonathan VanAntwerpen, 54–74. New York: Oxford University Press.

Drescher, Elizabeth. 2016. *Choosing Our Religion: The Spiritual Lives of America's Nones*. New York: Oxford University Press.

Eisenstadt, S. N. 2000. "Multiple Modernities." *Daedalus* 129: 1–29.

Hardacre, Helen. 1997. *Marketing the Menacing Fetus in Japan*. Berkeley: University of California Press.

Hunter, James Davison. 1983. *American Evangelicalism: Conservative Religion and the Quandary of Modernity*. New Brunswick, NJ: Rutgers University Press.

---

7 One issue that deserves further research is whether the category of "nones" or the "spiritual but not religious," which has become significant for understanding the changing religious landscape of North America and Europe, is a helpful one for understanding Asian communities as well. See Drescher (2016) and Zuckerman, Galen, and Pasquale (2016).

LaFleur, William. 1992. *Liquid Life: Abortion and Buddhism in Japan.* Princeton, NJ: Princeton University Press.

Madsen, Richard. 2010. "Secularism, Religious Change, and Social Conflict in Asia." In *Rethinking Secularism*, edited by Craig Calhoun, Mark Juergensmeyer, and Jonathan VanAntwerpen, 248–69. New York: Oxford University Press.

Nelson, John K. 2012. "Japanese Secularities and the Decline of Temple Buddhism." *Journal of Religion in Japan* 1: 37–60.

Porcu, Elisabetta. 2012. "Observations on the Blurring of the Religious and the Secular in a Japanese Urban Setting." *Journal of Religion in Japan* 1: 83–106.

Reader, Ian. 2011. "Buddhism in Crisis? Institutional Decline in Modern Japan." *Buddhist Studies Review* 28: 233–63.

———. 2012. "Secularisation, R.I.P. Nonsense! The 'Rush Hour Away from the Gods' and the Sense of Decline in Religion in Contemporary Japan." *Journal of Religion in Japan* 1: 7–36.

Stark, Rodney. 1999. "Secularization, R.I.P." *Sociology of Religion* 60: 249–73.

Sun, Anna. 2013. *Confucianism as a World Religion: Contested Histories and Contemporary Realities.* Princeton, NJ: Princeton University Press.

Taylor, Charles. 2007. *A Secular Age.* Cambridge, MA: Harvard University Press.

———. 2011. "Western Secularity." In *Rethinking Secularism*, edited by Craig Calhoun, Mark Juergensmeyer, and Jonathan VanAntwerpen, 31–53. New York: Oxford University Press.

Van der Veer, Peter. 2013. "Is Confucianism Secular?" In *Beyond the Secular West*, edited by Akeel Bilgrami, 117–34. New York: Columbia University Press.

Warner, Michael, Jonathan VanAntwerpen, and Craig Calhoun, eds. 2010. *Varieties of Secularism in a Secular Age.* Cambridge, MA: Harvard University Press.

Yang, Fenggang. 2012. *Religion in China: Survival and Renewal under Communist Rule.* New York: Oxford University Press.

Zuckerman, Phil, Luke W. Galen, and Frank L. Pasquale, eds. 2016. *The Nonreligious: Understanding Secular People and Societies.* New York: Oxford University Press.

CHAPTER 2

EMBRACING PLURALITY:
THE OPPORTUNITY OF SECULARIZATION

Shawn P. Behan

Secularization has become a buzzword in many churches, seminaries, and conferences due to the idea that more secularization in culture means less space for religion—or, more specifically, for the church. Combine this fear with the numerical reality that many churches in the West are in decline, then the word *secular* becomes a profanity uttered in hushed tones and behind closed doors. It is understandable, therefore, that many pastors, professors, and church leaders have come out in opposition to secularism, wanting to recover the prominent public place the church once had.

Yet the secularization[1] of American society today does not have to be a negative that we fear will destroy the church. Nor will we ever return to an idealized past of non-secularization. Instead it could be an opportunity for the church to grow, engage, and work within for the flourishing of our communities—if only we would embrace the plurality that secularization brings.

---

1 *Secularization* here is used in the sense of differentiation, as mentioned by Harold Netland in chapter 1 of this book. In that sense, the term *secular* will then refer to the institutions that have embraced the secularism of society.

In that spirit, I propose that secularization in a society is a good development because it provides a pluralism of belief options. This pluralism,[2] then, is an opportunity for the church to engage culture (and its members) on equal footing with other beliefs in the public sphere, critically self-reflect, bear faithful witness to the Bible's response to culture's key questions, and model an inner unity and acceptance unlike any other system of belief within the pluralistic society.

In order to fulfill this proposal, I will:

1. Survey some of the major academic Christian responses to secularism;
2. Reexamine secularization along the lines of Charles Taylor; and
3. Describe the opportunity that exists before the church in secularized situations in the West and hopefully around the world.

Christian Academic Responses to Secularization

Secularization is an important issue in contemporary Western culture. "It is generally agreed that modern democracies have to be 'secular'" (Taylor 2010, xi); and while this idea has come up for debate, secularization still must be engaged for the church to move forward in our culture and our call to be witnesses of Christ. The popular Christian responses have often largely viewed secularization as negative or even an attack upon the church. Academic responses take a more nuanced approach to understanding secularization and culture, and usually point out

1. that religion is not dying like it was predicted (as a matter of fact it is growing globally), and
2. the various ways in which to live in the reality of a secularized society.

While the first response tends to be directed toward the popular realm, it is the second type of response that has attracted more scholarly attention. It is important, then, to look at some of these proposed practical solutions.

In *Secularization and Mission*, Bert Hoedemaker seeks to unpack the relationship between mission and secular society, focusing on the point where these two meet and stressing the need for a new missionary ideal to address the complexities of secularization in society. He addresses the need to question the universal validity of the Christian story in the face of

---

2 As seen in Netland, chapter 1, pluralism is a positive outcome of secularization since it brings about the reality of multiple worldviews coexisting, side by side, in the ever-shrinking globalized world.

global secularization, showing that the only way to know is by assuming it is universal, continuing to test it in each context, and expect that "the basic thrust of the gospel responds to basic needs and problems of humankind"—thus removing the cultural context from witness and contextualizing within each specific secular context (1998, 59). Those who would engage this process can only hope to avoid the epistemological extremes of fundamentalism or syncretism, (ibid., 62) while truthfully and openly engaging the secular context God has called them to as witnesses.

Likewise, Graeme Smith's portrait of secularization in the West from *A Short History of Secularism* brings up the fact that 1) atheism has failed (2008, 14–15) and 2) Christianity has remained an important component of Western culture (ibid., 15–16). Smith shows that doctrine is that which was eliminated from public debates in the Enlightenment, thus turning religion from a public to a private matter (ibid., 16–17). All of this leads to his conclusion that secularization is not the end of Christianity; rather, it is the latest expression of Christianity (without its doctrine) within Western culture (ibid., 2). Thus, secularization is nothing to be feared or fought; rather, it is to be embraced and engaged as one seeks to understand the place of Christianity as the foundation of ethics for this society.

There is also the response of Craig M. Gay, whose book *The Way of the (Modern) World* regards how the church should function within a secular society. In his view, secularization is simply a new phase of Christianity, one that has privatized Christian faith by the removal of doctrinal discussions from the public sphere, much in the same way Graeme Smith does. In this context of practical atheism and secularization, Gay suggests that we focus our attention on redeveloping the personal aspects of God through the relationships of our lives. In this perspective, as opposed to Smith's, Christianity is about personal faith affecting how individuals view themselves in the context of their world (1998, 271–81). It is this working out of personhood in the divine-human relationship that then directs human-human relationships, while not directing the public sphere like in the age of Christendom.

Lastly, there is the example of Lesslie Newbigin, who wrote about secularization and plurality often, but in no more succinct location than his book *Honest Religion for Secular Man*. While taking the approach of understanding secularization, and critiquing the typical Christian response to the secularization of his day, Newbigin concludes with a discussion on living for God in a secular society. He states, "A secular style of life for the

Christian is described as one which does not turn away from the world to seek God, but finds God by involvement in the life of the world" (1966, 123). Thus, living out a life of seeking and following God draws us into the world, functioning as witnesses to God (sign, instrument, and foretaste, in Newbigin's language) and God's reigning kingdom in the world.

It is Newbigin's response—one that would draw us into the secular in order to seek God—that I would like to build upon, first by reexamining secularization (which I believe Newbigin would agree with—cf. Newbigin 1966, 123), and then by leveraging the opportunity that this new perspective affords us. My response is less concerned with specific practices or ways to respond, and it is more concerned with the mentality and attitude of the respondents living out this new perspective.

Reexamining Secularization

In recent years, there have been more critical engagements with the secularization theory from historians, philosophers, sociologists, and others—both Christian and not—several of which are of note. To name a few, Peter Berger has recanted some of his early assertions of secularization (1999, 2); Rodney Stark and Roger Finke have called for the end of the secularization theory (2000, 79); and Christian Smith (2017) has studied the place and importance of religion in the United States today, ultimately affirming its continued relevance to American society. Of all of the critiques and reconsiderations of secularization, the most helpful may be that of Charles Taylor, who reexamined secularization for better interaction among those who would strive to see the church have a public voice again within secular contexts.

What could be called Taylor's magnum opus, *A Secular Age*, deals with the reality of secularization that exists throughout the contemporary West. James K. A. Smith, in his condensed homage to Taylor's work, wrote his book to make Taylor's behemoth accessible for practitioners, "because I believe Taylor's analysis can help pastors and church planters understand better the contexts in which they proclaim the gospel. In many ways, Taylor's *Secular Age* amounts to a cultural anthropology for urban mission" (2014, xi).

Thus Taylor's defining of secularity[3] provides a foundation for understanding and engaging our culture with the powerful words of the gospel, calling for their message to be lived out by those who preach them. Smith argues, "At the same time, Taylor's account should also serve as a wake-up call for the church, functioning as a mirror to help us see how we have come to inhabit our secular age" (2014, xi). Providing a powerful tool for self-reflection and adjustment to living in this secularized age, Taylor's book is the foundation for understanding the opportunity of secularization as we seek to embrace it in the church today.

A philosopher by training, Taylor's approach is philosophical in nature, along the lines of his Hegelian epistemology and historical methodology. He identifies the philosophical movements over the centuries that have brought us to our current state of secularity in the contemporary West. He tracks three different paradigms of secularity that have existed in Western history. Secularism1 (S1) is the classic separation of sacred and secular (nonreligious), whereby the earthly or worldly things are set apart from the heavenly or spiritual things (Taylor 2007, 1–2). Secularism2 (S2) is the time period where public spaces have been completely drained of all things spiritual, religious, or metaphysical (ibid., 2–3). Both of these paradigms were most prominent in past ages of secularization, loosely associated with the Late Medieval (S1) and Enlightenment (S2) periods. Our current period of secularity, Secularism3 (S3), is one in which the conditions of belief have changed to allow for belief or nonbelief (ibid., 3).

It is this S3 paradigm that we currently live in, where belief in God is one of multiple options for how we understand and interpret the world. Thus we live in a period of beliefs, where a plethora of religious and nonreligious belief systems mutually exist and are accessible for investigation and decision by all members of society. We have a choice between God and not-God, with no choice being culturally determined or pressured. Within each choice, there are sub-choices that determine the depth and implications of our belief choice.

This cultural context by which choice for God or not for God, as in our current state, allows for the fully unencumbered exercise of our free will.[4]

---

3 Taylor's preferred terms are "secularity" and "secularism." In this section, I will respect Netland's terminology, established in chapter 1 of this volume, so that Netland's "secularism" is equivalent to Taylor's "secularity," and Netland's "secularization" to Taylor's "secularism."

4 This idea of free choice can best be equated with what Timothy C. Tennent termed the "freed Will," whereby God has prepared the stage for humans to freely exercise their will to choose God or not God (Tennent 2019).

By this, I mean that we have the opportunity to act as an independent agent in freely deciding whether or not to believe in God, and in what manner that belief will manifest in our life. For free choice to truly be a free exercise of the will, there must not only be no blockades to the exercising of that choice, but there must be viable options by which we can choose from freely. These viable options must be available to us, which does not happen culturally outside of an S3 society. S1s and S2s bind this choice by cultural pressure and parameters. This means that in Taylor's freedom of choice existent within the S3 culture we have the opportunity to exercise our free choice, unencumbered by cultural expectations to make a certain choice. This is unparalleled in Christian history.

When regarding Christian history in a general sense, free choice was limitedly exercised in the ancient Western world, in that persons could choose their faith as long as that faith did not interfere with the state faith. The cultural context only allowed for private exercising of free choice. When it entered the public realm, however, that is when political reactions against religions occurred—e.g., banishing the Jews from Rome, martyrdom, etc. After Constantine, the Christendom era of Western society did not allow the exercise of free choice; rather, the cultural conditions necessitated only a decision of belief in God. (Though some may have privately resisted, publicly they could never admit to this.)

There was then an in-between period, Taylor's S1, when secularity entered the public discourse and the sacred and secular began to be separated, but belief in God still had a public forum—thus free choice was still culturally restricted. During the Enlightenment, Taylor's S2, faith was again restricted to the private realm, though adding the element where belief had no public space (unlike the previous period). Throughout these periods, similar cultural conditions hindered the free exercise of choice. Though the sub-conditions of each era changed, the overarching condition had not. In S3, the cultural conditions for choice of belief now exist. These cultural conditions allow for a plethora of faiths to exist side by side, so that the choice for God or not can be made, along with how that choice will function within our lives.

This plethora of belief options works in tension with each other across the public sphere. Taylor describes it as a cross-pressure of beliefs (2007, 594–617), by which differing religious options push and pull each other, forcing these beliefs and their choices to be defended in the public spheres, where they can interact with one another. In this, they refine each other.

Ultimately, this is freedom of choice—a freedom we could associate with the operation of free will. Free choice is necessary for the gospel to be freely and truly heard in each and every society.[5]

Newbigin states, "Every human community must have the opportunity to hear, believe, and freely accept the true goal. That goal lies beyond history. Kingdoms will pass away. The earth itself and the visible cosmos will pass away. In the end Jesus Christ will be seen as the one to whom authority is given" (1989, 123). We now live in the condition of truly free choice, where the will can be noncoercively exercised by all members of the society.[6] It is in such conditions that we must now approach secularization in a new way, a way of embracing the plurality of choice that it brings. Otherwise, the church will continue to be relativized to the margins of society. Therefore, secularization is about entering into the exercise of free choice over religious belief, which must be shared openly in the public sphere with other belief choices in order for other members of society to make fully informed free-choice choices of their own. It is in this plurality that Christianity can begin to recover its public voice, alongside other belief systems, and express its truth and reality for others to evaluate and—God willing—choose to accept.

The Opportunity of Secularization

Having now seen some of the history of secularization and Taylor's reconsideration of it, we can turn toward the opportunity that secularization provides. The secularization of culture, while closely associated with modernism, does not have a causal link with it. Both secularization and modernity bring about a society of plurality, which can actually be a positive for the church, as Berger, Davie, and Fokas describe:

> Modernity does not necessarily bring about secularization. What it does bring about, in all likelihood necessarily, is pluralism. Through most of history, most human beings lived in communities with a high degree of homogeneity of beliefs and values. Modernity undermines such

---

5 The free will/predestination debate that may arise from this statement is beyond what can be discussed here. I understand predestination in Newbigin's form of election—whereby we are chosen to serve God, not to salvation (see Hunsberger 1998 and Newbigin 1989); and as such, I see the necessity of both free will and election holding each other in tension as necessary components of our life in God.

6 There is a small caveat when looking across an entire society. Subcultures within a society may still exert cultural pressure for certain belief decisions—for instance, a family may pressure a child to choose to follow the faith of the family. Culture at the national/societal level, however, is no longer placing those pressures on people, and that is what we are talking about here.

homogeneity—through migration and urbanization, by which people with very different beliefs and values are made to rub against each other. (2008, 12–13)

While secularization is not necessarily a part of modernity, the two have traditionally gone together. Whether together or separate, the point above holds true—societies that have either one or both now live in a time of reduced homogeneity and increased plurality. This plurality fits with Taylor's definition of secularization as a religious choice, and it is this plurality that provides the church with a great opportunity. Before we can fully embrace that opportunity, however, we must understand it. To understand the opportunity before us, we must study our context, critically self-reflect, then begin to witness into the plurality with a public voice, which also offers bridges toward unity among the body of Christ. To assert the positives of religious plurality in culture, we must first look to Scripture in order to see its perspective on pluralism.

Scriptural considerations of religious pluralism

Scripture shows many examples of religious pluralism as the world develops and God calls out Abraham to father his chosen people, as well as the Israelites' entire existence since Egypt. Jesus too lives in a religiously plural world, and Paul's entire ministry is interacting in religiously plural communities. Thus we begin this discussion of the opportunity of pluralism by looking at how the Bible treats religious pluralism in its pages.

Throughout the Old Testament, we see various contexts of religious pluralism. As early as the time of Noah, we find that "he walked faithfully with God" (Gen 6:9 NIV), meaning that people had the option not to walk with God (so at least two belief choices). Ab-raham models a relationship with God that appears to be unique to him—no other person is mentioned as having direct conversations or covenants with God. The Israelites lived among the Egyptians, who had different gods, yet the Egyptians knew about the Hebrew God and acknowledged his existence—though they still worshiped their own gods (Ex 4–14). From Joshua to Esther, there are times of other people worshiping other gods, acknowledging the God of the Hebrews, and some even coming to fear Yahweh. As well, we see in Daniel and a few other places in the prophets (Jonah, Isaiah, Zechariah) where other nations or peoples know and discuss the Hebrew God openly. All of these examples show what a pluralistic society, or even a pluralistic world, can look like; and they show how the example of the Hebrews can either help or hinder the spread of God's name.

One example of religious pluralism that stands out in the OT is that of Naaman (2 Kgs 5). Naaman, a military leader and prominent figure in Aram, is besieged with leprosy, casting him into isolation. Seeking cures, he is informed by a captured Israelite slave girl about a prophet of God (Elisha) who can heal him. He ventures to Israel seeking treatment and is finally directed to Elisha, who simply commands him to wash in the Jordan. In his own cultural smugness, he leaves unimpressed and does not wash, stating that the Jordan and Israel are inferior to Damascus and its rivers. Eventually he is convinced to go and wash. When he does, he is healed. This experience with the living God drives him back to Elisha and a confession of Yahweh as the only God. Yet he knows that he must return to Aram and once there complete his duties before the king—including helping the king worship the god of Aram.

While Naaman may not fully understand his confession or how to follow Yahweh, his experience of God has convinced him of the truth of Yahweh as the only God on earth, and he now seeks to find ways to practice this confession in the course of his life. We know little else about Naaman, though it is safe to assume that he still walked the king to the foot of Rimmon and he still led Aram into battle, possibly even battle with Israel. In this religiously plural situation, we see that God's name is not only known but also followed, based off of an experience of him.

We also see in the Gospels times when Jesus engages with those who are not part of Israel—the Magi who bring him gifts at his birth (Matt 2:1–2), the Roman centurion requesting healing for his servant (Matt 8:5–13; Luke 7:1–10), the demon-possessed daughter of a Canaanite woman (Matt 15:21–28), the Samaritan woman at the well (John 4:1–42), his healing of the demoniac among the Gerasenes (Matt 8:28–34; Mark 5:1–20; Luke 8:26–39), as well as his commissioning of his disciples to spread the gospel throughout all the earth (Matt 28:16–20; Mark 16:14–18; Luke 24:44–49; Acts 1:4–8). There are also points throughout Acts where the plurality of society is seen as the place of God's work: the work of Philip to spread the gospel in Samaria (4:1–8) and to the Ethiopian eunuch (4:26–40); Peter's interaction with the God-fearing Cornelius (10:1–48); the missionary journeys of Paul (13–20); and Paul's journey to and mission in Rome (23:23–28:31).

What makes the difference in the NT opposed to the OT, or to other faiths of the ancient world, is that after Jesus is resurrected, there is the Great

Commission. Here Jesus declares his message and salvation is meant for all people, not just a nation or culture; thus it is a transnational faith that must be spread around the world.

The most prominent example of this is Paul's message to the people of Athens in Acts 17. Paul has investigated Athens: observing, listening, and learning about its culture and beliefs. It is from this study that Paul contextualizes his presentation of the gospel, fitting it to connect with the major elements of Athenian society and showing how all of these "good" things ultimately point back to God. In this, Paul is engaging in a public witness with conviction, after having gained cultural knowledge and attempting to show the unity of the best of Athenian culture with the general revelation of God. It is these elements—studying cultural context, self-reflecting to connect that context with the gospel message, engaging in public witness, and seeking unity—that mark how we too should embrace the religious plurality that surrounds us. All of this is done in an effort to show God to people in our society, that they might experience God for themselves.

Context

The first thing that we have to do is study, taking the attitude of a learner. In a culture where there is religious choice, learning about the other options is essential for engaging in the public sphere of belief choices. We do this not solely so we can convert those of other beliefs (though we pray to that end), but so we can understand and dialogue with those adherents in mutuality. Newbigin describes it this way, "A person meets his or her (dialogue) partner with the expectation and hope of learning more of truth, but inevitably will seek to grasp the new truth by means of those ways of thinking and judging and valuing that he or she has already learned and tested" (1995, 168). Thus we enter into conversations with those of other beliefs with a learner's heart and mind-set, testing what they affirm by what we already know to be true—Scripture. Then we can begin to discuss their choice and ours, not in a combative way but in a way that exercises care for them and deep consideration of the beliefs that they hold.

Timothy C. Tennent explores this approach to the religious other in a dialogue of equal partners as well; when discussing interreligious dialogue, he brings up the assumptions of many liberal Christians[7] in such dialogues— suspension of faith commitments, conviction of no absolute truth, and no

---

7 As Tennent explains, many evangelicals and other conservatives have avoided such dialogue, so liberal Christians are the only ones who have a history in these dialogues.

concern for conversion (2002, 13–16)—calling all of these into question as false dichotomies for conversation. He argues that a truly equal conversation between people of differing religious choices is one where both come fully convinced of their faith, holding to that conviction, and desire to convert the dialogue partner, yet willing to accept that they may not convert (ibid.).

To engage in such a dialogue requires the heart of vulnerability that Newbigin discusses on the topic, as follows: "A real meeting with a partner of another faith must mean being so open to him or her that the other's way of looking at the world becomes a real possibility for us" (1995, 184), if we did not have our own faith belief. It is then in this context of plurality that we can freely talk about God, understanding that others will freely talk about their beliefs as well. Thus other viable belief options must be open to us and we must humbly seek to understand them at their deepest level—that we might believe them, if not for God and our experience of him that proves our belief correct.

This combination of Newbigin and Tennent shows that not only is plurality an acceptable place for the gospel to function in society but it can be a beneficial component for discussion and public engagement. Before we venture into such a dialogue, however, we must enter into critical self-reflection to make sure that we are representing the gospel properly and respecting our partner fully.

Critical self-reflection

Personal self-reflection has been viewed as a beneficial component to individual growth, but to engage our pluralistic culture we must embark on corporate self-reflection within the local congregation and the larger body of Christ. Such an engagement will necessarily require looking at the differences of the religious choices before us. Jesus remarks, "How can you say to your brother, 'Let me take the speck out of your eye,' when all the time there is a plank in your own eye?" (Matt 7:4 NIV). As the church, we must take a critically self-reflective attitude before we begin voicing our side of the dialogue in a pluralistic society. This approach ensures that we truly understand our faith, as well as truly understand the faith of the other—preparing us to critically contextualize the gospel within the dialogue.

Self-reflection, besides providing the preparation we need to engage with a pluralistic society, also combines with Taylor's view of secularization to help us gain a better understanding of our identity. Terry Muck describes just how identity and Taylor's secularization intersect,

Where he (Taylor) defines "secular" not as the absence of religion in a culture (its usual definition) but as the absence of compelling social forces mandating a specific choice of religion. The "secular" age we live in, according to Taylor, is one in which an almost bewildering variety of religious choices are available to us—including the choice of "no religion." The lack of social constraints on religious choice has an overall effect, perhaps, of devaluing religion overall. But its more compelling implication is what it does to individual religious identity, a topic written about in some detail by British sociologist of religion Zygmunt Bauman.

Bauman (2000) writes about what he calls "liquid modernity," a term that means in part that individual identity formation is no longer the once-for-all, hard-and-fast creation of personal identity (religion included) but a situation where identity formation (religion included) is a dynamic, fluid endeavor that may last a lifetime. Everything about our lives changes regularly—residence, occupation, family situation, and more—successfully navigating such cultures requires one to be flexible and multi skilled. In fact, says Bauman, flexibility has replaced solidity as the most desired characteristic of successful identity formation. (2014, 8–9)

This identity formation, developed in the context of critical self-reflection for engagement in a pluralistic society, brings us back to a few foundational truths about ourselves as children of God.

First, we are created in and to bear the divine image (Gen 1:26–30). Though we marred this image with sin, Jesus came to save us and restore us to our rightful place as God's children. Second, our election to be children of God redeemed by Christ's sacrifice was not only for our benefit, but also that we might be witnesses to that salvation. As George Hunsberger points out multiple times (most succinctly in *Bearing the Witness of the Spirit*, 1998, 45–112), in Lesslie Newbigin's search to understand the purpose of election, he unpacks that we are not elected to something (salvation) but rather for something (service to salvation as witnesses). This leads to the third point: understanding this identity naturally draws us into engagement with a world that operates within its free choice to accept or reject God. It is a freedom of choice necessitated by free will and that functions in the plurality that is needed for the church to honestly engage its neighbors in a dialogue of equal partners.

Thus, critical self-reflection is the groundwork and mentality needed to move into our next key component of this opportunity of plurality: witnessing with a public voice.

Public witness

Once we have a grasp on our context—learning as we go along—and critically self-reflect to have a better hold on our identity and the beliefs of others, we can begin to witness to our faith on mutual ground in the public sphere. The first two pieces give us the credibility, exhibit the respect we have for the beliefs of others, and allow space for us to speak openly about our faith commitment. Hence, with those two clearly demonstrated, we can begin to speak openly in the public sphere about God, Jesus Christ, and the implications of Christian faith.

It is important to note in this stage that the public sphere is not the place for disputes about hermeneutics, theology, or doctrine; these are internal discussions that should be had within the body of Christ and not when interacting with those to whom we are witnessing. With that said, there are two key elements to this public witnessing: what narrative we tell, and countering the predominant worldviews/mentalities (both in us and in our culture).

We exist in a culture of narratives. Even as some may dismiss the metanarrative, they are still telling a narrative, albeit an anti-metanarrative one (Grenz 1996, 162–66). In this context, we must seek to tell our own narrative in the midst of a plurality of narratives. This plurality of narratives is the context that we must engage in order to exert a Christian voice into the complex public sphere of our culture. "The complex plurality of faith stories cannot be reduced to a clean competition of truths, for the simple reason that this plurality is part of an even more complex network of interactions between religion and rationality" (Hoedemaker 1998, 54).

This plurality is complex and encompasses the relationships and beliefs that surround and interact with our lives on a daily basis. Newbigin, in his discussion of history and Jesus as the linchpin by which all of history turns, points out that the Bible is not just God's story to us but also God's story about us—giving us identity, direction, and purpose (1989, 89–115). The narrative of Jesus, what he has to say about history and about us, is what we are supposed to bear witness to before the eyes of a world searching for answers.

In this witness, we take on the identity not only of God's children, but also as his instruments of revelation to the world. This revelation is not something that can be done alone; rather, it requires that we are part of a community of revelation, as seen in the incarnational church (though not always in the physical one). It is, then, in our community of revelation lived out in culture that the incarnation is made known to each society through God's chosen people. "In our incarnational understanding of the mission of the church, we assert that God intended to have his grace known through human instruments in the events of human history" (Guder 1985, 116). Thus, the narrative we tell is the narrative of God, active in the world, through God's chosen people.

When a choice is made to believe in God, it must be made in reasonably full knowledge of what we are choosing and what we are intentionally not choosing. While we can study other belief choices to know about them, the only way to truly know God is to experience God. Intellectual knowledge about God can be debated, but experiential knowledge of God provides a new plausibility structure by which Christians are enabled to engage the plural societies in which we live. Our job, then, is to build relationships and through those relationships expose others to the experience of God and what it is like to live in a personal relationship with God. In other words, we live incarnationally in order to begin discipling all nations—that we might baptize them in the names of the Trinity, teaching them all that we have learned from Jesus, as we go about our lives (Matt 28:19–20). It is with this witness that we also approach the two mentalities that have so long existed within the church in Western culture: society of the church (Taylor's S1) or society without the church (Taylors S2).

Recent history has trapped most churches in one of two mentalities: either they are still existing in the Christendom mentality, where the church is a major component next to government in orchestrating the daily lives of the community, or the Enlightenment mentality, where the church has no place in the public realms of daily life. The reality of today is that neither of these mentalities is true—the church neither operates fully in the public nor fully in the private spheres, but partially in both. Contrarily, in our embracing of plurality we can begin to operate as the church is intended—fully in both.

The Christendom mentality, inaugurated by Constantine and generally serving as the foundation of Western culture from the fourth century until the modern period (sixteenth century and beyond), was a time when the church and the state worked side-by-side for the general operation of society—dictating matters of life for men and women all over Europe. There was no room for choice since the church was the dominant religious force (part of what created problems in the Protestant Reformation). In Ryan Bolger's book, *The Gospel after Christendom*, he begins with the assumption that Christendom is no more (2012, xxvii–xliv). Yet many churches still operate with the mentality that the church has a central place in the public sphere to the point that they would not allow any other forms of belief to have a public voice. This mentality is a barrier to the fully free exercise of the will. Our present culture of plurality is one of multiple belief choices. It is in this choice that the public voice of the church is to be exercised, alongside the voices of other belief choices. It is the option between Christianity and other religions within the public sphere that makes any choice of Christianity an exercising of free will. Thus, we must eliminate the mentality of Christianity as the only public choice (as existed within Christendom).

The other mentality, the Enlightenment, would disassociate Christianity from any public discourse. This mentality would see the church relegated to the private sphere, depending on the state to secure our "rights" and allowing it to subsume our faith (Meadows 2018, 34–36). This idea of the Enlightenment—that faith is a private matter—has so consumed our psyche that we often leave our faith inside the church building, visiting it only at the scheduled times. Yet when we engage the world on matters of beliefs without bringing our faith into the matter, then we have entered a conversation unevenly. We have seceded the ground of faith and belief to others, failing to respect both the Lord who gave us this faith and the other who seeks to know our faith and make their faith known. We cannot enter into proper conversation or dialogue on these grounds, nor does it allow us to engage other Christians as brothers and sisters in Christ, for we have abdicated our authority and voice for the sake of a false narrative of the Enlightenment.

In toto, we must fight the mentalities of Christendom and the Enlightenment that exist within our churches, reaching into the world with a public voice based upon the incarnational witness of God's story for all of creation. Doing such will bind us together with those of like spirit in Christ.

Unity

As briefly mentioned above, many disputes about issues of hermeneutics, theology, or doctrine exist throughout the body of Christ—as seen in the major traditions and the various denominations. In the embrace of plurality in the public sphere, we take on the mentality of acceptance of the theological other within the body of Christ. This means taking the same process—learning about them, critically self-reflecting with what we have learned, and then telling them about our position—in order that we may discuss these differences rather than argue about them. In this, we can begin to embody the image of God's people living united (Ps 133). As well, it provides ground on which to seek, find, and unite with the good elements of God's general revelation that exist within culture.

While our divisions may seem important to us, they are issues of human construct[8] and concern (until they fall into heresy, of which disunity is one). Christ prayed for the unity of his followers, mirroring the unity of the Father and Son. So too should we be united to the Father through the Son and with each other, so that we may fulfill his call to witness of him throughout the world (John 17:20–26). This unity of all of the followers of Christ comes about as we have all been made equals in Christ, called to service and love of each other and the world (Matt 23:8–12).

Likewise, Paul picks up on this path toward unity in Christ repeatedly throughout his letters. Whether in the image of the body united and working together for the sake of Christ (Rom 12: 3–8; 1 Cor 3:12–31), or as children of God (Gal 3:23–4:7), or the concept of reconciling our differences and working out maturity in Christ (Eph 2:11–22; 4:1–16), all these various examples bear the mark of siblinghood in Christ that we all must wear. This will bring us to forgiveness, peace, and unity in love for one another out of the love of Christ. Like Paul said, "Bear with each other and forgive one another if any of you has a grievance against someone. Forgive as the Lord forgave you. And over all these virtues put love, which binds them all together in perfect unity" (Col 3:13–14 NIV).

Paul isn't the only one to preach unity. Peter discusses unity in one of his letters, saying, "Finally, all of you, be like-minded, be sympathetic, love one another, be compassionate and humble" (1 Pet 3:8 NIV). This whole epistle is about how we should live when in relationship with each other and engaging the work that God has directed us to complete. Likewise, John tells us that we know we are in God and God is in us when we exercise love; and when we see love in others, we are seeing God in them as well (1 John 4:7–21). Thus, being marked by love and persevering in relationship is how we are to live together as brothers and sisters in Christ throughout the world.

All of these Scripture references point to unity being an essential part of the life of the body of Christ and its public witness. If we take on the same

---

8 Berger and Luckmann (1966) argue "that reality is socially constructed," and thus all the phenomena of that reality are of social construction as well (1). Therefore, the phenomena of hermeneutical, theological, and doctrinal differences are constructed elements of the reality in which we live today. While this does not negate their importance to us today, it does force us to think of these differences within the larger kingdom of God, not just within our own times. This larger vision should put these differences in perspective as importance issues of our day, but not something that should destroy the unity of the body of Christ.

mentality we use to engage the watching world, we can begin to recover the unity that has alluded us for so long. The world will then know that we are Christ's disciples by our love for one another (John 13:35).

In summary, what we have here is an attitude of humbly respecting our mutual partners in the public sphere of religious discussion. This respect comes from studying our context (necessitating a learner's heart), a critical self-reflection (developing a firm identity), a public witness (based in a foundation of conviction), and a unity that speaks to the truth of God's Word for all of creation. This leads us to a mentality of embracing the plurality of religion that surrounds us, in the same manner as our scriptural heritage would model for us, so that the witness of Jesus Christ may be seen and heard by all, and they too may experience the life-changing relationship with God.

Implications and Applications

While this new mentality of embrace is good in theory, we must consider what it means for our churches and how to actually apply it to our interactions with the rest of society. In order to do that, we must turn our attention to some implications and applications of this embracing of plurality.

Implications

First off, the implication of such an embrace is the development of a new mentality toward society and the place of the church in culture. No longer can we fear the plurality of belief and fight against secularization, for the reality of our culture is that both of these are present. Instead, if we can start looking at this plurality as an opportunity to regain ground in the public sphere that was seceded during the Enlightenment, then we can look at the plurality of belief as a beneficial component of our society. Here is how we must begin: study the Bible as the preparation we need to be fully invested in the public discourse of our communities, see religious choice (choice to belief or nonbelief) as a good thing, and view the theological other as my sibling in Christ and the religious other as a partner in dialogue.

Such an embrace then requires that we be open and honest about our faith choices and struggles—that we be vulnerable. This vulnerability exposes us to being publicly hurt, but we must take solace in the fact that Christ too was publicly betrayed and bears the marks of his vulnerability on the Cross. It is the Cross that we must turn to in our vulnerability in order to endure and humbly forgive those that may hurt us.

As well, this embrace requires that we have a deep conviction of our own beliefs. We must be prepared to give an answer for the hope we have in Christ Jesus (1 Pet 3:15b), approaching society with the conviction and assurance of our beliefs. Such conviction may be met with questions. In the embrace of plurality, however, questions are a welcome component of relevance in the public sphere. This embrace requires that we be engaged in society, which is what drives us now to the consideration of applications.

Applications

While a new mentality full of humility, vulnerability, openness, and conviction is an important part of embracing plurality in society, it is meaningless without specific ways of applying this new mentality to the church as it reestablishes its voice in the public sphere.

For the church to embrace plurality, it must first be publicly informed and engaged with culture. This means that congregations must be taught how to read the news more fully—watching or reading from different perspectives to get a fuller picture of the relevant stories of society. Once we know how to gain a fuller picture of the situation, we must be taught how to investigate Scripture to learn what God says about the relevant issues and topics of society.

This then drives us toward communal discernment, in small groups and even as the larger congregation, to determine what God is doing and how God is leading the church to be engaged with its society. Only then is the church ready to march into the public sphere and engage important topics and issues within the larger society. While this process may seem long and complicated, with practice it will happen faster and faster, to the point where it becomes the natural process by which a congregation and its individual members engage the surrounding world.

Since we are no longer in a pre-Reformation Christendom period, where one church (Roman Catholicism) controls all of Western Christianity, a problem exists with this process when congregations or Christian organizations reach differing biblically based conclusions on the same issue—for instance, Liberty University and Sojourners engaging the public sphere on an issue like immigration. Both have biblical foundations for their arguments and both have a vested interest and relevance to share their positions publicly. But the public sphere is not the place for them to debate these positions; rather they should acknowledge the other as their fellow laborer in Christ, though they disagree on the issue at hand.

It is much like when my brother and I disagree over sports (usually our hometown St. Louis Cardinals or Blues). We fight about it (in the private spheres of our homes or personal communications), we may even yell at each other, but at the end of the day we hug and go home because we are still brothers and that supersedes any disagreement we may have. This fact of our mutual siblinghood in Christ must outweigh our disagreements, especially in the public sphere (failure in siblinghood leads to a diminishing of the gospel, as disunity is a sin). Thus, when Christians disagree on issues in the public sphere, the disagreement should be discussed in private conversations and interactions, while publicly we acknowledge our difference of opinion but keep primary the reality that we are all part of the same body of Christ.

A second application point concerns specific dialogue on issues of belief choice. While beliefs will be exercised in the engagement of society on key issues—like public initiatives and working together on projects—a time will come when the formal conversation about belief choice will happen. We must bind together with others (both other Christians and other religions) to assert our right to state our belief choice and defend the rights of all to do the same. In these conversations, it is essential that the church exercise a listening-before-speaking approach, showing the love and respect of the other by giving them space first to express their belief choice. In kind, it is then our turn to speak with conviction about our belief choice, not solely in order to contradict their perspective or to convert them (though we pray this will happen), but to tell the story of God.

It is in telling this story that we pray they will experience God too and begin to move closer to a relationship with God. The Holy Spirit convicts and converts; it is our job to bring others into contact with the Holy Spirit. For such a dialogue, then, we must develop language that is understandable by all—negotiating with our conversation partner about what we mean by certain words and eliminating language that is too Christendom-focused or Enlightenment-focused.

The last application point is specifically for the leaders of churches in the move to embrace—we must model and teach this embrace throughout our lives and ministries. This means that we must first practice both the mentality and the activity of embracing religious plurality in society, showing people through our lives that the opportunity of secularization exists right before us. We must humbly and vulnerably be engaged in mutual dialogue with those of other belief choices, doing so for all the rest of the church to see. Once we have modeled this in our own lives, then we have the right to teach about it from the pulpit and lecture halls of our churches and schools.

It is only in the adopting of the mentality of embracing plurality, specifically applying it to our lives and churches, that we will regain our place of prominence in the public sphere and again bear fruitful witness before the West and the rest of the watching world.

References

Berger, Peter L., ed. 1999. *The Desecularization of the World: Resurgent Religion and World Politics*. Washington, DC: Ethics and Public Policy Center.

Berger, Peter L., Grace Davie, and Effie Fokas. 2008. *Religious America, Secular Europe? A Theme and Variations*. Burlington, VT: Ashgate Publishing.

Berger, Peter L., and Thomas Luckmann. 1966. *The Social Construction of Reality: A Treatise in the Sociology of Knowledge*. Garden City, NJ: Doubleday & Company.

Bolger, Ryan. 2012. *The Gospel after Christendom: New Voices, New Cultures, New Expressions*. Grand Rapids: Baker.

Gay, Craig M. 1998. *The Way of the (Modern) World: Or, Why It's Tempting to Live as if God Doesn't Exist*. Grand Rapids: Eerdmans.

Grenz, Stanley J. 1996. *A Primer on Postmodernism*. Grand Rapids: Eerdmans.

Guder, Darrell L. 1985. *Be My Witness: The Church's Mission, Message, and Messengers*. Grand Rapids: Eerdmans.

Hoedemaker, Bert. 1998. *Secularization and Mission: A Theological Essay*. Harrisburg, PA: Trinity Press International.

Hunsberger, George R. 1998. *Bearing the Witness of the Spirit: Lesslie Newbigin's Theology of Cultural Plurality*. Grand Rapids: Eerdmans.

Meadows, Philip R. 2018. "Christian Freedom in a Post-Christendom Society." *Wesleyan Theological Journal* 35 (1): 19–42.

Muck, Terry C. 2014. "The Christian Study of World Religion." In *Handbook of Religion: A Christian Engagement with Traditions, Teachings, and Practices*, edited by Terry Muck, Harold A. Netland, and Gerald R. McDermott, 3–10. Grand Rapids: Baker Academic.

Newbigin, Lesslie. 1966. *Honest Religion for Secular Man*. London: SCM.

———. 1989. *The Gospel in a Pluralist Society*. Grand Rapids: Eerdmans.

———. 1995. *The Open Secret: An Introduction to the Theology of Mission*. 2nd ed. Grand Rapids: Eerdmans.

Smith, Christian. 2017. Religion: *What It Is, How It Works, and Why It Matters*. Princeton, NJ: Princeton University Press.

Smith, Graeme. 2008. *A Short History of Secularism*. New York: I. B. Tauris.

Smith, James K. A. 2014. *How (Not) to Be Secular: Reading Charles Taylor*. Grand Rapids: Eerdmans.

Stark, Rodney, and Roger Finke. 2000. *Acts of Faith: Explaining the Human Side of Religion*. Berkeley: University of California.

Taylor, Charles. 2007. *A Secular Age.* Cambridge, MA: Belknap Press of Harvard University.

————. 2010. "The Meaning of Secularism." *The Hedgehog Review* 12, no. 3 (Fall).

Tennent, Timothy C. 2002. *Christianity at the Religious Roundtable: Evangelicalism in Conversation with Hinduism, Buddhism, and Islam.* Grand Rapids: Baker Academic.

————. 2019. "Biblical Faith and Other Faiths: Examination of Historical Views of Universal Revelation, General Revelation, and Prevenient Grace Operative in the Context of Other Religions." Presentation at the E. Stanley Jones School of World Mission and Evangelism Missiology Seminar, Asbury Theological Seminary, Wilmore, KY, February 6.

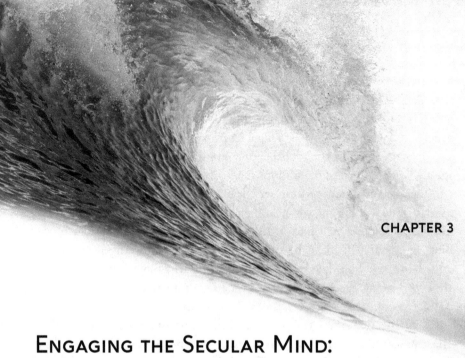

Engaging the Secular Mind:
An Urgent Call to the American Church

Raphael Anzenberger

Is the American evangelical church engaging the secular mind? If so, how? I must confess that, as a French-European, I have found much confusion on this topic in America. As such, I welcome the initiative of the EMS to revisit missions and evangelism in a secularizing world. It is urgent that we define exactly what we mean by "missions in a secularizing world." In this chapter, I will quickly frame the conversation, moving then to an assessment of current issues in cultural engagement with secularization. I will especially call the American church to focus its engagement in four areas: (1) telling the story of secularism correctly, (2) avoiding the culture wars, (3) moving beyond missiological theory, and (4) rediscovering the power of the gospel. I will conclude this chapter with a model of cultural engagement for a secularized world from Scripture.

Framing the Conversation

Secularization is a historical process with both positive and negative aspects. The secularization process started in the pre-Reformation age and continues to this day. The result of the secularization process is secularity—a snapshot, if you wish, of the secularization process at a specific time. Charles Taylor, in *A Secular Age* (2007, 4), defines secularity around three modes: one, as that which is retreating in the public space (plurality of beliefs); two, as a type of belief and practice which is or is not a regression (decline of religious beliefs); and three, as a certain kind of belief or commitment whose conditions in this age are being examined (conditions of religious belief).

The secularization process will lead to different stages of modes of secularity depending on which milieu of the West you find yourself. For instance, an atheist will find it difficult to defend his belief system in the Bible Belt, but will likely be at ease in Harvard. An evangelical, on the other hand, will find the reverse to be true. Both the Bible Belt and Harvard are experiencing the secularization process, but at different speeds, which translate to different stages or modes of secularity.

Secularization, then, is a process, while secularism is a system of belief. The two cannot be used synonymously. This process leads to pluralism (Thuswaldner 2014), which in itself modifies the state of secularity (plurality of beliefs, decline of religious beliefs, modification of the conditions of belief).

Our theme here, "Missions and Evangelism in a Secularizing World," seeks to assess the modes of secularity of the world in which we wish to engage, as well as the relevance of our cultural engagement. Talking about the latter, let us move now to an honest look at current issues regarding the way we engage the secular mind in the United States.

An Urgent Call!

I see four issues that are hampering our effectiveness in properly engaging the secular mind in the US: telling the story of secularization correctly, avoiding the culture wars, moving beyond missiological theory, and rediscovering the power of the gospel.

Telling the story correctly

The first issue arises with the way the story of secularization is told, both from the secularist and evangelical perspectives. Some secularists in the US wish that the classical secularization theory was true. To quote one of its proponents, Sam Harris, in his *Letter to a Christian Nation*,

> This letter is the product of failure—the failure of the many brilliant attacks upon religion that preceded it, the failure of our schools to announce the death of God in a way that each generation can understand, the failure of

the media to criticize the abject religious certainties of our public figures—failures great and small that have kept almost every society on this earth muddling over God and despising those who muddle differently. (2008, 91)

I would argue that the failure Harris refers to is not *a lack of* cultural engagement from the secularists, but another proof that secularization will not produce secularism but rather pluralism. Europe, for instance, is moving into a "post-secular age, which refers to the persistence of religious beliefs and practices in a society that has undergone a long process of secularization, in other words, European countries are becoming more secular and more religious, which Bérengère Massignon refers to as a 'second era of secularization.'"[1]

Why do Harris and other likeminded secularists fail to correctly asses the current situation? Put simply, they are not telling the story correctly. In the words of Taylor, Harris subscribes to the "subtraction story."

Concisely put, I mean by these stories of modernity in general, and secularity in particular, which explain them by human beings having lost, or sloughed off, or liberated themselves from certain earlier, confining horizons, or illusions, or limitations of knowledge. What emerges from this process—modernity or secularity—is to be understood in terms of underlying features of human nature which were there all along but had been impeded by what is now set aside. (2007, 22)

A common "subtraction theory" in vogue in the US attributes everything to disenchantment. Taylor explains:

First, science gave us "naturalistic" explanation of the world. And then people began to look for alternatives to God. But things didn't work that way. The new mechanistic science of the seventeenth century wasn't seen as necessarily threatening to God. It was to the enchanted universe and magic. It also began to pose a problem for particular providences. But there were important Christian motives for going the route of disenchantment. Darwin was not even on the horizon in the eighteenth century. (ibid., 26)

It would be too easy at this point to shift the blame squarely onto the secularists for not telling the story correctly. In his movie *God's Not Dead*, director Harold Cronk seeks to offer a sound apologetic by embodying secularism in the discourse of a philosophy professor who declares God a prescientific fiction. The evangelical believer will identify himself or herself

---

1 For more on the state of secularization in Europe, see Van De Poll (2013).

with the hero of the story, Harper, who delivers a solid rebuke of atheism amid an amphitheater full of students who are won over by the professor's secularism. Pause. Is this really how things are happening in the academic world? Are all philosophy professors in secular universities disciples of Christopher Hitchens or Michel Onfray?[2]

As Taylor rightly argues, we need to

> avoid the naïvetés on all sides: either that unbelief is just the falling away of any sense of fullness, or the betrayal of it (what theists sometimes are tempted to think of atheists); or that belief is just a set of theories attempting to make sense of experiences which we all have, and whose real nature can be understood purely immanently (what atheists are sometimes tempted to think about theists). (2007, 14)

We need to tell the story correctly on both sides of the equation by avoiding simple caricatures.

Avoiding the culture wars

The second issue in our cultural engagement with the secular mind lies in lumping that conversation with the current culture wars raging in some segments of the church. As Taylor rightly discerns,

> It seems that the fusion of faith, family values, and patriotism is still extremely important to one half of American society, that they are dismayed to see it challenged, both in its central values (e.g., the fight over abortion or gay marriage), and in the link between their faith and the polity (fights over school prayer, the phrase "under God," and the like). (2007, 527)

Effective missions praxis in a secularized age requires great care to resist blurring the lines between cultural engagement and political engagement. As Bruce Ashford rightly acknowledges,

> Over the course of the past half-century, many American evangelicals have put their eggs in the basket of short-term political activism—with the emphasis on the political and the short-term.... We reduced culture to politics, and politics to short-term activism, assuming a large part of the remedy to our social and cultural ills lies in a quick political fix. Repeatedly, we've treated each presidential election or midterm election as the one that—despite all historical evidence to the contrary—will finally deliver our hopes and ease our fears. (2017, 96)

---

2 Leading voices of the New Atheism movement.

It is urgent to redefine the condition of our predicament, to recreate space in our structure of plausibilities for fresh articulation of secularity and religion. As Newbigin rightly asserts,

> There are at least three ways in which the opposition between religion and the secular is referred to in current Christian writing. Firstly, a secular *society* is described as one in which the citizen is not subject to pressure from the state, or from the organs of society, to conform to a particular set of beliefs. Secondly, a secular *ethic* is described as one which does not subordinate the actual concrete decision to an alleged supra-natural law or standard but permits it to be made on the basis of the empirical realities of the situation in each case. Thirdly, a secular *style* of life for the Christian is described as one which does not turn away from the world to seek God but finds God by involvement in the life of the world. I hope that the discussion of these three issues will help us make more precise distinctions, and to indicate the sense in which a Christian must still be a religious man and a secular man at the same time. (1996, 123)

Secularization, better understood in both its positive and negative outcomes, can help us seek ways to be whole—both a secular man and a religious man at the same time without giving in to secularism or retreating into our evangelical fortresses.

Moving beyond missiological theory

A third issue with our current engagement with the secular mind is looking at the different facets of secularism (be it atheism, hedonism, naturalism, or any other "ism") on the pure plane of theory and, as a result, developing an apologetics that engages only the mind on a rational level. Some call it "worldview comparison." The idea is simple: probe the secular worldview, push it toward its logical conclusion, and urge that Christianity is a better—nay, a superior—worldview.[3] But will this translate into effective evangelism and missions? What is the link between worldview and the proclamation of the gospel, which is at the core of our biblical mandate? Jacques Ellul explains,

> The word is of the order of truth; it is located in the sphere of truth. It can also at the same time be falsehood if it does not speak this truth. For me,

---

3 I am not disregarding the importance of this contribution to the field of apologetics by Francis Schaeffer. His approach was anchored in hospitality and relationships, which were conducive to bringing the seeker to a fuller understanding of the call of God on one's life (propositional truth imbedded in relational truth). Disembodying Schaeffer's approach to a pure confrontation of worldviews would not do justice to the legacy of L'Abri.

this possibility results precisely from the fact that the human word is a response to the Word of God. In this response it can lie. It is never dictated by God's Word. It has its own autonomy as we ourselves do, and thus it can say things different from what it hears in God's Word.... Seeing is of the order of reality and is indispensable if we are to grasp the world. It sets us in the world and incites us to act in it. It does not lead to truth, and it does not give meaning. The word is what can give meaning to what we see. Seeing enables me to apprehend at a stroke all that reality presents to us and that the word is ill-equipped to describe. But the word (I am thinking of poetry), with reference to the real, can bring out what is hidden in it. The two things cannot be separated. Truth must incarnate itself in reality; reality is empty without truth. If truth is the unfolding of meaning, this is the meaning of what we see to be real and not phantom. This is how it is with us. (1989, 23–24)

The word is of the order of truth; seeing is of the order of reality. What is the link between the two? The *word* is what can give meaning to what we see. In other words, Christianity is foremost a voice that speaks into *worldviews*, and calls humans to repent for having assumed that they know what truth is all about. "He who is of the truth listens to my voice," says Jesus to Pilate. Remaining on the plane of worldview comparison will never lead us to confrontation with truth, but only to perspective about reality. Proclamation, on the other hand, will either lead to obedience or rebellion. Pilate opted for rebellion. "This is how it is with us," says Ellul.

So how shall we address the different facets of secularism? Not as competing worldviews (or theories about reality), but as lived conditions. As Taylor argues,

In order to get a little bit clearer on this level, I want to talk about belief and unbelief, not as rival theories, that is, ways that people account for existence, or morality, whether by God or by something in nature, or whatever. Rather what I want to do is focus attention on the different kinds of lived experience involved in understanding your life in one way or the other, on what it's like to live as a believer or an unbeliever. (2007, 4)

Taylor goes on to describe the modality of this lived condition in a secular society:

There is a kind of stabilized middle condition, to which we often aspire. This is one where we have found a way to escape the forms of negation, exile, emptiness, without having reached fullness. We come to terms with the middle position, often through some stable, even routine order in life, in which we are doing things which have some meaning for us; for instance, which contribute to our ordinary happiness, or which are fulfilling in various ways, or which contribute to what we conceive of as the good. Or often, in the best scenario, all three: for instance, we strive to live happily with spouse and children, while practicing a vocation which we find fulfilling, and also which constitutes an obvious contribution to human welfare. (2007, 6)

The different facets of secularism are all just a fruitless attempt by humans to find fullness, meaning, and happiness, while running away from negation, exile, and emptiness.

As a result, missions and evangelism in the secularizing West must move beyond the theory stage to address the particular lived condition of that stage—whether it is deep ecology or the American dream. We speak truth into visions of realities that assume to know the whole story. Evangelism is about calling the secular human to repentance of dead works and to faith in the living God, where true fullness awaits.

Rediscovering the power of the Gospel

The fourth and last issue related to our current engagement of the secular mind lies in the gospel itself. Do we still believe that the gospel is the power of salvation for those who will hear it (Rom 1:16)—even the secularist? As a French evangelist, let me tell you that I have every reason to believe it still does![4] Let me also tell you how surprised I am to hear some who are skeptical about the possibility of evangelizing secularists! Despite what your preferred news media tells you, there is still hope in the gospel!

There is nothing new under the sun. Secularism is just another take on what it means to live *sicut Deus*, in the likeness of God, rather than *imago Dei*, in the image of God. As Bonhoeffer rightly argued in his lectures at the University of Berlin in the winter semester of 1932–33,

Thus, for their knowledge of God human beings renounce the word of God that approaches them again and again out of the inviolable center and boundary of life; they renounce the life that comes from this word

---

4 Currently, France has the second-fastest rate of growth in evangelicalism in Europe. A new church is planted every ten days. See the 2017 statistical report on church planting compiled by the National Council of French Evangelicals (http://www.1pour10000.fr/download.php?fil_id=29&nom=livret_2017_statistiques_cnef_daniel_liechti.pdf&fichier=public_files/file/livret_2017_statistiques_cnef_daniel_liechti.pdf).

and grab it for themselves. They themselves stand in the center. This is disobedience of service, the will to be creator in the semblance of being a creature, being dead in the semblance of life. (1997, 117)

Truth against truth—God's truth against the serpent's truth. God's truth tied to the prohibition, the serpent's truth tied to the promise, God's truth pointing to my limit, the serpent's truth pointing to my unlimitedness—both of them truth, that is, both originating with God, God against God. And this second god is likewise the god of the promise to humankind to be *sicut deus*....*Imago dei*—bound to the word of the Creator and deriving life from the Creator; *sicut deus*—bound to the depths of its own knowledge of God, of good and evil. (ibid., 113)

Now humankind stands in the middle, with no limit. Standing in the middle means living from its own resources and no longer from the center. Having no limit means being alone. To be in the center and to be alone means to be *sicut deus*. It now lives out of its own resources, creates its own life, is its own creator; it no longer needs the Creator, it has itself become creator, inasmuch as it creates its own life. Thereby its creatureliness is eliminated, destroyed. (ibid., 115)

The issue is that humans live in the middle of the story and think that they are both *alpha* and *omega*. Secularism is only another take on this agelong pattern of humans being *sicut Deus*. Amid this certainty resounds God's question to humanity: "Adam, where are you?" This is what drives evangelism and missions. The gospel story reminds us that fullness and exile are only reconciled at the Cross, where both become center: "Christ redeemed us from the curse of the law [exile] by becoming a curse for us—for it is written, 'Cursed is everyone who is hanged on a tree'—so that in Christ Jesus the blessing of Abraham might come to the Gentiles, so that we might receive the promised Spirit through faith [fullness]" (Gal 3:13–14 ESV).

"Adam, where are you?" This was God's question to Adam in the beginning. It is still God's question to humans today, and it will continue to be until the end of this age. There is power in the gospel to save those who are trapped in their middle condition—not only to the secularists outside the church but also to the secularist Christians inside the church. As Jen Pollock Michel rightly observes,

> ...secularism is not the problem "out there." Instead, every Sunday morning, it is "secular" people filling our pews. They attest to loving Jesus—but accept "no final goals beyond human flourishing, nor any allegiance to anything else beyond this flourishing." They pray for God's

kingdom to come—and imagine the advent of their own happiness. In the secular age, God becomes the guarantor of our best life now. (2017, 117)

Perhaps the church would be wise to first clearly retell the story of the gospel inside its walls before venturing outside and potentially confusing the world with its erroneous articulations of belief.[5]

Four praxis that we must urgently recover in order to carry missions and evangelism well in a secularizing West include telling the story correctly, avoiding the culture wars, moving beyond missiological theory, and rediscovering the power of the gospel. Now that we have framed the conversation, defined the terms, and assessed issues in current cultural engagement toward secularism, Scripture will help us find our way home.

An Example of Cultural Engagement

The missional hermeneutical spiral encourages us to bring our ideas, or lack thereof, to the text of Scripture—from context to text to context. We surveyed the context; we now turn to the text before returning to our context, hence cultivating what John Stott describes as "double listening": called to listen both to the Word of God and to today's world.

Let us listen to the words of our Lord Jesus, as he engaged a skeptical Nathanael about the reality of the kingdom to come.

> The next day Jesus decided to go to Galilee. He found Philip and said to him, "Follow me." Now Philip was from Bethsaida, the city of Andrew and Peter. Philip found Nathanael and said to him, "We have found him of whom Moses in the Law and also the prophets wrote, Jesus of Nazareth, the son of Joseph." Nathanael said to him, "Can anything good come out of Nazareth?" Philip said to him, "Come and see." (John 1:43–46 ESV)

I would argue that Nathanael embodies three marks of secular humanity: individualism, cynicism, and pragmatism. Let's see how Jesus reaches out to him, and how this can in turn inform our praxis for missions today.

Individualism: "I see you!"

The story of Nathanael starts with him sitting under a fig tree, watching the world. Alone. What is he thinking about? We do not know. The text does not say. He may be wrestling with questions about origin (Where do I come

---

5 The reader will find helpful insights in *Our Secular Age: Ten Years of Reading and Applying Charles Taylor* (Ashford 2017).

from?), meaning (What am I doing here?), or purpose (Where do I go from here?). He may be questioning his lived condition (What is fullness? How can I experience it?). The fact of the matter is that Nathanael is alone, and he frames reality from the vantage of what he can see, under the fig tree.

Taylor reminds us that our current epoch is characterized by the "age of authenticity"—an age of "expressive individualism" (2007, 299).

> And, crucially, this is a culture informed by an ethic of authenticity. I have to discover my route to wholeness and spiritual depth. The focus is on the individual, and on his/her experience. Spirituality must speak to this experience. The basic mode of spiritual life is thus the quest, as Roof argues. It is a quest which can't start with a priori exclusions or inescapable starting points, which could pre-empt this experience. (ibid., 507)

Nathanael is on a quest. But Jesus precedes him in his quest: "Before Philip called you, when you were under the fig tree, I saw you" (John 1:48b ESV). I saw you! Before you were, I am. Before you saw, I see— from all eternity.

What does it mean for today? Nothing but the obvious: *missio Dei* precedes *missio ecclesiae*. We teach this to those who seek the person of peace among unreached people groups. We remember that Jesus precedes us also here in the West. He sees secularists, such as Harris, and is neither taken off guard or unable to speak into their predicament. He sees them. He sees us!

Cynicism: "I know you!"

The second mark of the secular mind is *cynicism*.

> Philip found Nathanael and said to him, "We have found him of whom Moses in the Law and also the prophets wrote, Jesus of Nazareth, the son of Joseph." Nathanael said to him, "Can anything good come out of Nazareth?" Philip said to him, "Come and see." (John 1:45–46 ESV)

"Can anything good come out of Nazareth?" From Nathanael's worldview, nothing good can come out of Nazareth. Jerusalem perhaps; Rome surely. But Nazareth? Nathanael is trapped in his own story, his vision of reality defined from under the fig tree. Disconnected from history, he does not remember another story, the great story—that of old time, that of the coming of the Messiah announced by Moses and the prophets. Nathanael forgot the story. His vision of the possible is reduced to what he sees. For only what he can see is real (*individualism*). He judges Philip for failing to see the obvious. In a spirit of *sicut Deus*, Nathanael infers that he knows and that Philip does not. Nothing good can come out of Nazareth—everybody knows this...but Philip! Yet Philip remains confident that Nathanael wants more and needs more.

What does this mean for today? Jean-Paul Sartre once famously said that even if God existed, that would make no difference (1996, 77). But how does he know? Has he come and seen for himself? Trapped in the immanent frame, the secular mind concludes that the *default* option is unbelief. Yet, as Taylor rightly demonstrates, this is not the *only* logical option. Some are open to transcendence, and some move to closure (Taylor 2007, 566, 595). The buffered-self operates in both directions. Individualism combined with cynicism might lead us to think that the situation is so desperate that no one can reach the secular mind. Are we growing cynical by the same token?

As Taylor argues, lumping together the spiritual quest of the age of authenticity with

> invitations to self-absorption, without concern for anything beyond the agent, whether the surrounding society, or the transcendent...is an illusion which arises from the often-raucous debate between those whose sense of religious authority is offended by this kind of quest, on one hand, and the proponents of the most self- and immanent-centered forms, on the other, each of which likes to target the other as their main rival. (ibid., 508)

The church needs more visionaries like Philip who will see beyond the offense of credulity to invite the secular humanity to pursue his quest. "Come and see" for yourself—move beyond your cynicism and explore other possibilities! The church needs to be the place where today's Philips invite the Nathanaels to come and see fullness embodied. As Newbigin rightly argues,

> The Gospel offers an understanding of the human situation which makes it possible to be filled with a hope which is both eager and patient even in the most hopeless situations.
>
> It is only as we are truly "indwelling" the Gospel story, only as we are so deeply involved in the life of the community which is shaped by this story that it becomes our real "plausibility structure," that we are able steadily and confidently to live in this attitude of eager hope....That is why I am suggesting that the only possible hermeneutic of the Gospel is a congregation which believes it. (1989, 232)

Missions and evangelism can occur in a secularizing West—but not alone. They need to occur together, in missions! Newbigin's statement raises a profound question about the nature of the church as embodying and indwelling the gospel story. The conversation is not finished. There is still much to say about how the church can be *missional*, in the true sense of the term.

Pragmatism: "I call you!"

Rather than being offended, Philip boldly invites Nathanael to come and see Jesus. And Nathanael is happy to accept. His curiosity is piqued. In the words of Newbigin, Philip remembers that

> ...skepticism is not the active principle in the advance of knowledge. The active principle is the willingness to go out beyond what is certain, to listen to what is not yet clear, to search for what is hardly visible, to venture the affirmation which may prove to be wrong, but which may also prove to be the starting-point for new conquests of the mind. In the traditional language of Christianity, the name for that active principle is faith. (1996, 84)

As Nathanael, not knowingly, started his journey of faith (*pragmatism*), "Jesus saw Nathanael coming toward him and said of him: 'Behold, an Israelite indeed, in whom there is no deceit!' Nathanael said to him, 'How do you know me?'" (John 1:47–48a ESV). How strange it is for our Lord to compliment the cynic individual! Yet this affirmation of Jesus opens up a new reality for Nathanael. "I see you and I know you! Welcome, Nathanael!"

> Nathanael answered him, "Rabbi, you are the Son of God! You are the King of Israel!" Jesus answered him, "Because I said to you, 'I saw you under the fig tree,' do you believe? You will see greater things than these." And he said to him, "Truly, truly, I say to you, you will see heaven opened, and the angels of God ascending and descending on the Son of Man." (John 1:49–51 ESV)

Nathanael confesses that he does not know anymore. What suddenly appears evident is that "you are the Son of God!" This is the heart of repentance. "You are God, and I am not." From the spirit of *sicut Deus*, which knows it all, to the spirit of *imago Dei*, which confesses that only God knows it all. Nathanael repents from dead works and through faith in Jesus discovers that there is more to come: "You will see greater things that these"

(John 1:50b ESV). Jesus calls Nathanael to more—to life to the full. At last Nathanael becomes what he was predestined to be: *imago Dei*—a gift of God, a gift from God, to the world.

What does this mean for today? Taylor reminds us that

> …many young people are following their own spiritual instincts, as it were, but what are they looking for? Many are "looking for a more direct experience of the sacred, for greater immediacy, spontaneity, and spiritual depth," in the words of an astute observer of the American scene. This often springs from a profound dissatisfaction with a life encased entirely in the immanent order. The sense is that this life is empty, flat, devoid of higher purpose. (2007, 506)

There is hope! Many Nathanaels are looking for a more direct experience of the sacred, for greater immediacy, spontaneity, and spiritual depth. They are looking for a fullness that they are unable to find in their lived condition. "Come and see" for yourself, is as relevant of an invitation today as it was to Nathanael two thousand years ago. The personal encounter with Jesus will lead them to see greater things!

But what about transcendent truth? Is this pragmatic view of missions a concession to postmodernism? Not at all. Missions and evangelism in a secularizing West do not the end of the journey. If missions and evangelism do not lead to spiritual formation through solid disciple-making within community, it is neither biblical missions nor biblical evangelism. As Brett McCracken reminds us,

> Christianity requires the submission of one's individual will to the lordship of Christ. It is impossible to simultaneously assert the sovereignty of one's subjective spiritual path and the supremacy of Jesus Christ. We are either in Christ on his terms and by his grace, or we aren't. Christianity doesn't work on the terms of consumerism. (2017, 80)

As Nathanael journeyed through faith, he discovered not only the one who is truth (relational truth), but trusted that his words were true (propositional truth. Requiring a firm commitment to propositional truth as a necessary condition to encounter the living truth, however, tells us more about our philosophical presuppositions than what Scriptures requires.

We have now moved from context to text to context. Double listening requires us to listen to the world well, but also to the Word well. In this passage we see the evangelist John giving us a brilliant example of culture engagement, well suited for the secular mind. To the individualist, Jesus says: "I saw you before you saw me." You are not alone in your quest. To the cynic, Jesus declares: "I knew you before you ever knew me." You do not know the whole story. To the pragmatist, Jesus promises: "I call you to see greater things!" You can experience fullness in Jesus.

What better place than the church to offer a solid hermeneutic of the gospel to the secularist, so that he may receive life to the full. God asks, "Adam, where are you?" Jesus sees you, knows you, and calls you to see greater things!

Conclusion

After carefully framing the conversation, we assessed issues in current cultural engagement toward secularism to include (1) telling the story correctly, (2) avoiding the culture wars, (3) moving beyond missiological theory, and (4) rediscovering the power of the gospel. We have offered a model of cultural engagement from Scripture which reminded us that (1) Jesus precedes us in our cultural engagement, (2) the church is *still* the best hermeneutic of the gospel, and (3) evangelism within the continuum of spiritual formation in community can lead the skeptic to true discipleship.

God asks, "Adam, where are you?" Jesus responds, "I see you, know you, and call you to see greater things!"

It is urgent that the church in America recaptures the urgency of evangelism and missions in a secularizing West. Of course, many, if not all, would subscribe to the necessity of carrying the biblical mandate, but not all would define it as urgent. As a fellow evangelist speaking to other evangelists, I urge you to carry on the task of an evangelist. The fields are white for harvest (John 4:35). I pray that the church will see it. May the Lord bless the church in America!

References

Ashford, Bruce Riley. 2017. "Politics and Public Life in a Secular Age." In *Our Secular Age: Ten Years of Reading and Applying Charles Taylor*, edited by Collin Hansen, 87–98. Deerfield, IL: The Gospel Coalition

Bonhoeffer, Dietrich. 1997. *Creation and Fall: A Theological Exposition of Genesis 1–3*. Minneapolis: Fortress.

Ellul, Jacques. 1989. *What I Believe*. Grand Rapids: Eerdmans.

Harris, Sam. 2008. *Letters to a Christian Nation*. New York: Vintage Books.

McCracken, Brett. 2017. "Church Shopping with Charles Taylor." In *Our Secular Age: Ten Years of Reading and Applying Charles Taylor*, edited by Collin Hansen, 75–86. Deerfield, IL: The Gospel Coalition.

Newbigin, Lesslie. 1989. *The Gospel in a Pluralist Society*. Grand Rapids: Eerdmans.

———. 1996. *Honest Religion for Secular Man*. London: SCM Press.

Pollock Michel, Jen. 2017. "Whose Will Be Done? Human Flourishing in the Secular Age." In *Our Secular Age: Ten Years of Reading and Applying Charles Taylor*, edited by Collin Hansen, 113–24. Deerfield, IL: The Gospel Coalition.

Sartre, Jean-Paul. 1996. *L'Existentialisme est un Humanisme*. Paris: Gallimard.

Taylor, Charles. 2007. *A Secular Age*. Cambridge, MA: Harvard University Press.

Thuswaldner, Gregor. 2014. "A Conversation with Peter L. Berger: 'How My Views Have Changed.'" *The Cresset* 77 (3): 16–21. http://thecresset.org/2014/Lent/Thuswaldner_L14.html.

Van De Poll, Evert. 2013. *Europe and the Gospel: Past Influences, Current Developments, Mission Challenges*. London: Walter de Gruyter.

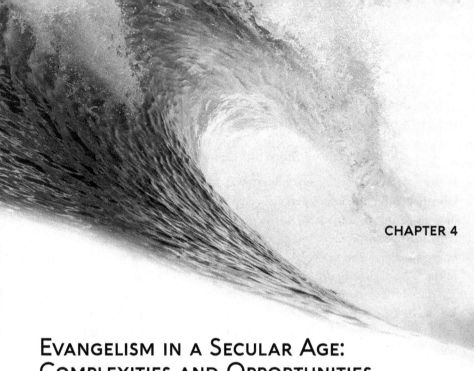

CHAPTER 4

Evangelism in a Secular Age: Complexities and Opportunities

W. Jay Moon

A farmer from Iowa went to visit a farmer from England recently. As expected, they compared notes on crop yields, soil productivity, weather patterns, etc. When–– the topic of the size of their respective farms came up, the Iowa farmer did not want to embarrass his English friend. A farm in Iowa may need two thousand acres for the farm business to be viable, whereas England simply does not have enough land to typically allow such large farms.

Trying to be subtle, the Iowan described the size of his farm by saying, "If I get in my truck in the morning and drive the perimeter of the farm, then I will not reach my home again until it is time for lunch."

The British man thought a minute and then responded, "I understand. I used to have a truck like that!"

The process of secularization, like farming, is complex, with multiple threads attached. When we simplify the discussion too quickly, we may talk past each other like two farmers comparing the size of their farms based on acreage or truck speed. In this chapter, I will discuss some of the complexities for evangelism in the twenty-first century.[1] In doing so, we will recognize that secularization is indeed an important topic for the church, but it is attached to other complexities.

Lack of Spiritual Conversations

If these complexities are not understood and addressed, then the average Christian is often confused about where to start sharing his or her faith or how to address questions in an increasingly secular and pluralistic world. A recent Barna survey found that "the average [American] adult says they only have about one spiritual conversation in a year.... For most Christians in the U.S., topics of faith come up less than once a month" (2018, 7).

This lack of evangelism is typified by John, a seminary student in the US, as he is about to cross the stage to receive the paper that would now call him a "Master of Divinity." While his church and parents are beaming with joy and pride at his achievement, he still has lingering doubts about his next step after graduation. In the back of his mind, he often asks himself, "Do I have the ability to rise up to the challenge that this first church ministry assignment is asking of me?"

The church is in decline and needs help. One of the major duties the church elders asked of John was to assist the church in evangelism. John muttered under his breath, "How can I teach others to evangelize if I don't know how to do it very well myself? The seminary prepared me to preach by giving me three preaching opportunities in class with feedback from peers and professors, but I never had three evangelism 'practice sessions' in class with any feedback!" To make things worse, when John tried outdated evangelistic practices, the encounters weren't pleasant, so he concluded, "I guess that means that I'm not called to be an evangelist, so I will simply let others do it!"

John's angst could be multiplied many times over in seminaries around the country. In this chapter, I will draw upon the results of a three-year research project with Knox Fellowship and Asbury Theological Seminary to help people like John understand the complexities of evangelism amid

---

1 Portions of this chapter are drawn from (and used with permission) *Practical Evangelism for the Twenty-First Century*, edited by W. Jay Moon (Nicholasville, KY: GlossaHouse and Digi-Books, 2017). This is available in print or Digi-book (a video-enhanced digital book available on the iBooks app on Mac devices).

secularization and then equip them both to share their faith and to train others to do the same.[2]

To describe this process, I will:

1. Sketch six complexities, and the resulting opportunities, for faith sharing in a secular world.
2. Focus on the complexity of pluralism.
3. Describe an emerging worldview in secular contexts.
4. Explain a training approach to help individuals practice evangelism as well as equip others to evangelize.

Starting with an understanding of these complexities in the twenty-first century will lay a foundation for equipping folks like John.

Six Complexities and Opportunities: SPIRIT

The beginning of the twenty-first century reveals a very different and more complex cultural landscape than the beginning of the twentieth century. The forces of globalization, immigration, and technology (to name a few) have created a very different environment for evangelism than when Bill Bright first created the "Four Spiritual Laws" and Billy Graham started his crusades. In order to discuss these complexities, I will group them under the acronym SPIRIT: Secularism, Pluralism, Individualism, Relativism, Identity, and Technology.

Like a Russian doll with smaller dolls stacked inside in successive layers, these six complexities are interconnected. Once we uncover these layers and respond appropriately to these complexities, the exciting discovery is that there are now new opportunities for evangelism that did not exist before! This provides fresh approaches to help John gain confidence to both practice and equip his church for evangelism.

First, I will briefly survey these complexities and resultant opportunities, one at a time.

Secularism

The Western world has sharply divided concerns that are regarded as sacred versus secular. In everyday life, then, secular discussions are often much more prominent for the average person in the public sector than discussions about

---

2 Knox Fellowship, established in 1991, is an interdenominational nonprofit corporation that "integrates work of evangelists, academics, and supporters to advance evangelism throughout U.S. Christianity" (knoxfellowship.com).

ultimate issues of heaven and hell. As a result, many do not perceive the church as relevant to their everyday needs and concerns. The rise of the de-churched population testifies to this.[3] Amid this onslaught of secularism that has pushed out religion from public discourse, the irony is that postmoderns now have a hunger for spirituality to address their deeper needs and concerns. In short, the scientific method does not address the deeper longings, pains, and desires that linger long after scientific theories have reached their limits (Motak 2009).

For the most meaningful aspects of life that include deep values and emotions, secular solutions are simply insufficient. For example, what scientific formula can be used to prove that you love someone or that your life has purpose to it? This provides an opportunity now to address these issues through "alternate plausibility structures," such as narratives (Newbigin 1989). While laws (based upon scientific plausibility structures) are often insufficient, narratives are robust enough to carry the weight of deeper values and meaning. Secularism now provides an opportunity for evangelists to consider the role of narrative for conveying the gospel, such that evangelists are now regarded as good storytellers who portray true stories that address the longings of the soul.

Like unstacking a Russian doll, the use of alternative narratives to reveal truth is connected to another complexity—pluralism.

Pluralism

In a previous century, evangelism was likened to a revival meeting, whereby people were called to return to their faith with new vigor. Evangelists assumed a largely Judeo-Christian background, such that appeals were made to "come home" to the faith of their fathers. In the twenty-first century, though, a Christian is likely to encounter a Hindu, Buddhist, Muslim, or atheist in his or her workplace or neighborhood. Evangelism, then, is not simply awakening people from their spiritual sloth; instead, the evangelist needs to address the assumptions of entirely different systems of both faith and culture.

Pluralism now provides an opportunity for evangelists to consider how they may have limited the gospel by their own cultural assumptions. Evangelists in the twentieth century assumed that the problem of sin

---

3 For an overview of recent research, see "Secularism Grows as More U.S. Christians Turn 'Churchless,'" Religion News Service, October 24, 2014, http://religionnews. com/2014/10/24/secularism-is-on-the-rise-as-more-u-s-christians-turn-churchless/.

resulted in guilt that separated humans from God. Jesus addressed this sin problem, accordingly, by becoming a sacrifice to restore the justice of God through his substitutionary atonement. This is true and biblical, yet it will not necessarily resonate with the plausibility structures of other worldviews. When encountering people from other religions who hold different worldview assumptions, we find that Jesus addresses a different set of problems based on fear/power or shame/honor worldview assumptions. Evangelists may, for the first time, understand how the gospel is much larger than they ever imagined, once they are willing to remove their own cultural limitations.[4] I will return to this shortly.

In a secular society, pluralism leads to new choices and options for religious faith, such that some parents are even hesitant to inculcate a faith in their children since they want to let their kids decide. Once again, we can unstack the Russian doll and notice the deeper connection between pluralism and another complexity—namely, individualism.

Individualism

The concept of the autonomous self was a seed planted in the soil of the Enlightenment that eventually came into full fruition in the twentieth century. Evangelistic approaches were often geared to offer salvation as largely an individual and personal transaction. Darrell Guder notes that this "has made salvation a private event by dividing 'my personal salvation' from the advent of God's healing reign all over the world" (1998, 92). Evangelists focused on merely individual decisions and personal faith journeys.

The irony of living in a hyper-individualistic world is that this creates a yearning for belonging in a community where everyone knows your name. A recent survey (Cigna 2018) of more than twenty thousand adults ages eighteen years and older revealed that nearly half of Americans report sometimes or always feeling alone (46 percent) or left out (47 percent). In addition, Generation Z (adults ages eighteen to twenty-two) is the loneliest generation and claims to be in worse health than older generations.

Postmoderns are yearning for community, since they want to be reassured in a fragmenting world and society that they belong to a family (Stott 1988). This yearning for community now offers twenty-first-century

---

4 For example, consider how a highly trained Western missionary had to relearn how to present the gospel when engaging African traditional religion, as described in Blaschke (2001).

evangelists an opportunity to express their faith through hospitality that is offered in small groups.

To engage individualism a bit deeper, though, the evangelist must also understand the natural connection to another complexity—relativism. Once again, the Russian doll reminds us that there is another layer underneath the present one.

Relativism

In the age of modernity (born out of the Enlightenment experiment), the scientific method of reasoning trumped all other approaches to truth. As a result, the "Four Spiritual Laws" were developed by Bill Bright in the twentieth century to articulate defensible laws that were circulated across university campuses with significant results. Today's students, though, often eschew this formulaic approach. The postmodern turn has made them skeptical of simplistic black-and-white answers that are universal, objective, and reliable (Bazargani and Larsari 2015, 90). While postmoderns often reject objective truth, they may adopt the other extreme of subjective truth, typified by the expression "Whatever!" This shift from a naive realist epistemology (everything is black and white) to an instrumentalist epistemology (everything is gray) results in postmodern Christians who are less confident to share their faith due to fears that they may be perceived as intolerant, extreme, or "imposing their faith" on others.

This complexity of relativism also provides an opportunity for evangelists to consider and appreciate the dangers in both extremes of the totally objective or totally subjective positions (as if these were the only options). This now provides an opportunity to describe and appreciate a third mediating option called a critical realist epistemology (there is an objective reality, but our understanding is limited; therefore we are labeling this "pinstripe") that avoids the extremes of the other two positions (Hiebert 1999). The "pinstripe" foundation, then, reinvigorates evangelists to have a bold humility (or a humble courage) as they share their faith.

To dig underneath the complexity of relativism, however, we must unstack the Russian doll again and find inside another complexity—identity.

Identity

In a previous century, people often found their identity based on geographical and familial ties. Evangelism, then, focused on engaging your neighbors and other "close by" acquaintances. Evangelism was often conducted by canvasing a neighborhood, and churches were formed based on the demographics of those living around the church.

In the twenty-first century, the acceleration of the above complexities has increased such that individuals often find their closest connections and identity based on networks tied to social media, workplace, or "third spaces" (e.g., gym, aerobics class, coffee shop, etc.). Geography does not often define identity as it once did. For example, millennials often feel more closely connected to those whom they regularly contact on social media who live fifty miles away as opposed to their neighbors who live fifty feet away! This now provides an opportunity to explore evangelistic opportunities through these new "bridges of God" (McGavran 1981) in their places of work, play, and social media.

The whole discussion of social media, once again, is undergirded by another layer of complexity in the twenty-first century—namely, technology. For the last time, we now unstack the Russian doll to describe how these shifts in identity are inherently connected to technological shifts.

Technology

The burgeoning of digital media has given rise to a pedagogical shift whereby people increasingly receive information through digital sources instead of print sources. Jonah Sachs (2012) calls this a "digitoral" learning preference, which recognizes that learners prefer to receive information and are most likely transformed when learning comes in oral forms (as opposed to merely print forms), mediated through digital media. For example, students are less likely to read books or tracts; rather, they greatly prefer more experiential learning approaches such as videos, role plays, skits, mealtime chats, and group discussions that address everyday encounters and struggles.

A conversation often attributed to Abe Lincoln, though likely spoken much later, says, "A woodsman was once asked, 'What would you do if you had just five minutes to chop down a tree?' He answered, 'I would spend the first two and a half minutes sharpening my axe!'"[5] Twenty-first-century millennials preparing to chop down a tree would likely spend the first two and a half minutes watching a YouTube video demonstration! Technology has drastically changed how we receive, process, remember, and then pass on information (Madinger 2013).

---

5 The first recorded evidence of this story appears in C. R. Jaccard, "Objectives and Philosophy of Public Affairs Education," in *Increasing Understanding of Public Problems and Policies: A Group Study of Four Topics in the Field of Extension Education* (Chicago: Farm Foundation, 1956), 12.

This learning-preference shift provides an opportunity for evangelists to learn and teach churches effective communication approaches from this "oral renaissance." Digital tools provide creative ways to share the gospel through images, videos, symbols, etc., in ways that were unimaginable in the twentieth century. Leonard Sweet describes the twenty-first century as the most poised generation to ignite revival due to the TGIF—Twitter, Google, iPhone, and Facebook (2012).

New opportunities for faith sharing have arisen via technological innovations like phone apps developed by Cru to help believers recognize this learning shift and engage people in spiritual discussions. For example, the Voke app is a "video-sharing app that uses short videos to help you start spiritual conversations with your friends," and the Soularium app uses a set of fifty images and five questions "that help people talk about their life and spiritual journey."[6]

Summary of Complexities/Opportunities

Table 1 summarizes the above-mentioned six complexities and resultant opportunities for evangelism in the twenty-first century.[7]

Complexity	Opportunity
Secularism	Narrative as alternate plausibility structure
Pluralism	Multi-worldview dimensions of the gospel
Individualism	Faith shared through hospitality in community
Relativism	"Pinstripe" understanding of truth
Identity	New bridges of God
Technology	Digit-oral learning approaches

Table 1: Complexities and Opportunities for Evangelism in the Twenty-First Century

---

6 "Apps & Tools," Cru website, www.cru.org/us/en/digitalministry.

7 The Knox/Asbury Seminary cohorts walk students through each of these complexities and then provide activities to engage the opportunities over a period of eight weeks. The detailed weekly curriculum is available at Moon, *Practical Evangelism*. In addition, a six-part video series is available at https://www.logos.com/product/148329/practical-evangelism-opportunities-for-the-21st-century. A trailer to the series is available at https://www.youtube.com/watch?v=Y-5FT3LUsFY&feature=youtu.be.

Each of these complexities are interconnected, as described above. For example, Peter Berger, who has spent a lifetime studying the process of secularization, argues that pluralism is the major change resulting from secularization.

> Our main mistake was that we misunderstood pluralism as just one factor supporting secularization; in fact, pluralism, the co-existence of different worldviews and value systems in the same society, is the major change brought about by modernity for the place of religion both in the minds of individuals and in the institutional order. (2014, ix)

Let us now turn our attention to this complexity of pluralism and focus on the new opportunities this provides for evangelism. This discussion will then provide a training approach to help John increase his competence and confidence for evangelism in a secular age.

Pluralism: Opportunities for Evangelism

To consider how to present the gospel in a pluralist society, New Testament theologian Brenda Colijn contends that there are various starting points to describe salvation in the New Testament.

> The New Testament does not develop a systematic doctrine of salvation. Instead, it presents us with a variety of pictures taken from different perspectives.... The variety of images attests to both the complexity of the human problem and its solution. No single picture is adequate to express the whole.... Each image is a picture of salvation from one perspective, posing and answering one set of questions. When seen together, they balance and qualify one another. We need all of them in order to gain a comprehensive understanding of salvation. (2010, 14–16)

To identify the starting point for evangelism in various contexts, Colijn develops twelve images of salvation from the New Testament that are theologically appropriate for various contexts. If the context is not taken into consideration, though, students will likely start with the image of salvation that is most resonant with their own culture. For example, someone from a guilt/justice worldview will likely connect with the penal-substitution image of salvation—which will likely fall on deaf ears, though, when evangelizing people from a shame/honor or fear/power worldview.[8]

Craig Ott notes that "one can begin with a biblical analogy that has the most common ground with the hearer's worldview, experience, and frame of reference" (2014, 359). Ott identifies four starting points for four different cultural contexts. Jayson Georges simplifies this to three worldviews, as he states, "Each cultural worldview is a unique blend of guilt, shame, and fear" (2016, 16).

To address the complexity of a pluralistic society, students need to be aware of and then address the worldview assumptions of these contexts. As summarized in table 2, each worldview considers differently the result of sin, solution in Jesus, and image of salvation.[9]

Worldview	Guilt/Justice	Shame/Honor	Fear/Power
Typical Location	West (North America, Europe)	East (Middle East, North Africa, Asia)	South (Sub-Saharan Africa, Tribal, Caribbean)
Sin's Result	Separation/Guilt	Shame	Fear/Curse/Bondage
Solution	Payment/Substitute	Restore/Cleanse/Honor	Deliverance
Image	Courtroom/Justice	Relationship/Cleansing	Power/Freedom

Table 2: Evangelism Differences amid Three Worldviews

As Georges recognizes, "Although guilt, shame, and fear are three distinct cultural outlooks, no culture can be completely characterized by only one. These three dynamics interplay and overlap in all societies" (ibid., 15). As a result, evangelists should be aware of all three cultural contexts and then be ready to adapt presentations of the gospel accordingly. Students now have the opportunity, for the first time perhaps, to understand how the gospel is larger than they ever imagined—once they are willing to remove their own cultural

---

8 This was my own experience of early attempts at evangelism in Ghana, West Africa, among the Builsa people, who largely held a fear/power worldview while I was from a guilt/justice worldview. They were not as interested in a gospel that addressed guilt; rather, they were extremely interested in Jesus' power to overcome spiritual forces. (See Moon 2009.)

9 This table draws from (modified slightly) Ott 2014, 357-74.

limitations. A brief understanding of each of these three worldviews is then necessary for twenty-first-century evangelists.

Guilt/justice worldview

In modern America, as well as in much of the West, the predominant worldview was characterized by guilt/justice. We engage in numerous jokes about the dishonesty of lawyers, but in truth we place a high value on legal order. Theologically, this worldview regards the problem of sin to create guilt, and the answer that Christ provides is justice or a restored right standing before God. Westerners may be moved by the biblical image of being judicially set free from our sins and offenses, like in a courtroom drama—so we've chosen the apostle Paul as our favorite narrator of the biblical story. He drops the gavel and proclaims, "You are absolved!"

Many in the world, however, do not see through the lenses of guilt and justice like so many Westerners do. There are other ways of perceiving the world, which we will call majority worldviews or "mega-traits." How others perceive the problem of sin and how they regard Jesus' solution to sin may be much different than your own worldview, but it makes sense to *them*.

Shame/honor worldview

Those who live in shame/honor societies are not likely to conceive of sin in the same way a Westerner does. Shame/honor societies are often collectivist cultures in which every person has an assigned role that is understood by the community. People's status is assigned or affirmed by the group based upon who they are—not upon what they do. Maintaining honor is the highest value to which individuals ascribe. The community functions as a kind of a personal credit service, assigning individuals particular ratings. Severe consequences are associated with violating the norms of the society (Georges 2016, 20–22). Both the strengths and the offenses of the society are interpreted more as collective actions. Thus a prominently recognized activity such as "honor killing" may be tolerable if it addresses communally accrued shame, restoring honor to the community, which views itself as a wounded party (ibid., 23).

The point is that evangelists among those with a shame/honor worldview need to recognize that they regard the effect of sin (shame) and the solution in Christ (honor restored as children of the King) very differently than those from a guilt/justice worldview. This will then result in a very different, yet contextual, approach to evangelism.

For example, in a shame/honor culture, evangelists may highlight that, before the fall of humanity, the Bible declares, "Adam and his wife were both naked, and they felt no shame" (Gen 2:25 NIV). One of the results of sin, then, was shame, as evidenced by Adam and Eve's first response after the fall: "Then the eyes of both of them were opened, and they realized they were naked; so they sewed fig leaves together and made coverings for themselves" (Gen 3:7 NIV). A gospel response may be more appropriately derived from a biblical story like the prodigal son, which portrays how God can remove shame and restore honor as a child of the Father again.

Fear/power worldview

Another large block of the world's peoples live in communities where supernatural engagement with the spirit world is commonplace. These are considered to be fear/power cultures. Major pockets of societies embrace this particular worldview all across the globe. Some adherents reside in shamanic societies or practice indigenous religious beliefs that we might refer to as primal or folk religion. In these settings, humans live in a world inhabited by spiritual forces; therefore they are in need of protection to overcome their fear.

Western evangelists ministering in these regions have traditionally spoken in terms of "high religion," often referring to theoretical principles. Their explanations didn't resonate with people who were wondering, "Why did I get sick?" "Why is there a drought?" "How can I get him to love me?" "How do I protect myself from harm?" (Hiebert, Shaw, and Tienou 1999). The point is that evangelists among those with a fear/power worldview need to recognize that they regard the effect of sin (fear) and the solution in Christ (power) very differently than those from guilt/justice or shame/honor worldviews. This will then result in a very different, yet contextual, approach to evangelism.

For example, the Builsa people in Ghana, West Africa, were excited to hear stories of Jesus' power over sickness, and even death, to break free of the fear of spiritual forces holding them in bondage. This resonates with the fall of humanity, as well, since one of the results of sin was fear, evidenced by Adam's response to God's call: "I heard you in the garden, and I was afraid..." (Gen 3:10 NIV). The gospel addresses this need by being "the power of God that brings salvation to everyone who believes" (Rom 1:16 NIV).

Fourth worldview

While the three worldviews discussed above have been identified by anthropologists for years,[10] growing secularization seems to be producing another worldview system that is qualitatively different than the other three. Based on research conducted with over four hundred participants (largely millennials) in the last four years, their response to sin is not often guilt, shame, or fear. Instead, their response to sin is often indifference. Steve Bruce points out that the end point of secularization is not atheism but religious indifference (2002, 42). While the religious landscape of secular contexts is by no means homogeneous, indifference is a prevailing worldview that needs to be understood in contemporary Western culture.

This response to sin also has precedence early in the Bible. For example, in the time of Noah, "The LORD saw how great the wickedness of the human race had become on the earth, and that every inclination of the thoughts of the human heart was only evil all the time" (Gen 6:5 NIV). There was no hint of the normal results of sin—namely guilt, shame, or fear. Rather, they were indifferent.

Just as with the other three worldviews, the gospel provides a unique response to indifference. Instead of offering justice, honor, or power, the gospel addresses the needs of those who are indifferent by providing "belonging with purpose." This response is typified by the story of Zacchaeus (Luke 19:1–10). Since Zacchaeus was a chief tax collector, he was an outsider to the Jewish religious community; therefore he was indifferent to the Jewish faith. Jesus, though, responds to his need by visiting his house with his disciples, such that Zacchaeus recognizes that he belongs in their community and then finds new purpose for his work. Jesus then replies, "Today salvation has come to this house, because this man, too, is a son of Abraham. For the Son of Man came to seek and to save the lost" (Luke 19:9–10 NIV).

After interviewing several millennials who have come to faith, they often replied that this sense of belonging with purpose is what drew them to Christ and to be a part of a Christian community. John Stott (1988) noted that postmoderns are often yearning for three things:

---

10 A history of the development of shame/honor theory is available at Simon (2018).

1. Community—a sense that in a fragmenting world and society they belong to a family.
2. Significance—a sense that they are meaningful, have purpose, and make a difference.
3. Transcendence—a sense or a connection with what is beyond immediate and material things and beings. (Pocock, Van Rheenen, and McConnell 2005, 116)

Jesus offers community, significance, and transcendence as they are invited to belong with purpose, like he did with Zacchaeus. To put the two halves of this worldview together, this worldview can be summarized as "indifference/belonging with purpose."[11] Table 3, then, expands the previous worldview summary to include another column to the far right that describes how different worldviews regard sin's result, the solution in Jesus, and the image of salvation.

Worldview	Guilt/ Justice	Shame/ Honor	Fear/Power	Indifference/ Belong with Purpose
Typical Location	West (North America, Europe)	East (Middle East, North Africa, Asia)	South (Sub-Saharan Africa, Tribal, Caribbean)	Post-Christian
Sin's Result	Guilt/ Separation	Shame	Fear/Curse/ Bondage	Indifference
Solution	Payment/ Substitute	Honor restored, cleansed	Deliverance	Belonging with Purpose
Image	Courtroom/ Justice	Relationship/ Cleansing	Power/ Freedom	Homecoming

Table 3: Evangelism amid Four Worldviews

While the information in this table may seem intimidating at first glance, our research found that training using gamification greatly helped students to recognize these worldviews and then respond with biblical stories that were

---

11 This worldview is emerging and needs further research. Several university Christian groups that I visited affirmed that they often find students that fit this "indifference/ belonging with purpose" worldview. For example, the website for the Chi Alpha Christian group at American University in Washington, DC, states, "Jesus. Purpose. Community"–which indicates Jesus' offer to belong (in community) with purpose. See www.auchialpha.org.

appropriate for the various worldviews. This training approach was engaging, memorable, and effective at teaching the various evangelistic approaches available in the four worldviews. This resulted in increased competence and confidence to evangelize in a pluralist society.

Teaching through Gamification: Faith Sharing Card Game

The term *gamification* has recently appeared in the field of education to help incentivize students to learn in an engaging and memorable manner. In short, this term refers to the use of game elements that are applied to non-game contexts (Huotari and Hamari 2012). From the US military to large companies like Unilever or online sources such as Khan Academy, gamification is gaining increased interest and usage. Creating a game to teach skills can increase student participation, course relevancy, and knowledge retention. Since 2010, gamification has gained traction in the online computer software world (Mangalindan 2010). It makes sense that this concept would find its way into seminaries to address the changing learning preference of missiology students in the twenty-first century.

To give students confidence for evangelism amid the complexity of pluralism, the Digit-Oral Publishing Services recently developed a card game that provides a practical approach to various evangelistic encounters using different images of salvation.[12] The Faith Sharing Card Game is designed to "remove the fear and return the story" for evangelism in the twenty-first century. Research demonstrated that it helped students think about different images of salvation to address different cultural contexts.

---

12 This game is available at digitalbiblecollege.com.

Here is how the game works:

1. Break players into groups (six players maximum) to play the Faith Sharing Card Game.
2. Place the four card types in separate piles in the middle of the players and ask each player to draw one card from each pile: 1) Person; 2) Place; 3) Problem, and 4) Presentation. Every player will now have a set of four cards in their hand.
3. The object of the game is to use these cards to form a story to share with the group concerning an encounter where they met this person at this place who had this problem and they presented a relevant biblical story.
4. The complexity is that the Problem cards are based on one of four worldviews; therefore they need to match an appropriate Presentation card that is suited to the same worldview.
5. For example, when a student drew a Problem card that read "Ashamed of outburst, resulting in broken relationships," the bottom of the card indicated that this relates to a shame/honor culture. Eventually, she drew the Presentation card that read "Shame/Honor" at the bottom and the rest of the card read "Relational Image" with "Jesus restores family relationships" based on the biblical story of the "Prodigal Son." When she shared her story using the character and setting, she described both the

problem of sin and the presentation of Jesus using this biblical story that was appropriate for a shame/honor audience.

6. As I observed the various storytelling groups, there were immediate learning opportunities. Several students noted how it stimulated their thinking about complex contextual problems they hadn't been aware of. It enabled them to address the concerns of other cultural contexts through more empathetic lenses. The card game helped them to think through how the contextualization process might interface with the presentation of various biblical narratives. Students also commented that this game was both enjoyable and taught them how to think biblically to share God's story. It helped them think about what the sin problem is in various contexts and how to address it. It also forced them to think on their feet and share their faith in creative and different ways. They realized that they did not need to attack other faith systems (e.g., Islam, Hinduism, Buddhism, atheism); rather, they can start with the worldview upon which these faith systems arise in order to engage them meaningfully.[13] In the end, the use of gamification became a creative way to engage students, resulting in a memorable learning experience about new opportunities for evangelism resulting from pluralism.

---

13 Comments are from "Results of the Faith Sharing Card Game Prototype," an unpublished twelve-page document by W. Jay Moon, Joshua Moon, and Irene Kabete, 2017.

Conclusion

Whether discussing farming or evangelism, the twenty-first century provides complexities that need to be understood and addressed. These complexities provide multiple challenges, but they also provide new opportunities to help the church regain its voice for evangelism.

Research and discussion on evangelism amid secularization comes at a critical moment in the life of the church. A recent Barna survey (2018, 18) noted a significant decline in the church's effectiveness in evangelism training over the last twenty-five years, as 57 percent agreed that their church did a good job of training people to share their faith in 2018 compared to 77 percent in 1993. What can be done to prevent this same rate of decline to continue for another twenty-five years, such that the church's public voice gets gradually muted?

To address this question, this chapter presented the following conclusions, based upon a four-year research project with the Knox/Asbury partnership:

1. *Evangelism is more complex now than in the twentieth century, such that simple formulaic approaches are less effective.* We cannot simply rely upon simple formulas for a "one size fits all" approach in a secular society. It is helpful to understand and address these complexities since they actually provide creative opportunities for evangelism.

2. *The gospel addresses various worldview concerns differently, thereby encouraging contextual evangelistic approaches.* The gospel has been likened to a multifaceted diamond, whereby various cultures highlight different aspects of the gospel from within their own culture (Wax 2014). Pluralism can help us, perhaps for the first time, understand how we have put a cultural straightjacket upon our own understanding of the gospel.

3. *In a secular society, the effect of sin is not solely guilt, shame, or fear (even though these may occur to some degree); rather, an emerging response to sin in secular contexts appears to be indifference. Jesus responds to this worldview by offering "belonging with purpose."* This understanding was very evident as people playing initial versions[14] of the Faith Sharing Card Game would say, "What about

---

14 The initial prototype only included the guilt/justice, shame/honor, and fear/power worldviews. It was only through beta testing that this fourth worldview emerged so that the game was changed to add indifference/belonging with purpose.

my sibling who doesn't seem to experience guilt, fear, or shame? How does Jesus address their situation?" This emerging worldview of indifference seemed to fit within many of the students' own evangelism contexts.

4. *Evangelism training needs to consider these complexities and opportunities in a secular world. Gamification should be considered as one approach to train the church to share their faith in a secular society.*[15] At the completion of the eight-week cohorts, 100 percent of the students affirmed that they knew how to practice evangelism in most contexts (compared to only 25 percent at the beginning of the eight-week sessions). In addition, 62 percent affirmed that they *felt confident* to practice evangelism in most contexts (compared to only 30 percent at the beginning). The students' self-evaluations represented a significant increase in both their competence (300 percent increase) and confidence (107 percent increase) to practice evangelism.

At the end of one of the Faith Sharing Card Game sessions, a leader of a worldwide ministry to university students commented, "I have experienced a lot of evangelistic training over the years, but this has been the most helpful and the most fun!" I wish that every evangelistic training and encounter were that way. After all, secularization makes evangelism more complex—but even a slow truck will get you there, if you know the way.

References

Barna Group. 2018. *Spiritual Conversations in the Digital Age: How Christians' Approach to Sharing Their Faith Has Changed in 25 Years*. Ventura, CA: Barna Group.

Bazargani, Davood Taghipour, and Vahid Noroozi Larsari. 2015. "'Postmodernism': Is the Contemporary State of Affairs Correctly Described as 'Postmodern'?" *Journal of Social Issues & Humanities* 3 (1): 89–96.

Berger, Peter. 2014. *The Many Altars of Modernity: Toward a Paradigm for Religion in a Pluralist Age*. Boston: Walter de Gruyter.

Blaschke, Robert. 2001. *Quest for Power: Guidelines for Communicating the Gospel to Animists*. Ontario, Canada: Guardian.

---

15 This approach has become so popular that the Digit-Oral Publishing Services recently created a board game that leads participants through each of the six complexities so that they engage the opportunities for evangelism.

Bruce, Steve. 2002. *God Is Dead: Secularization in the West*. Oxford: Blackwell/Cigna. 2018. "New Cigna Study Reveals Loneliness at Epidemic Levels in America." https://www.cigna.com/newsroom/news-releases/2018/new-cigna-study-reveals-loneliness-at-epidemic-levels-in-america.

Colijn, Brenda. 2010. *Images of Salvation in the New Testament*. Downers Grove, IL: IVP Academic.

Georges, Jayson. 2016. "The 3D Gospel: Ministry in Guilt, Shame, and Fear Cultures." Unpublished. HonorShame.com.

Guder, Darrell L., ed. 1998. *Missional Church: A Vision for the Sending of the Church in North America*. Vol. 1, *The Gospel and Our Culture*. Grand Rapids: Eerdmans.

Hiebert, Paul G. 1999. *Missiological Implications of Epistemological Shifts: Affirming Truth in a Modern/Postmodern World*. Edited by A. Neeley. Harrisburg, PA: Trinity Press International.

Hiebert, Paul G., R. D. Shaw, and T. Tienou. 1999. *Understanding Folk Religion: A Christian Response to Popular Beliefs and Practices*. Grand Rapids: Baker.

Huotari, K., and J. Hamari. 2012. "Defining Gamification—A Service Marketing Perspective." In Proceedings of the 16th International Academic MindTrek Conference. Tampere, Finland.

Jaccard, C. R. 1956. "Objectives and Philosophy of Public Affairs Education." In *Increasing Understanding of Public Problems and Policies: A Group Study of Four Topics in the Field of Extension Education*, 12. Chicago: Farm Foundation.

Madinger, Charles. 2013. "A Literate Guide to the Oral Galaxy." *Orality Journal* 2 (2): 13–40.

Mangalindan, JP. 2010. "Play to Win: The Game-Based Economy." *Fortune*, September 3.

McGavran, Donald. 1981. *The Bridges of God*. 2nd ed. Pasadena, CA: Fuller Seminary Press.

Moon, W. Jay. 2009. *African Proverbs Reveal Christianity in Culture: A Narrative Portrayal of Builsa Proverbs Contextualizing Christianity in Culture*. Vol. 5 of *American Society of Missiology Monograph Series*. Eugene, OR: Pickwick Publications.

———, ed. 2017. *Practical Evangelism for the Twenty-First Century*. Nicholasville, KY: GlossaHouse and Digi-Books.

Moon, W. Jay, Joshua Moon, and Irene Kabete. 2017. "Results of the Faith Sharing Card Game Prototype." Unpublished twelve-page document.

Motak, Dominika. 2009. "Postmodern Spirituality and the Culture of Individualism." *Scripta Instituti Donneriani Aboensis* 21: 149–61.

Newbigin, Lesslie. 1989. *The Gospel in a Pluralist Society*. Grand Rapids: Eerdmans.

Ott, Craig. 2014. "The Power of Biblical Metaphors for the Contextualized Communication of the Gospel." *Missiology: An International Review* 42 (4): 357–74.

Pocock, Michael, Gailyn Van Rheenen, and Douglas McConnell. 2005. *The Changing Face of World Missions: Engaging Contemporary Issues and Trends*. Vol. 2 of *Encountering Mission Series*. Grand Rapids: Baker Academic.

Sachs, Jonah. 2012. *Winning the Story Wars: Why Those Who Tell (and Live) the Best Stories Will Rule the Future*. Boston: Harvard Business Review Press.

Simon, Walter Bud. 2018. "Honor-Shame Cultural Theory: Antecedents and Origins." Global Missiology 1 (16). Available at http://ojs .globalmissiology.org/index.php/english/article/view/2189.

Stott, John. 1988. "The World's Challenge to the Church. Part 1. Griffeth Thomas Lectureship at Dallas Theological Seminary, on Christian Missiology in the Twenty-First Century." *Bibliotheca Sacra* 145 (578): 123–32.

Sweet, Leonard. 2012. *Viral: How Social Networking Is Poised to Ignite Revival.* Colorado Springs: WaterBrook.

Wax, Trevin. 2014. "The Multifaceted Diamond of Christ's Atoning Work." *The Gospel Coalition, U.S. Edition* (blog). April 17. https://www.thegospelcoalition.org/blogs/ trevin-wax/the-multifaceted -diamond-of-christs-atoning-work/.

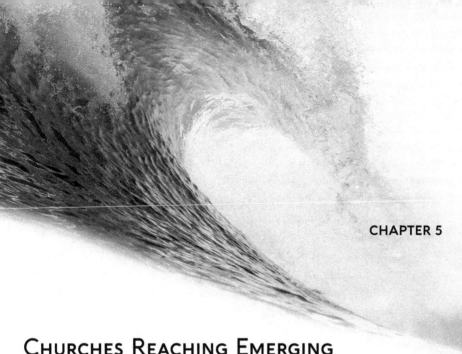

CHAPTER 5

Churches Reaching Emerging Adult "Nones" and "Dones" in Secularizing North America

Beth Seversen

Churches reaching young adults in North America are rare. Researchers report that "emerging adults,"[1] especially between the ages of eighteen and twenty-three, are both the least reached and least churched age group in the United States and the least serviced by the church. Pew Research Center (2015) finds the drop in religious affiliation to be highest among millennials, especially the youngest millennials. Twenty-three percent of Americans in general, and 35 percent of eighteen- to twenty-nine-year-olds in particular, identify as unaffiliated religious "nones"—which includes people who answer "atheist," "agnostic," or "nothing in particular" when asked for their religious preferences (Pew Research Center 2012). The increase in older millennials (age twenty-five to thirty-three) who say they have no religion is up 9 percent since 2007. The rate of decline in religious affiliation is similar among college

---

1 The term is ascribed to Jeffrey Arnett and refers to the prolonged transition from adolescence to adulthood (Arnett 2015; Arnett and Taber 1994; Wuthnow 2007, 18). I use it as a social descriptor of young adults in the United States between the ages of eighteen and thirty-five.

graduates and those who did not attend college.[2] College does not currently appear to have an "edge" on secularizing young adults.

Likewise, as Christian Smith (2009; 2015) shows, the number of young adult church dropouts, or "dones," is growing. Young adults between the ages of eighteen and twenty-nine—even those who attended church during high school and intend to continue after graduation (LifeWay 2007)—are increasingly absent from mainline, evangelical Protestant, and Catholic churches,[3] most of which are losing more emerging adults than they are reaching. Pastors and laypeople frequently express their frustration over losing these young adults; as well, they bemoan their inability to reach unchurched emerging generations. In this context, the church, which is moving toward the twenty-first century, urgently needs to discover successful models of outreach and retention of young adults.

Evangelizing the Secularized: A Study of Churches Reaching Emerging Adults

This chapter investigates the key practices and evangelistic approaches of churches that are successfully reaching and incorporating emerging adults aged eighteen to thirty-three. It is based on findings from qualitative research carried out in 2015 and 2016 among nineteen North American Evangelical Covenant churches effectively reaching and retaining young adult "dones" and "nones." The purpose of this research was to identify the cultural, social, and organizational features of evangelistically effective churches and explore their influence on young adult conversions, with the goal of helping to increase the number of churches that reach young adults in our secular and pluralistic post-Christian Western context.

Three factors will increase the number of young adults in the church: (1) retention, (2) evangelism/recruitment, and (3) incorporation. While all three factors are necessary to understand church absenteeism and affiliation among emerging adults, we will focus here primarily on evangelism and incorporation. In addition, I identify common pathways to faith and

---

2 Pew Research Center (2015b) reports the percentage of college graduates who identify as Christian has declined since 2007 by 9 percentage points, from 73 percent to 64 percent, and at about the same rate as those without a college education–down 8 percentage points, from 81 percent to 73 percent.

3 Young adults between the ages of eighteen and twenty-nine are increasingly absent from churches when compared to their presence when they were in high school (Uecker, Regnerus, and Vaaler 2007, 1667; Wuthnow 2007, 231; White 2014, 14; Pew Research Center 2015b. Smith unpublished research used by permission of Christian Smith in email correspondence dated October 19, 2015, and sent to me in 2015).

explore how churches can welcome and incorporate young adults into faith communities. These conclusions are drawn from ethnographic interviews of both pastors and formerly unchurched converts.

Over the course of my research, I found that non-Christian emerging adults connect to the church early in their faith journeys. Most often these young adults connect through the invitation of a Christian friend to weekend worship services or "portal" events such as sports, social, or service activities. They are, then, formally or informally assimilated into the church community.

Moreover, lead pastors of those churches play a major role in emerging adults' faith journeys by establishing an evangelistic and invitational ethos and acting as cultural informants who make Christian faith plausible in culturally relevant ways. As cultural brokers, pastors help emerging adults navigate new experiences by making the unfamiliar familiar. Emerging adults' journeys to faith follow pathways consisting of *compelling* Christian community, *service* that makes a difference, and *mentoring and leadership* development providing accountability.

Churches facilitate emerging adults' pre-conversion process through the following means, which will be explained further in the "Findings" section:

1. Initiating, inviting, including, involving, and investing in them—immediately;
2. Encouraging emerging adults to engage in Christian community and behave like Christians before they believe and commit;
3. Incorporating and retaining emerging adults before or during the evangelization process;
4. Evangelizing inside the church;
5. Promoting retention activities, such as service projects, outside the church;
6. Blending evangelism and retention strategies;
7. Serving as compelling and mentoring communities in which like-minded friends support, legitimate, and help maintain faith; and
8. Orienting emerging adults in a collective Christian identity that provides meaning, belonging, and expectancy, and helps them navigate the tension of remaining both culturally distinct and culturally engaged.

These findings show that the church needs a new set of practices to reach emerging adults. To that end, I propose here five "I's" that present a fresh methodology to reaching and retaining emerging adults: initiating, inviting, including, involving, and investing in them—and doing so immediately. This approach will work well with millennials both inside and outside a church-saturated culture.[4]

Against the backdrop of the growing secularism evidenced in the increasing number of "nones" among millennials born between 1981 and 1997 (Pew Research Center 2015), churches that stand out for reaching emerging adults are ones in which non-Christians are swiftly *engaged, invited, included, involved*, and *invested* in by the church. Newcomers are not left to navigate unfamiliar church culture on their own, but are connected with cultural informants and mentors who communicate the credibility of Christian faith with cultural fluency and help them "jump in."

New paradigms of evangelism and incorporation reflect the fact that emerging adults often become incorporated into the church community before or during the evangelization process. Churches reach younger generations by giving them opportunities to "try on" Christian identity before making a commitment. In doing so, they facilitate the pre-conversion process by providing for the type of identity construction that characterizes young adults' lives.

Methodology

This study was based largely on thirty-four one-to-two-hour qualitative interviews. After identifying churches that are effectively reaching and retaining emerging adults,[5] I interviewed nineteen of their pastors about their leadership culture and organizational and social ethos. I also interviewed fifteen emerging adults between the ages of eighteen and thirty-three who came to faith in these churches. I wished to learn their motivation to commit to Christian faith as well as to become active in church. I was surprised to discover that *most of these emerging adults became active in their churches before they committed to faith in Christ.*

Churches. Nineteen Evangelical Covenant Church (ECC) congregations are represented in the research. My selection process took into account church

---

4 Additional findings related to life stages, expectancy theory, and church culture will be in my forthcoming book with IVP (2020).

5 Demonstrated by their retention of eight or more eighteen-to-thirty-three-year-olds who had made new faith commitments within the previous twelve months.

size, geographic location, environment (suburban or urban), age, and ethnic makeup, aiming to include a broad range of ECC congregations. Aside from the omission of Hispanic/Latino churches, the study reflected the ethnic composition of the ECC by including eight multiethnic, nine white, one African American, and one Asian church. It also included eight suburban and eleven urban churches, representing all geographic regions in the ECC except Alaska and the southeastern United States. One Canadian church was included; the rest were American.

The study included two churches with over 10,000 attendees, three with over 1,000 attendees, three with 500–999 attendees, and nine with 175–499 attendees. The number of new young adult faith commitments required to qualify for the study precluded smaller churches.

Pastors. Pastors varied in age, ethnicity, gender, training, gifts, philosophy of evangelism, and leadership style. The group included one African American, four Asian Americans, and fourteen white pastors, for a total of nineteen. Seventeen men and two women participated. Both women and one man were associate pastors, while the rest were lead pastors. The group included one director in her twenties, six pastors in their thirties including one female, eight pastors in their forties, two in their fifties, and two in their sixties. This age range suggests that millennials are not necessarily drawn to churches with millennial-aged lead pastors.

Emerging Adults. All the pastors I interviewed were asked to provide the name and contact information of a previously unchurched young adult who had made a first-time faith commitment to Jesus Christ in their church. The fifteen young adult interviewees differed in church background, marriage and parenting status, education, gender, vocation, and ethnicity. The group included one African American, five Asian Americans, and nine white participants. Nine reported unchurched religious backgrounds, while six identified as church dropouts (four from Catholic churches, one from a Korean Protestant church, and one from a traditional black Protestant church). All fifteen young adults were unmarried when they first connected to their church (one was engaged, and one was dating someone who attended the church), indicating that most of the participants did not connect to church for traditional markers of marriage and family formation.

All emerging adults gave permission for their names to be used, but I have chosen to provide only their pseudonyms. Note that eight of the fifteen young adult participants had been attending church for less than one year at the time of their interviews.

Findings: Three Ways Young Adults Connect to Church

Young adults described their pre-conversion journeys toward faith in Christ in terms of three distinct but relatively similar trajectories. The first and most common involved friendships with Christians. The second involved personal crisis or complexity during which a Christian friend pointed to their church or pastor for guidance or a solution. The third, which was only pursued by a few participants, involved an Internet search for a church due to crisis or relocation. Significantly, most of these young adults initially connected to church by way of relational bridges provided by close friends and family members whom they admired. Almost all of the young adults first attended church accompanied by a friend or family member. These findings highlight the power of close, supportive, intentional, and enduring friendships with unchurched young adults.

Once unchurched young adults began attending church, what led to their conversions? The next interval in their faith journeys included one or more of the following pre-conversion pathways: (1) experiencing compelling community; (2) making a difference through service or leadership; and (3) receiving mentoring (including pastoral care and accountability) or leadership development. The findings of this study suggest that the sooner any of these steps were taken, the more likely young adults were to become active in their churches. Every emerging adult in the study followed at least one of these pathways, and most experienced two or more.6 Interestingly, every emerging adult on Pathway 2—making a difference through service or leadership—was very connected to church.

The two interviewees who did not follow any of these pathways were the least connected to church and most vulnerable to dropping out. Their attendance was very infrequent, and although they both met occasionally with their lead pastors, they did not experience regular community, service, or mentoring. It should be noted that both of these young adults faced extremely challenging life circumstances.

Pathway one: Community

Communities such as small groups or more informal gatherings of friends helped young adults avoid becoming isolated in their faith exploration. The most significant of these were compelling communities in which previously

---

6 Zoë experienced only one factor, meeting with her pastor, and that was interrupted by her relocation. Although Tyler has two factors, his lengthy addictions obstruct his growth and church attendance.

unchurched young adults not only experienced belonging but also were challenged in their thinking, behaviors, allegiances, and idols, and propelled forward in their progress toward faith commitment.

Small groups were where young adults experienced Christian love, acceptance, support, and optimism. They often formed friendships and experienced a casual but intentional sort of "group mentoring" in their new communities. Garrett's description of his small-group experience contains several common threads: (1) he felt accepted, supported, and loved; (2) his identity was affirmed; and (3) he received direction.

> They were all very strong with God, and they're all very supportive. It didn't matter what my past was, they accepted me for who I am and saw the positive things in me; and I really feel like they've surrounded me with a lot of love. They taught me basically how to love, just love on everyone.... They're just there for community—actually caring, like a family.

Garrett's community met many of the needs North Americans experience during emerging adulthood, a period of time in which they explore their identities, experience instability, are self-focused, and feel in-between, yet are optimistic about future possibilities (Arnett 2004, 8; Arnett and Tanner 2006).

Reaching aspirations

Emerging adults looked to their church for healthy relationships and support in establishing healthy behaviors. Small groups provided the relational support and encouragement they needed to sustain their early efforts to uphold the ethical standards to which they aspired. Seversen and Richardson (2014) note the evangelistic importance of helping emerging adults succeed in achieving the moral standards they hope to attain.

Brooke was one of many young people who said church provided alternatives to weekend clubbing, partying, drinking, and other destructive behaviors.

> Saturday nights are important because when you have a group at church, we're able to say, "Hey, let's all go grab dinner afterwards." So then you're...expanding your community and you're building relationships....A lot of people struggle with Saturday nights...[but] we have...a way for them to have fun, without going out with friends that

maybe aren't the healthiest for them. So after Saturday night service we always play volleyball.

Spiritual transformation

Emerging adults also observed that their Christian communities were a place where God began to do something within them. Shea explained it this way:

> Finding a Life Group was a big thing for me. Finding that community. Meeting girls my age who were struggling and were honest with each other. They didn't even know me, and it was like they loved me and cared about me, and they were interested in who I was and what was going on in my life and what God was doing in my life.... My first time I went to this Life Group, I was like, this is it, this is what I've been looking for. Some people say when they meet Christ it's like overnight, but for me it was gradual. Then I started serving, and that was around my baptism as well.

Shea began to experience inner transformation as she explored Christian community, serving, and following Christ among new friends. Just three months passed between her first visit to Life Church Broken Arrow and her baptism. Shea's pathway to faith commitment was based on genuine, caring friendships that pointed her to Christ and challenged her to make a new beginning.

Church strategy one: Intentional community

Churches that effectively reach emerging adults are doing so intentionally. One important strategy for reaching and retaining young adults is funneling visitors into Christian community. Pastors across the nineteen participating churches agreed that their church's *core* evangelism strategy involved encouraging church attendees to build relationships with non-Christians, invite those non-Christians to church, and include them in communities— usually small groups—where they can safely explore faith in Christ, observe Christians up close, and develop deepening relationships with Christians.

Pastor Aaron Cho commented on the critical importance of community in emerging adults' faith journeys and the connection between community and evangelism:

> I find that a part of the evangelism process, part of getting people to be on that journey, is "Are there others who are with me?" And those are the questions that are often asked. They feel like this spiritual journey is often isolated and alone—they feel alone in it. I think that there are

things that happen when we do things together in community. Questions are asked, questions are answered. Sometimes questions are asked and questions aren't answered; and I think the phenomena, or the miracle, is that people are not opting out to leave. They're opting to stay, and they still are wrestling with unanswered questions. They may not say it this way, but you're still on this journey; God is doing something in you, and you're still staying and sticking with it. Getting plugged in to the life of the church through small groups is kind of the main way.

Pastor Peter Hong outlined a similar strategy of "kingdom relationships leading to invitation." This involves training congregants to form relationships with non-Christians "not necessarily for the sole purpose of converting them, but just loving them." Or, in Pastor Alex Rahill's words, "We are incredibly intentional about connecting with people who are far from God, building relationships with millennials outside the church, inviting them into safe environments, and explaining the full life that God created everybody for" and which cannot be experienced outside of Christ.

Strategy One can be pictured this way:

Build Relationships + Invite to Church + Include in Safe Community = New Commitment (NC)

Community is a powerful agent for transformation. Sociologists observe that change occurs only when some sort of crisis or challenge exerts pressure on a person. Significant personal relationships can exert this kind of pressure. Smith (2009, 209) writes, "Rarely do people's thinking and feeling and behaving change dramatically (or stay the same) without significant social relationships exerting pressures to do so and facilitating these outcomes." The power of being embraced by the church community catalyzed these emerging adults' spiritual transformation, kindling their new faith commitments and counteracting the pressures of secularization.

In sum, my findings suggest that churches can facilitate emerging adults' pre-conversion journeys by helping them experience compelling Christian community, whether experienced in young adult programming or small groups. In such communities, emerging adults (1) found friends to validate their faith; (2) asked questions and found answers without feeling judged or pressured; (3) experienced the deconstruction and reconstruction of their views of Christians and church; (4) met companions for their faith journey; (5) began to experience God at work in their lives; and (6) received challenge, mentoring, and support as they practiced new beliefs and behaviors aligned with their aspirations and identity formation.

Pathway two: Serving that makes a difference

Service is at the core of the second way emerging adult participants came to faith. Both emerging adults and pastors linked serving to "making a difference" and "giving to their community." Brooke commented, "It was easy for me to work in the children's ministry because I already work with children and I love it, so I thought I could help there as well giving back to the community."

Young adults wanted to contribute where they belonged, and they identified their experience of serving was significant and transformative.

Serving accompanied by investment

We should also note that as the emerging adult participants invested their time, talent, creativity, and energy by serving in their churches, church leaders—including pastors, staff, and lay supervisors—simultaneously invested in the emerging adults. The young adults I interviewed volunteered as nursery workers, Sunday school teachers, youth leaders, college ministry leaders, church interns, worship leaders, camera and sound operators, and leadership board members. As they did so, they were supervised, trained, appreciated, and often mentored; and some were developed as leaders.

Serving leads to relational networks

Emerging adults who served in their churches formed relational bonds through their volunteerism, developing connections with supervisors, fellow volunteers, and the people they served. As emerging adults contribute to their churches, they receive the "benefits" of religion (Stark and Finke 2000).

Serving leads to faith commitment

While serving, young adults often began to act like disciples of Jesus in the sense that they practiced Christian enactments and participated in church community. Among the emerging adults interviewed, those who became involved in serving at church within a few weeks or months of first attending were relatively quick to come to faith in Christ. Katelyn, for example, attended a class focused on identifying one's spiritual gifts after just a few Sundays at church. A staff member then reached out and invited her to join a church leadership team. In Katelyn's words, "That is how I got super involved in my church." She was baptized a few weeks after first attending Life Community Church, and she started a new small group for millennials, with a church staff member, seven months later.

These findings suggest that meaningful service that allows emerging adults to "contribute where they belong" may function as an antidote against the pressure of secularization.

Church strategy two: Service as means of reaching emerging adults

Many pastors observed that encouraging emerging adults to contribute to the church community through service and leadership is a significant means of outreach. Asked how they were reaching young adults, pastors described providing opportunities to "get involved," "serve," and even "lead." Pastor Craig Groeschel, for example, asserted that giving millennials a way to contribute may be at least as important as providing compelling community.

> Getting them connected relationally really matters. But I think that getting them contributing matters even more. That generation wants to make a difference more than they want to make a living. If the church isn't missional, or serving in the community, or making a difference, that's a real turnoff. If the church is missional and making a difference, that's a plus. If there's a place they can use their gifts and help make a difference, that's a plus. If they can lead it, that's a hundred times better.

Pastors like Groeschel understood that millennials want to "make a difference," so they offered opportunities to get involved. Campus life director Dena Davidson explained that Bayside Church staff and leaders are intentional about immediately inviting first-time visitors to serve.

Pastor Will Barnett described service as part of the pathway to faith in Christ for young adults.

> We want to invite everyone to serve, even if they don't even fully identify as a Christian. In fact, that's one of the ways of learning the culture and learning who Jesus is about.... So actually, a number of them—who it's still a question for me where they're at spiritually and with Jesus—serve in our Kids Rock ministry, or our hospitality ministry, or some other ministry. We've had some who were really wrestling with their faith, but they're serving on the worship team. In terms of leadership, I'm more careful about who we select as our leaders and want them to be in a more established place in their faith.

Emerging adult respondents confirmed these pastors' observations by expressing their desire to contribute and make a difference. Shea, who attended Groeshel's church, made the point that emerging adults are far more interested in contributing and serving than in simply attending church. "I think everyone wants to be part of something. And so when someone says, 'Come with me to be a part of this, like serve with me in high school ministry,' you are more inclined to do it."

Most of the emerging adults described how their churches affirmed them and helped them grow. As a result, the young adults began to believe the tenets of the Christian faith, and in time most made faith commitments to Jesus Christ.[7] These churches helped emerging adults find belonging and identity in a satisfying and morally orienting subculture (Smith 1998, 89–119). That Christian subculture is distinct from other social groups while at the same time engaging the cultural trends offered in their secular emerging adult world. Service may thus help counteract secularism.

Pathway three: Mentorship and accountability

Another step along many emerging adults' journey to faith—the decisive step, for some—was mentorship and accountability. This often involved meeting one-on-one with lead pastors once every four to six weeks. Pastor Aaron Cho, for example, indicated that he and other Quest pastors see it as part of their role to "stay with, disciple, walk with, and mentor the young adults." He described meeting regularly with emerging adults in the early stages of their journey toward faith in Christ, "checking in on life, spiritual questions they may have."

Surprisingly, many of the pastors I interviewed described investing time to meet regularly with emerging adults who were not fully embedded in the life of the church and had no history of meaningful contact with other churches. This highlights their commitment to building meaningful relationships with non-Christians.

Following up with unchurched emerging adults to administer pastoral care, answer faith questions, and track spiritual progress encouraged them to attend church and get more involved. Furthermore, meetings with pastors may become the juncture where non-Christians made faith commitments. Michael, for example, discussed his questions about God and Jesus with Pastor Peter Hong on a regular basis. He described their one-on-one relationship as follows:

---

7 Jane was an exception, as she was still undecided at the time of her interview.

Peter, he was amazing throughout the entire process. Guiding me to ask the right questions, thinking about the right things, and letting me take my time in the process. We had coffee probably once a month....After I asked another pretty big, meaty question I struggled with for a while, he finally said, "You know, Michael, you can ask all the questions you want to; apologetics is a great field, and it's a wonderful subject to be smart in, especially as a Christian."

But he said, more than anything else, the only evidence that he needs—and he said that I should need in time—is personal experience and personal transformation. And he said, but God has done so much work in him...that there doesn't need to be more evidence than that for him. That was a really powerful statement and something that stuck with me even when I still struggle sometimes. That's a good summary of where I was when I first started pursuing Jesus, or felt like he was pursuing me, and I was finally acknowledging it.

A significant finding of this study is that pastors tracked the spiritual progress of young adults who were moving toward Jesus and provided regular accountability and mentoring for those who needed help making progress toward faith commitments to Christ. A few pastors, including Larry Kim, also made themselves available to speak at campus fellowship events. Students have responded well to his messages, but Tessa, who attended Kim's church, explained that one-on-one time with him was more significant in her journey to faith.[8] Tessa also noted that Kim attended Urbana, led discussions, and was generally very present in students' lives: "He's just...very present, but also really good at knowing how to direct you to resources. So I just...really trusted his spiritual leadership. [He] played...a huge role inv...the first time I kind of connected with a church and a pastor." The few pastors located near universities seemed to have an impact on secular campuses.

Other emerging adults were invited into mentoring relationships with pastors and staff due to their volunteer work. Again, it is notable that many lead pastors invited young adults into service, mentoring, and leadership development before they made faith commitments. Some even invited emerging adults to live with church staff members, giving them the opportunity to observe more mature disciples living out their faith day-by-day.

---

8 Pastor Kim takes time after each message to meet personally with students. He also makes time to pray for students and provide counsel on faith questions and life issues after he speaks on campus.

Church strategy three: Churches invest in emerging adults

So far, we have observed that non-Christian emerging adults receive many benefits from Christian community and that pastors of effective churches were key mentors to them. Once young adults began to serve in their churches, the churches reciprocated by investing in them. This might include giving young adults curriculum; inviting them to team meetings or one-on-one conversations; providing supervision, training, or mentoring; helping them envision reaching their potential; and recognizing their service, teaching, or outreach abilities. In today's secular culture, effective churches are helping fulfill young adults' longings for mentorship and growth.

Emerging adult leadership investment: There are others like you on the journey here

Pastors articulated that emerging adults need to identify with other emerging adults on a journey toward faith in Christ. Many pastors commented that young adults need to see others like themselves in order to feel welcome and incorporated into the life of the church, and most mentioned intentionally including and integrating emerging adults throughout their church ministries and leadership. Andrew Mook, Bill Johnson, and Larry Kim were among many pastors who said that "emerging adults are leading everything" at church. Emerging adults confirmed their pastors' reports.

In contrast to Robert Wuthnow's assessment (2007), the pastors in this study did not stress the importance of specific programming for young adults, but they did agree that emerging adults need an opportunity to meet one another. As Pastor Rahill commented, "Once they know you are not a cult, they're looking for people like them. 'Who can I build friendships with? Who can I do life with?'"

A few pastors recognized that two of emerging adults' needs are in tension: they need the church to provide structure to keep them together in relationship with others similar to themselves, but they also need enough freedom to create something that they can invest in and enjoy. It seems that one key to young adult evangelism and retention is letting them help build young adult ministry rather than providing something ready-made. This finding may be a version of Wuthnow's theory (2007) that churches need to provide scaffolding and community for emerging adults to help them find and recognize each other.[9] A few pastors in the study asked young adults to organize something for young adults and then began working with those who showed interest, identifying leaders among them and helping those leaders get something organized.

Pre-conversion pathways summary

The results of this study suggest that churches facilitated the second part of the emerging adult respondents' pre-conversion process by inviting them into Christian community, service, and mentoring—often within weeks of their first church visit. In all these cases, emerging adults were invited to belong before they believed. This allowed them to try on Christian roles before they committed to faith in Christ. Many emerging adults took advantage of this openness and began to practice belonging and behaving like Christians before they accepted Christian beliefs.

The steps on the pathway to faith described in this section are common to many emerging adults' stories, but they are not necessarily followed precisely or in a particular order. The journeys varied, but two or more of the core elements of community, service, and mentorship appeared in almost all of the emerging adults' stories, supporting Stark's thesis (1996, 18) that "conversion tends to proceed along social networks formed by interpersonal attachments." These three elements contribute to churches' retention of emerging adults in the broader context of a secularizing society by helping them become embedded in the life of the church and cultivate strong ecclesiological visions and commitments.

What We Learn from the Findings

Most of the churches in this study used a combination of the three evangelism strategies discussed above. The picture that emerges can be depicted as a pattern of steps that may be followed either sequentially or nonsequentially. (1) Non-Christians are *invited*, or ask to be invited, to church in the context of relational connections. (2) Once they begin attending church, non-Christians are *included* in Christian community, often immediately. (3) Non-Christians are invited to *get involved* and *contribute* through service or leadership. (4) The church *invests* in non-Christians through informal or formal mentoring or leadership development and one-on-one meetings with

---

9 This finding should not be taken to support Stark's theory (Stark, 1996, 18) that providing services and programming for emerging adults is not necessary because churches are competing for each other's emerging adults and emerging adults will return to church when they marry and have stable careers.

pastors or small group leaders. (5) Non-Christians are invited to repent and commit to following Christ, then encouraged to stay active in the churches where they have already been incorporated. Again, note that incorporation and retention often precede or occur simultaneously with what is traditionally thought of as evangelism. (6) The church encourages emerging adults to invite others to church, and the cycle begins again. The church's role in this process is to initiate, invite, include, involve, invest, and encourage the continuation of the cycle.

Church ethos

The churches in this study shared a number of characteristics. (1) They were radically welcoming, hospitable, friendly, and nonjudgmental toward non-Christians and the unchurched. (2) They expected non-Christians to be present in significant numbers, and congregants regularly invited friends. (3) They provided settings for conversations with non-Christians and engagement with subcultures and cultural issues. (4) They immediately invited young adult newcomers into community and service. (5) They presented regular opportunities to make faith commitments and become disciples, not always in that order.

I suggest that the experiences of the emerging adults in my study are in some ways very similar to those of Jesus' disciples, who followed Jesus before fully understanding and committing to him. In a postmodern context, churches are providing young adults with radically hospitable, authentic, and personal engagement with community, service, and mentoring—strong deterrents to secularization.

Asked what attracts them to their church community, young adults described church as engaging, compelling, stimulating, and fun, but also as a place where they are challenged to wrestle with their thinking, behaviors, allegiances, and idols. They mentioned activities such as rich and spiritually directed conversation, meaningful prayer, Scripture reading, book and sermon discussions, and table fellowship. They also referred to the presence of the Holy Spirit. All these things are part of the texture of communities in which emerging adults deconstruct their understanding of church and Christian stereotypes and reconstruct church and faith as they are exposed to and begin to practice Christian enactments. Old scripts, narratives, practices, and identities are set aside, and new ones are "tried on."

Effective church communities support the emerging adult life stage as described by Jeffrey Arnett and Jennifer Tanner (Arnett 2004; Arnett and

Tanner 2006). They support young adults by helping them reach their ethical goals through holding them accountable and providing alternative activities to clubbing, partying, drugs, alcohol, and promiscuous sex. They encourage young adults to pursue their dreams of making the world a better place (Parks 2011). They often facilitate experience or encounter with God. Garrett and Maddy, for example, said that being prayed for by their small group was significant in their spiritual journey. For almost every interviewee, the community of Christians was a powerful agent of transformation in an age of skepticism.

Churches that are reaching young adults are communities of service. Volunteerism inside and outside the church is a central part of their ethos, and they expect all community members to contribute in some way. In return, church leaders, pastors, and participants pour into young adults' lives—helping them learn, grow, and flourish in their new ministry roles. Young adults like Megan learn that they are capable leaders ("I always wanted to volunteer before, but my involvement in the church has helped me feel like I am capable"), encouraged by their importance to the church and their church's belief in them.

Five practices of churches reaching unchurched emerging adults: Initiate, invite, include, involve, invest

Findings reveal that relational evangelism and inviting people to church play a key role in the success of the churches in this study. The qualitative data demonstrate that bridging and building relationships with non-Christians, inviting them to church, and engaging them in evangelistic conversations combine to form a strong three-legged stool that serves as the foundation for evangelizing young adults. Although "one-size" evangelism does not fit all, several common patterns can be observed in the study participants.

Once bridges are built and invitations extended, emerging adults are welcomed into participation and service at church. Many serve and some lead in multiple capacities before their faith is fully developed, or even before they make faith commitments. Churches then begin to invest in them, and young adults receive what Stark (2011) refers to as religious "benefits" as they experiment with Christian identity in a culture of high expectancy and engagement. In this process, incorporation, retention, and evangelization take place simultaneously. The resulting pathway is pictured in Figure 1.

Initiate　　Invite　　Include　　Involve　　Invest　　Faith Commitment

Figure 1: Evangelism Approach and Pathway for Effective Churches Reaching Young Adults

Belonging and behaving before believing

The data on where people are experiencing conversion present an interesting cultural phenomenon, and perhaps a theory to be tested on a larger sample. Over the past two decades, George Hunter (2000) and others have stressed the importance of relationships and Christian community as powerful evangelism tools in a postmodern context. Based on the results of this study, I propose that the model be expanded to embrace another antecedent to Christian commitment.

Emerging adults belong to compelling Christian communities, practice Christian enactments, and serve in the church before they fully believe and make faith commitments. Churches facilitate young adults' pre-conversion process by giving them space to struggle and ask their questions, places to make meaningful contributions, mentors to guide them, and leadership development to help them grow. Non-Christians were also given the opportunity to behave like Christians—practicing enactments of faith such as prayer, worship, Bible study, and church participation—as a precursor to Christian faith. These enactments enhanced the journey to belief and gave emerging adults opportunity to experiment with Christian identity.

As the data showed, the emerging adult participants were invited to receive the benefits of the church community before they believed in Christ. Belonging and behaving like Christians was part of "trying on" Christian identity, a step in the process of committing to the church and eventually to Christ. Churches that offered the benefits of belonging increased their attractiveness, leading young adults to invite friends and family to church to receive what they received. The emerging adults' journey thus comes full circle, forming a "wheel of attraction."

Conclusion

Churches that are effectively reaching and incorporating emerging adults facilitate new attendees' pre-conversion journeys using approaches that share some commonalities yet differ from approaches to evangelism that were prevalent in earlier generations. These new approaches can be similar to traditional friendship evangelism, but they go further to cultivate an invitational culture and accessible pathways leading from church to faith in Christ. Emerging adults in effective ECC churches are typically evangelized *inside* the church, and they are frequently incorporated and retained before or at the same time as they are evangelized. The characteristics and approaches of churches that are effectively reaching and retaining emerging adults appear to be particularly missionally persuasive within the current secular climate of North America.

References

Arnett, Jeffrey Jensen. 1996. "Learning to Stand Alone: The Contemporary American Transition to Adulthood in Cultural and Historical Context." *Human Development* 41: 295–315.

———. 2004. *Emerging Adulthood: The Winding Road from the Late Teens through the Twenties.* New York: Oxford University Press.

———. 2015. *Emerging Adulthood: The Winding Road from the Late Teens through the Twenties.* 2nd ed. New York: Oxford University Press.

Arnett, J. J., and S. Taber. 1994. "Adolescents Terminable and Interminable: When Does Adolescence End?" *Journal of Youth and Adolescence* 23: 517–37.

Arnett, Jeffrey Jensen, and Jennifer Lynn Tanner, eds. 2006. "Emerging Adults in America: Coming of Age in the 21st Century." In *Emerging Adults in America: Coming of Age in the 21st Century.* New York: American Psychological Association.

Hunter, George G., III. 2000. *The Celtic Way of Evangelism: How Christianity Can Reach the West...Again.* Nashville: Abingdon.

LifeWay Research. 2007. "Reasons 18- to 22-Year-Olds Drop Out of Church." August 7. https://lifewayresearch.com/2007/08/07/reasons-18-to-22-year-olds-drop-out-of-church/.

Parks, Sharon Duloz. 2011. *Big Questions, Worthy Dreams: Mentoring Emerging Adults in Their Search for Meaning, Purpose, and Faith.* San Francisco: Jossey-Bass.

Pew Research Center. 2012. "'Nones' on the Rise." Religion and Public Life. http://www.pewforum.org/2012/10/09/nones-on-the-rise/.

———. 2015a. "America's Changing Religious Landscape." Religion and Public Life. http://www.pewforum.org/2015/05/12/americas-changing-religious-landscape/.

———. 2015b. "Millennials Are Less Religious Than Older Americans, but Just as Spiritual." Fact Tank. http://www.pewresearch.org/fact -tank/2015/11/23/Millennials-are-less-religious-than-older -americans-but-just-as-spiritual/.

———. 2015c. "U.S. Public Becoming Less Religious." Religion and Public Life. http:// www.pewforum.org/2015/11/03/u-s-public -becoming-less-religious/.

Seversen, Beth, and Rick Richardson. 2014. "Emerging Adults and the Future of Evangelism." *Witness* 28: 31–51.

Smith, Christian. 1998. *American Evangelicalism: Embattled and Thriving.* Chicago: University of Chicago.

———. 2009. *Souls in Transition: The Religious and Spiritual Lives of Emerging Adults.* With Patricia Snell. New York: Oxford University.

———. 2015. October 19 mail correspondence with author.

Stark, Rodney. 1996. "Why Religious Movements Succeed or Fail: A Revised General Model." *Journal of Contemporary Religion* 11 (2).

———. 2011. *The Triumph of Christianity: How the Jesus Movement Became the World's Largest Religion.* New York: HarperOne.

Stark, Rodney, and Roger Finke. 2000. *Acts of Faith: Explaining the Human Side of Religion.* Berkeley, CA: University of California.

Uecker, Jeremy E., Mark D. Regnerus, and Margaret L. Vaaler. 2007. "Losing My Religion: The Social Sources of Religious Decline in Early Adulthood." *Social Forces* 85 (4): 1667–92.

White, James Emery. 2014. *Understanding and Reaching the Religiously Unaffiliated.* Grand Rapids: Baker.

Wuthnow, Robert. 2007. *After the Baby Boomers: How Twenty- and Thirty-Somethings Are Shaping the Future of American Religion.* Princeton, NJ: Princeton University.

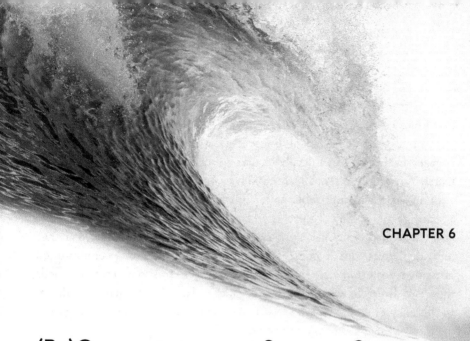

CHAPTER 6

(Re)Connecting with Secular Society

Steve Thrall

Several years ago I was attending the opening of an art show at our gallery in Paris. The artist, a friend of mine, introduced me to his new girlfriend, Marie,[1] who worked as a movie director. My artist friend presented me by saying, "This is Steve. He is a pastor and the director of this gallery."

Surprised, Marie stepped in close and whispered, "Are you really a pastor?"

I stepped back to allow more personal space and assured her that I was indeed a pastor. Again she moved in close, still whispering, "We need to talk!"

This time I held my ground and did not move away, since it seemed important to her to keep our conversation private. Speaking quietly, Marie told me that she grew up in an atheist family and hardly ever had a thought about God until a few months earlier, when things suddenly changed.

"Now I *know* God exists," Marie stated, "and I don't know what to do about it."

I expressed my excitement about what she had just told me, and then I said, "I have to ask why we are whispering about this."

---

1 Marie is not her real name.

Marie looked quickly in both directions, and then responded, "This room is full of people who work in the film industry. If they heard me say that I believed in God, I might lose my job."

This experience is not as unusual as it might sound for those of us engaged in ministry in a deeply secular culture. Secularism casts religion as merely private and personal, a question of conscience and personal reflection with no bearing on any public role, influence, or responsibilities. Those with a heart for the mission of the church have a problem, because the good news is public truth and not just a private concern. The gospel does indeed change individual lives, but it goes on to transform families and communities, bringing transformation to society. How are we, as missionaries, to reconcile these two divergent views when we are called to labor in a secularized culture? In this chapter, I offer a path toward tackling this dilemma by drawing from my thirty years serving as a missionary in France.

To many astute observers of French society, the staunch secularism that has defined France's progress since the eighteenth century ironically appears as somewhat of a modern state religion (Astier 2004). Today the angry anticlericalism of past generations has been replaced by what the French call *je-m'en-foutisme*, a general "I don't give a damn" attitude. The process of secularization has seemingly inoculated the French against the gospel. Traditional evangelistic efforts are often met with boredom and total indifference. This has been a major reason why so many missionaries have become discouraged.

France is not the only Western nation to experience these phenomena. In spite of centuries of Christian history, the current population across Europe has virtually no knowledge of the good news and up until now has shown little willingness to even ask questions concerning the Christian gospel (Sherwood 2018). Yet there are encouraging signs of change.

The Roots and Development of Secularized Society

Scholars are agreed that "secularism's history is inextricably bound with that of Western Christendom" (Berlinerblau 2017, 86). The roots of secular society can be traced back centuries to a theological separation between what was considered the *secular* part of life from what was considered *sacred*. That which was deemed secular was focused on the mundane, profane, everyday parts of life. The sacred, however, was held to be of much higher importance, touching anything related to the church—whether it be a building, music, visual art, vocation, etc. This distinctly Western thinking, anchored in Greek philosophy (Makolkin 2015) rather than Scripture, became a cornerstone of Christendom during the Middle Ages. The hegemony of Western Christendom began to show its weakness with increasingly sharp criticism of the church coming from both Protestant Reformers and Enlightenment thinkers. Although dualistic thought continued to hold firm, it shifted to a dualism between the role of the church and the role of the state. In this new view the state now had the preeminence in public discourse, while the church was obligated to accept a secondary role in the private domain.

Western society embraced this perspective, putting its faith in government to care for its citizens and keep the peace between rival religious groups. Compartmentalization between public and private sectors, as well as between state and religious beliefs and practice, has proved fairly useful in maintaining peace and order in religiously pluralistic societies, but the cost has been the privatization of faith with little, if any, public influence in society.

In each Western nation, the process of secularization has been experienced a bit differently in response to its own cultural and historical context. The United States, one of the first countries to adopt the idea of the separation of church and state, interpreted the idea as a protection of the church from control of the government because of the large number of religious refugees fleeing to the New World. In Europe, concerns focused primarily on the protection of the government from undue control of religion, particularly that of the Roman Catholic Church. The 1689 English Bill of Rights assured the English that the Roman Catholic Church would not control the laws in England. In order to have a proper understanding of the separation of church and state in each country, one must understand the historical and cultural events that have been the precursors to its development.

French secularism, known as *laïcité* (which some translate as "secularity"), is a way of framing the philosophical debate concerning church and state in order to respond concretely to concerns about the practice of religion in society. The laws on *laïcité* took effect in 1905, but the roots extend much further back into France's history. Bloody battles between Roman Catholic and Protestant groups (Knecht 2002) and later merciless attacks on the Roman Catholic Church by anticlerical revolutionaries, beginning in 1789 (Religious Literacy Project 2018), were paramount in the lawmakers' minds. French Enlightenment thinkers worked hard to put distance between the dominance of the Roman Catholic Church and the newly emerging form of government, which was to be "of the people, by the people and for the people" (French Constitution 1958, article 2).

Although the word *laïcité* was not coined until a century later, the concept was already found in "The Declaration of the Rights of Man and the Citizen," published in August 1789, a month after the start of the French Revolution. Article 10 proclaims, "No one shall be disquieted on account of his opinions, including his religious views, provided their manifestation does not disturb the public order established by law" (Declaration of Human and Civic Rights of 26 August 1789). By the time of the writing of the 1958 French constitution, the term *laïcité* was front and center, a key to understanding the French Republic today. Article 1 states, "France shall be an indivisible, secular (*laïque*), democratic and social Republic. It shall ensure the equality of all citizens before the law, without distinction of origin, race or religion. It shall respect all beliefs. It shall be organized on a decentralized basis" (French Constitution 1958, article 1).

In France, the divide between public and private, church and state, has been deep. The process of secularization led to whole generations being insulated from the challenge of robust Christian thinking and practice. French populations began to be inoculated against what they perceived as the old Christian myths and their dominance over life. By World War II, the Roman Catholic Church proclaimed that France had become a mission field (Godin and Daniel 1943).

The way that *laïcité* is interpreted is constantly shifting, all the while it is asserted to be timeless. The need to respond to religious diversity in cities today, particularly to recent threats of radical Islamic terrorism, has thrust *laïcité* back into the forefront of the French political debate. French president Emmanuel Macron has often reminded his people that in France, "The République is secular, but (French) society is plural" (Lhaik 2018). The diverse pluralistic societies in which we live produce differences in values that are sometimes profound and incompatible. They push the limits of human rationality and political capacity to provide a solution that will accommodate most people in society (Maclure and Taylor 2010, 17–27).

French sociologist and historian Jean Baubérot is the foremost French specialist on the question of *laïcité*. He began one of his recent books by observing that "a large majority of the French are very attached to *laïcité*," but in the current confusion the risk is that "no one knows what it really consists of" (Baubérot 2015, 13). Baubérot points to a panoply of seven different understandings of *laïcité* coexisting in France today. They range from openly anti-religious and anticlerical to the Concordat system in Alsace-Moselle, where, for historic reasons, the French state officially recognizes and collaborates with the Roman Catholic, Reformed, and Lutheran churches, as well as the Jewish community.

Protestant evangelicals in France have experienced *laïcité* as a double-edged sword. At the turn of the twentieth century, when Protestants were an embattled minority, the 1905 laws protected churches, pastors, and missionaries and allowed them the joy of freedom of worship. However, it also put limitations on the scope of their missionary activities in public spaces such as schools, hospitals, and prisons (DILA 2017). Today the Muslim experience of *laïcité* is similar because of heightened tensions and amalgams with the militant Muslims. Moderate Muslims who are well integrated into French society have sought shelter under the laws of *laïcité*, as the Protestants did over one hundred years ago.

Some well-known political figures in France have suddenly "discovered" France's historic Christian identity and are attempting to interpret the laws of *laïcité* in ways that would block Muslims from entering the country and integrating into French society (Maurot 2012). Historically in France, the concept of *laïcité* was most strongly promoted by the left wing of the political machine, but recent events have prompted a sudden shift from left to right (Baubérot 2014, 7). That being said, virtually no one in France expresses a nostalgic longing to return to a state-established religion, Roman Catholicism or otherwise.

One of the foremost scholars on secularization today is Canadian philosopher Charles Taylor. In his masterpiece, *A Secular Age*, Taylor attempts to give new direction to thinking on secularism. He begins by asking, "Why was it virtually impossible not to believe in God in, say, 1500 in our Western society, while in 2000 many of us find this not only easy, but even inescapable?" (2007, 25). We need better responses than we have yet been given to the question on why secularization has become so deeply rooted in Western society.

Taylor begins on a new track and offers a three-pronged definition of secularity. The first two mirror the traditional understandings. The *first* definition is the separation of church and state, where the church no longer dominates life. The *second* definition is the decline of faith and practice. It is Taylor's *third* understanding, or definition, of secularity that becomes the focus of his attention in his nearly nine-hundred-page book and also connects with my own experience as a missionary in France. Taylor sees the third understanding as the logical conclusion of the slow but steady development of secular thought. Secularity is where society in general embraces nonbelief as the most intelligent, most viable option. "Belief in God is no longer axiomatic. There are alternatives" (ibid., 3). In this secular world we have permission, even encouragement, to not believe in God (Smith 2014, 4). It has become the age of "self-sufficing humanism" (Taylor 2007, 19). Belief in God has no connection with everyday life, and even thinking about it is a waste of time.

Traditional understandings of the process of secularization have run into difficulties in recent years. Back in the eighteenth century, many Enlightenment thinkers, like Voltaire, believed that "religion was on a diminishing road" (Erlanger and de Freytas-Tamura 2015). Scholars in the nineteenth century turned to science and away from Christian faith, believing that the end of organized religion was unavoidable in light of industrialization (Norris and Inglehart 2011, 8). In 1959, sociologist C. Wright Mills wrote confidently that the process of secularization had "loosened the dominance of the sacred. In due course, the sacred shall disappear altogether except, possibly, in the private realm" (Mills 1959, 32–33). Other sociologists in the sixties and seventies, such as Peter Berger, David Martin, and Bryan Wilson, agreed and promoted the *secularization theory*, claiming that modernity inevitably produces a decline of religion (Norris 2003, 4). As science advances in modern life, the theory goes, religion loses its plausibility and becomes privatized and marginalized, thus losing its significance. Because secularization is primarily a Western phenomenon, many have come to see it as practically synonymous with de-Christianization (Clark 2012, 161–94).

However, more recently sociologists, such as Rodney Stark, Roger Fink, and Peter Berger, as well as others, tell us that the data collected over the last decades does not support this theory. Stark and Finke wrote, "After nearly three centuries of utterly failed prophecies and misrepresentations of both present and past, it seems time to carry the secularization doctrine to the graveyard of failed theories" (2000, 79). Berger humbly came to the conclusion that "the assumption that we live in a secularized world is false. The world today, with some exceptions...is as furiously religious as it ever was, and in some places more so than ever" (1999, 2). Berger specified at the end of his life that there are only two areas in the world that are heavily secularized. One is geographical: the area of Western and Central Europe. The other is what Berger calls the international intellectual class, wherever you find them (Thuswaldner 2014, 16–21).

Berger went on to say:

I came to the conclusion some years ago that to replace secularization theory—to explain religion in the modern world—we need the theory of pluralism. Modernity does not necessarily produce secularity. It necessarily produces pluralism, by which I mean the coexistence in the same society of different worldviews and value systems. (ibid., 16–21).

British missiologist Lesslie Newbigin also sees pluralism as the central focus in the struggle to faithfully communicate the good news of the gospel. Europe is 73 percent urbanized (United Nations Report 2014, 8), and the cities of Europe all have populations of religious groups such as Muslims, Buddhists, Hindus, and Sikhs, as well as Christians. Emmanuel Macron's observation that "the French State is secular, but French society is clearly plural" (Lhaik 2018) seems to agree with Berger and Newbigin. While we may be willing to embrace the diversity of cultural pluralism, the questions raised by religious pluralism have led to doubt among believers and those who want to believe. Newbigin (1991) believed that the church in Europe has been very timid about public proclamation of the gospel. Christians struggle to find ways to present the gospel in an engaging way in a pluralistic context. Unlike science, religion is understood in secular society as something strictly personal—and unverifiable. No particular religious belief is perceived as truer than another. Newbigin points out that with the collapse of the theory of secularization there is a rise in new religious movements among the young and affluent in European society (1989, 212–13).

Twenty years ago, French social scientist Danièle Hervieu-Léger published a book based on her research on religion in French society. She wrote that there had been a resurgence of religion in France, but that many had missed it because it did not conform to classical understandings or denominational structures (Hervieu-Léger 1999, 29–60). The rise in religious interest is clear, but the expressions are widely diverse. Hervieu-Léger uses the word *exculturation* (2003, 91–132) to describe how French society has abandoned the church's sphere of influence. She writes, "Society having 'exited religion' eliminates even the footprints that the church had left in the culture" (ibid., 288).[2] The history, words, holidays, and images from Christendom have been emptied of their meaning and discarded. At the same time, believers no longer identify themselves with the surrounding secular culture. The sad result is that at the moment in history when there is a renewed interest in the

2 Translation is mine.

spiritual and the transcendent, neither group knows how to communicate with the other.

Even though predictions of the secularization theory have largely failed, it is true that in Western culture we are miles away from where our historical-cultural journey began. We have had radical shifts in how we understand human beings, our roles in society, and our identities. But in regard to Christian faith, modern Western society has gotten lost along the way and no longer knows where to turn, or even what words to use to describe its predicament.

Taylor's work is pertinent at this point. In a 2015 interview with Glenn Smith (Taylor 2015), he talked about why it was important to have a new narrative for our understanding of secularity. It is not enough to simply acknowledge that the secularization theory had failed; another story needs to become embedded in our history and our sociological understanding. Taylor proposes a narrative that explains the shifts in thought over the past several hundred years that allowed for radical changes in thinking to occur (ibid.).

According to Taylor, in the five hundred years since the end of the Middle Ages, in order for secularization of this kind to take hold, the "obstacles to unbelief" had to first be dismantled (Smith 2014, 28). An example is the process beginning with an "enchanted world," where all of society is keenly aware of the spiritual realm, to one of disenchantment. In our disenchanted world, we accuse each other of lazy, unintellectual thinking when we engage in any reflection on spiritual forces (Taylor 2007, 28–29). Taylor talks about Deism being a sort of halfway point in the long journey from belief to unbelief (ibid., 221). At this point, we have moved from Father God, the creator who evokes our worship through his creation, to an impersonal, distant creator. The focus shifts from worship to order, moralism, and the accomplishment of good as man's goal.

Today, at the end of this five-hundred-year journey, we arrive at what Taylor calls "exclusive humanism," where no reference to God is sought or required. He uses the metaphor of the "imminent frame" (ibid., 539–93) to describe the end result of our "disenchantment." The frame is a natural order, totally cut off from the spiritual, the supernatural (ibid., 542). The goal of Western humanity today is to find their own happiness and fulfillment in life—to "flourish," using Taylor's word (ibid., 16). This human flourishing, however, is totally unconnected to anything related to a god.

In the interview, Taylor reminds us not to waste time thinking that they (secular society) won the battle and we (Christians) lost. That is merely looking back wistfully at the model of Christendom. The gospel is heard differently when we stop fighting to "return to Christendom" to recover what we lost (Taylor 2015). He believes that leaving Christendom has some positive aspects for reflection. Christendom inevitably had a certain level of coercion. Now people are totally free to be seekers on a spiritual journey or pilgrimage. Another aspect is that we can have a different picture of doubt. "Doubt is not a threat to faith. Doubt helps us grow" (ibid.).

So what is the way forward in our secular age, as defined by Taylor's third definition? One of his strongest suggestions, surprisingly, is to take conversion seriously (ibid.). Converts are the ones who have broken out of the immanent frame (Taylor 2007, 728).

Taylor encourages Christians to self-define by reaching out in ways that others do not and would not think of doing. The model is Jesus, who surprised people by reaching out to publicans, prostitutes, Pharisees, and Samaritans—caring for all who were in need. Christians need to be known for the way they reach out and not for their sharp reactions to people who insult them, their faith, or their friends. Taylor cautions Christians to respond compassionately to angry reactions rather than to condemn. Kind responses become a *firebreak*, slowing or stopping the advancement of hatred (Taylor 2015).

Discouragement and Signs of Hope in Secular Europe Today

Missionaries, whether they have grown up in a Christian family or come to faith as adults, have a deep sense of personal gratitude for the gospel. They have experienced God's forgiveness, physical and emotional healing, and have seen families restored. They have encountered the Lord in some of their deepest personal struggles. They have seen whole congregations experience surprising renewal that only comes from the Spirit of our loving Lord. So, when leaving their nurturing environment to go out as missionaries, they expect the same Lord to reproduce the same results in their receiving country. Many do not adequately take into account the cultural, spiritual, and other contextual realities that make secular culture more resistant to the good news. Even when presenting the gospel with the best of intentions, this life-giving message is often met with stifled laughter or total indifference and boredom, resulting in deep disappointment among the missionaries. Discouragement of this kind has been common, leading many to dub France the graveyard of missionaries (Broussard 2012).

In addition, American mission boards have often focused on a revivalist approach to evangelism—a call to return to faith. In Europe, there is virtually nothing left to revive. When missionaries labor to invite people to church by stuffing mailboxes and speaking to people on the street in order to invite them to hear a preacher, they should be prepared for discouragement. They are not connecting in any way to the reality of our secular audience. Another reason for discouragement is that secular culture tells us that our faith has little or nothing to offer society—if we insist on practicing our faith, we must keep it private. Any public proclamation of the Christian gospel as *the* truth is perceived as intolerant, even arrogant and divisive.

At the same time, there is good news if one knows where to look. First, it must be noted that the dearly held theory of the unimpeded advancement of secularization has been judged and found wanting, primarily because of ample proof of increased religious practice everywhere. Evangelicals are certainly representative of this trend. Harvey Cox, author of *The Secular City* (1965), published *Fire from Heaven* in 1995, highlighting the role of Pentecostalism in the secular world's religious renaissance. Across Europe, church-planting efforts led by Europeans are seeing hard-won successes (Redeemer City to City). In France, new churches are being planted every ten days (France Mission). Although the overall total remains small, L'Institut Biblique de Nogent reports that the number of evangelical believers in France has doubled in the past ten years (Institut Biblique de Nogent). According to a France 24 television report, the number of evangelicals in France has gone from 50,000 in 1950 to 650,000 in 2018 (France 24 2018). In the report, church members cite the emphasis on personal conversion and meeting practical needs in modern society as reasons for evangelical church growth in France.

Secondly, there is an evident curiosity—even a new hunger—for the spiritual, the transcendent. This interest reveals itself, for instance, in various forms of artistic expression, particularly among the younger generation. Two recent examples are Pascal Obispo's musical, *La Fresque Musicale Jesus—De Nazareth à Jérusalem* (Obispo 2017), and Natasha St-Pier's newest album, *Thérèse de Lisieux—Aimer C'est Tout Donner* (St-Pier 2018). Believers need to learn to tap into this hunger creatively. Spiritual curiosity can also be seen in the number of young adults who are involved in Alpha courses (www.alpha.org), who visit the monastic community of Taizé (www.taize.fr/en), or who take pilgrimages on the Camino Santiago de Compostela (www.santiago-compostela.net) in Spain.

Thirdly, the call to mission has emphasized Jesus' call to go the ends of the earth. People from the ends of the earth have now come to our cities and become our neighbors and friends in our own urban environments. These future leaders of business, politics, and medicine from the emerging nations of the world have come to our Western cities for training and experience. The door to share the good news with these talented people is often wide open. An ironic example can be found in France's deep connections with the Islamic world, which has provided a very important open door into the Muslim world for the spread of the gospel. The secular press is watching carefully and reporting regularly on these events (Chambraud and Couvelaire 2017).

In dealing with secular society, the open doors for the gospel are not usually where one would expect. To quote Henry Blackaby, we must learn to "watch to see where God is working and join Him in His work" (2004, 70). This means moving outside of our comfort zone and learning to expect the unexpected from God. We don't expect to find God hard at work in our secular societies, so our thinking needs to be challenged and shaped by Scripture. There we can find stories of godly leaders in both the Old and New Testaments discovering open doors in in hospitable circumstances. Two examples come from the cities of Babylon and Athens. These stories do not occur in secular cultures, since secularization is a modern Western development, yet they are certainly set in pluralistic, pagan cultures.

Ministry in Babylon and Athens

We read in the first chapter of the book of Daniel that it was the third year of Jehoiakim's reign, or 605 BC, when Daniel and his three friends found themselves standing in Nebuchadnezzar's court. They were part of a remnant of Jews who had remained faithful to God after most had turned their backs on the Lord. These godly young men of Jerusalem had suffered the loss of their families, their home, their culture, and their noble status. God's city, Jerusalem, had passed into the hands of the enemy army and they were deported to the great pagan city of Babylon. Although Daniel lived a long life, he probably never saw Jerusalem again. Yet he remained faithful to God and served in the court of pagan kings until 539 BC (Dan 1:21).

As education for their work began, Daniel and his Jewish friends were taught the language and literature of Babylon (Dan 1:4), which was known for its poetry and stories, both humorous and bawdy. It was filled with the mythology of Babylonian gods in rich detail. In this culture, which prized divination, God gave Daniel the special ability to interpret the meanings of visions and dreams. He became known for his "unusual aptitude for understanding every aspect of literature and wisdom" (Dan 1:17 NLT), which brought him the respect of his pagan peers.

The wealth, beauty, and power of Babylonian culture can still be attested to by visiting a number of the world's great museums. Yet idolatrous practices were linked to every aspect of life in Babylon. Daniel was required to study Babylonian culture and did not seek to be disconnected from it in order to be protected from the confusing evil world around him. Instead, Daniel prayed (Dan 6:10) and relied on God. It was God's heart and God's word that helped him sift through his thoughts and daily experiences, retaining and applying the values of God's kingdom.

The ability of humans to create culture is part of God's plan, as outlined in what we call the *cultural mandate* (Gen 1:28). It was God's intention for humans to work alongside of God, using God's gifts and resources for the ongoing development of the world God called into existence (Edgar 2017, 26). Today, in our fallen world, there are beautiful and fascinating parts of all cultures; significant aspects of French, Ethiopian, Afghan, and Chinese cultures all testify to the wonder of God's creative genius. Cultures are developed by human beings—created in God's image, following God's design. Sadly, they also reflect the damage of human sin. The process of secularization draws attention away from God, focusing on humanity as an end in itself, leading to an increasingly sterile life. Healthy development of culture is the opposite, opening up creative possibilities and drawing us to our Lord, the author of all that is "very good" (Gen 1:31). Likewise, Daniel grew and flourished in the midst of Babylonian culture, not outside of it.

Daniel was not the only one learning these lessons. About twelve years after Daniel's arrival in Babylon, Jeremiah the prophet sent a letter from Jerusalem to the whole Jewish community in exile (Jer. 29), exhorting the people to learn how to flourish in that hostile society through "outward-looking cultural engagement" (Edgar 2017, 207). God asked them to be fruitful—to multiply and build. God asked them to pray for Babylon and seek its *shalom*. If God's word is true, then putting the cultural mandate into practice in Babylon was just as possible as it was in Jerusalem.

Six hundred years after Daniel, the apostle Paul entered the great city of Athens for the first time. This polytheistic city was the center of learning for the whole Roman Empire. Paul, who was raised as a Pharisee, had not even been permitted to read literature written by pagans, much less study their gods. Like any serious Jewish scholar, Paul knew the depth of evil that the worship of false gods represented. The books of the Law and the Prophets spoke very harshly about any compromise with idolatry. When Paul, now an apostle of Jesus, arrived in Athens, he was still deeply distressed by the rampant idolatry (Acts 17:16), but his approach had changed radically form his early upbringing. Paul engaged with both Jews and Greeks freely, and treated them with equal respect (Acts 17:22). He actively explored their culture and read the inscriptions on the idols. When invited to present his views to a group of Greek philosophers, Paul eagerly accepted. What is striking is that Paul did not quote from Scripture, as one would expect; instead he cited an inscription he found to an "unknown god." Showing his familiarity with Greek poetry, Paul quoted verses from two different poets, Epimenides and Aratus. With this foundation, Paul taught about the "unknown god" being the creator and sustainer of life. At the mention of the resurrection, the meeting broke up with both dismissive laughter and curiosity.

Paul's approach shows a freedom to engage with pagan culture, which put him in direct opposition to his early training. Conservative Jewish groups and other believers in Christ from a Jewish cultural background were in constant conflict with him over this point. Paul had learned that "the way we hear the Gospel is through our culture, not in spite of it" (Lausanne Occasional Papers No. 2 1978, 7). He taught us that it is not the idolaters and sexually immoral people of this world whom we are to avoid, but rather those within the church who act in such a way (1 Cor 5:9–11). Those on the outside need to hear the good news from a friend who cares for them.

We must avoid the individualistic tendencies of secular culture. The cultural context is not the threat to our spiritual life. It is how our hearts respond to those cultural elements, those false values that reveal our deepest desires. To borrow an image from Tolkien, we need to avoid the risk of becoming a loner like Gollum—harboring covetous desires, saying "My precious" in regard to the money, lifestyle, and politics of this world (1 John 2:15). What are we willing to keep and what are we willing to give up?

We need communities of believers who are willing to help one another learn how to be engaged in this world while not becoming a part of it. Together, we must lead each other into a transformative encounter with God (Rom 12:2). The decisions we make are rarely simple or easy, but when we allow ourselves—for the sake of convenience—to make decisions that are simplistic, black and white, all or nothing, then the salt of the earth becomes insipid. Jesus did not pray that we would be taken out of this world, but that we would be protected from evil while active in it (John 17:15). He told us that we, as his disciples, are being sent out on mission in the same way God the Father sent him: fully human and fully equipped with God's Spirit (John 20:21–22).

In God's mind, there is no room for dualistic thinking. There are not two worlds, a sacred/religious world and a secular world. There is only one world, which God created. We have been given one life in this world in which we can make a difference. Like Daniel and Paul, we are to be envoys of the kingdom of God, active agents of change. Paul uses the metaphor of an "ambassador" to describe our responsibility (2 Cor 5:20). We are to be fully connected and engaged with secular society in order to correctly represent God's interests in this world that he loves.

(Re)Connecting with Secular Society

In Europe, the tide of religious sentiment continued its retreat unabated for several generations, giving credence to the secularization thesis. However, the tide is turning. The idea of a continuous advance of secularization has been proven faulty. Interest in the spiritual is once again on the rise. The problem today is that the younger generations who have been nurtured in secular thought have been *exculturated*, to use Hervieu-Léger's word. The disconnect means that although they may have the instinct to explore the ideas or the notion of transcendence, they do not have the tools or even the words to describe what they are seeking. Christians must also admit that we do not feel much affinity for their secularized culture.

Those of us who have answered a call to ministry within a deeply secularized Western culture develop tempered expectations of what God will do. We feel a bit like Jesus' disciples when he asked them to throw their nets in again after fishing all night without catching anything (Luke 5:5). Missionaries need to find ways to reconnect concretely with culture for the sake of the gospel, and to respond to Jesus' call by faith to throw the nets in once again.

Reconnecting with culture in a secularized society requires that we respond by humbly taking the first step and *entering the broader world with eagerness to learn*. Missionaries have normally excelled in this kind of cross-cultural challenge, but we have come to somewhat believe that our private religious world is where we are supposed to be and we seem to have forgotten how to connect with the public sector. We must remember that our host culture has facets of beauty and vestiges of creation, which reflect the glory of the Creator. It is a gift to be able to learn the language and culture, to enjoy the food, the art and ideas, and to explore them thoroughly.

Learning a language takes time. Learning a culture takes even more time, but they are linked. It is absolutely essential for the success of mission to learn the language well in order to appreciate and fully enter into that new culture. American missions have sometimes not allowed enough time or money for this essential step in Western nations where English is a strong second language. This is a serious mistake, which makes it very difficult for young missionaries to properly connect with people on a deeper level. A surface-level connection is not enough.

In addition to time and money, learning a language and a culture requires humility and a willingness to show weakness. Adults despise feeling dependent on others, like a child again. However, this is precisely what unlocks doors with secular culture. Learners are no longer perceived as a threat, and surprisingly the doors begin to open for a true friendship when one reveals weakness and asks for help.

For me, an example that comes to mind was learning how to hang art shows with professional artists in a gallery at the center of Paris. For a few years, I was "the student" again, with many different artists as my teachers. I would watch and ask many questions, working closely with them before gaining confidence in composing arts shows. Through this process I made many new friends, leading to fascinating conversations about art and about God. Experiences like this make clear that some of the significant barriers to outreach we have to overcome in this secular culture are actually within us.

Once launched on this new trajectory, we also realize that we will never be self-sufficient again. We will always be asking questions, always learning in our host culture. This new humility must become a permanent reality, our new normal. With the help of our new friends, we explore their culture and God's creation with them to find multiple points of connection. We explore together and engage them by asking many questions. In a secular culture, we must never begin by expecting people to come first to our church and ask the right questions. They won't. They will, however, be happy to answer honest questions and show us their culture.

Art is another key point of connection. Among artists from all disciplines there is a pronounced interest in the spiritual dimensions of life that appears regularly in their work. The church might not find many artists exploring links to a historic Christian worldview, but there is interest in a transcendent reality that breaks with the predominant secular thinking. In French culture, as with other European cultures, there is a tendency to honor the intellectual and ignore the religious. French culture has an appreciation for deep-thinking artists and good art of all kinds. Art is a well-established bridge between the spiritual world and the secular world, one that has been largely ignored by the church. It has a way of engaging that is significant, but this process does not happen with words (Thrall 2009).

Art is a language, which—although we have all been exposed to it—remains a foreign language to most of us. The "goal is to hand people a key to this world that is rich and fascinating yet sometimes hard to enter" (ArtWay). It communicates the deep thoughts and reflections of the heart. Jesus reminds us that the transformative changes he looks for happen on a profound, foundational level—that of the heart. Art is a natural form of communication with the heart, but it is never simplistic.

Taylor seems to have discovered the same idea and uses the example of poetry. He believes that our language today has been flattened, emptied and impoverished through its instrumentalization. He goes on to say that "through language in its constitutive use...we open up contact with something higher or deeper" (2007, 758).

Whether in music, painting, dance, drama, and the like, art is not a form of direct communication; it is indirect. Art tells stories, points, gives clues. Art beckons by asking questions. It refuses to give direct answers and explain. It piques people's curiosity and draws them further into their search. For many who are eager to communicate directly about the good news of the gospel, this seems like a distraction. In a secularized culture, however, an indirect approach tills soil, plants seeds, and nurtures curiosity that will lead to harvest later. For those of us who have never been trained in art, this will be another exercise in humility—but one that will prove to be fruitful.

In a society of self-sufficient individualism, a *healthy multicultural community* is another connection point, a novelty that attracts attention and raises questions. Those on the outside of the church may begin to wonder, "How did such a diverse group of people ever find one another? What holds them together? What are their core beliefs and values?"

The majority of congregations in Paris, both Catholic and Protestant, are culturally diverse. At one point, our family was involved in a new church where sixteen different nations were represented among the thirty-five regular attenders. At Christmas, we chose to honor those cultural differences by asking members of the congregation to prepare and share typical Christmas food and songs, representing their culture, at the church's Christmas celebration.

Our invited neighbors and friends were intrigued by the experience, which stimulated good conversations about our faith.

In spite of the many differences, Scripture affirms that every person we encounter is wondrously and marvelously created by our Lord (Ps 139). Even for believers, a culturally diverse community presents a myriad of challenges. Churches in multicultural communities must lead the way, learning to embrace the God-given opportunities to open their arms and welcome others warmly. We must learn how to express love in concrete terms, responding to each culture. The host culture needs to learn how to be the *servant*, giving away their "rights"[3] in order to warmly welcome as many as possible (1 Cor 9:19–22). For instance, in our Western world, which has become fearful of Islam, believers of the gospel need to show people how to love our Muslim neighbors as ourselves—to care for them as we care for ourselves. Actions of this variety become the firebreak to which Taylor refers.

Urban neighborhoods in the secularized West are filling up with migrants from all over the globe. When our churches are made up of members who are in deep relationship with other members representing the diversity of our communities, it becomes a powerful public testimony to the transformation of the gospel. Vibrant multicultural Christian communities caring for their members and their neighbors are the best antidote to the vapid privatization of faith promoted by *laïcité*.

The younger generation in our secular society is beginning to consider the "God option." They are looking for an authentic experience and community, and they need to see a clear *congruence between words and actions*. This longing for words leading to real action reaches far beyond the religious world. By this standard of congruence, the political world in the West has been judged and found wanting. If the church wants to connect and does not want to suffer the same fate as the old European political parties, we need to check our hearts and motives. Hypocrisy is not treated kindly. This is the time the Christian community can and must shine brightly.

Missionaries need to learn to *celebrate the small steps*, even the baby steps, people take in their walk toward the Lord. We must cultivate a willingness to be patient during their long journey to conversion. People may take years to come to deep faith. The patience necessary will require hard work, prayer, real friendship, and also celebration at appropriate times. I have an artist friend who introduced himself to me ten years ago as an atheist.

---

3 By "rights," I mean the host culture's privilege to employ the exclusive use of its language, food, worship style, and leadership style in all church-related activities.

As we have worked on many art-related projects together, he has become one of my closest friends. He has attended church services regularly, and Bible studies on occasion. I would like to see him continue to grow; but he clearly expresses faith in God, and for this I am extremely grateful.

We can become discouraged when we have little to report to mission agencies and supporters who are looking for quantifiable results. Thankfully, Jesus did not reason like this! In a deeply secularized society, we will find encouragement when we watch how people begin, tentatively at first, to move in the direction of God. We need to celebrate all along the route to a solid relationship with the Lord.

Reconnecting with our surrounding culture in a healthy way, as exemplified by Daniel and Paul, will require hard work. For too long, the church's fears and confusion about secular culture have coerced it into pulling back and disconnecting from any possibility of cultural engagement out of concern that secularization will subtly seep into our souls. At the same time, secular society has lost an ability to understand Christian spirituality and the core of the gospel message.

In recent years, there have been signs that change is happening in Western society. People are beginning to ask fresh questions about God. Responding requires meeting people in their cultural context. It is up to Christians to boldly take the first steps. We need to humble ourselves, learn, reconnect, engage, and act with integrity within secular culture for the gospel message to bring them to true conversion. Connecting involves an inclination to be a learner—to try new ways and learn from failures. It does require that our church communities step out of our comfort zones with a willingness to take risks. When we are willing to leave comfort and safety behind, we are most likely to find God already hard at work in the most unusual places.

References

ArtWay. "Vision." http://www.artway.eu/artwayphp?id=3&action =show&lang=en.

Astier, Henri. 2004. "The Deep Roots of French Secularism." *BBC News Online*, September 1. http://news.bbc.co.uk/2/hi/europe/3325285.stm.

Baubérot, Jean. 2014. *La Laïcité Falsifiée*. Paris: La Découverte.

———. 2015. *Les 7 laïcités Françaises*. Paris: Edition de la Maison des sciences de l'homme.

Berger, Peter. 1967. *The Sacred Canopy: Elements of a Sociological Theory of Religion*. Garden City, NY: Doubleday.

————, ed. 1999. *The Desecularization of the World: Resurgent Religion and World Politics*. Grand Rapids: Eerdmans.

Berlinerblau, Jacques. 2017. "Political Secularism." In *The Oxford Handbook of Secularism*, edited by Phil Zuckerman and John Shook, 85–102. Oxford: Oxford University Press.

Blackaby, Henry. 2004. *Experiencing God*. Nashville: Broadman & Holman.

Broussard, David. 2012. "What Nobody Is Saying about France." *Christian Headlines*, April 9. https://www.christianheadlines.com /news/what-nobody-is-saying-about-france.html.

Chambraud, Cécile, and Louise Couvelaire. 2017. "Quand les évangéliques s'emploient à convertir les musulmans." *Le Monde*, May 22. https://www.lemonde.fr/religions/ article/2017/05/22/quand -les-evangeliques-s-emploient-a-convertir-les-musulmans_5131740 _1653130.html.

Clark, J. C. D. 2012. "Historiographical Reviews: Secularization and Modernization: The Failure of a 'Grand Narrative.'" *The Historical Journal* 55 (1): 161–94. https://www.cambridge.org/core/services/aop-cambridge-core/content/ view/7B7C772F14A974F07AAEC4D8A13862C8/S0018246X11000586a .pdf/secularization-and-modernization-the-failure-of-a-grand-narrative.pdf.

Cox, Harvey. 1995. *Fire from Heaven*. Reading, MA: Addison-Wesley.

————. 2013 [1965]. *The Secular City: Secularization and Urbanization in Theological Perspective*. Rev. ed. Princeton, NJ: Princeton University Press.

Declaration of Human and Civic Rights of 26 August 1789, Article 10. https://www. conseil-constitutionnel.fr/sites/default/files/as/root/bank_mm/anglais/cst2.pdf.

DILA: Direction de l'information légale et administrative. 2017. "L'Etat, Garant de la Liberty Religieuse." Administration centrale des services du Premier Ministre. Last modified July 1. http://www.vie-publique.fr/politiques-publiques/etat-cultes-laicite/ liberte-religieuse/.

Edgar, William. 2017. *Created and Creating: A Biblical Theology of Culture*. Downers Grove, IL: IVP Academic.

Erlanger, Steven, and Kimiko de Freytas-Tamura. 2015. "Old Tradition of Secularism Clashes with France's New Reality." *New York Times*, February 5. https://www. nytimes.com/2015/02/06/world/old-tradition-of-secularism-clashes-with-frances- new-reality.html.

France 24. 2018. "The Surprising Growth of Evangelical Churches in France." Reported by Juliette Lacharnay. March 19. Video, 6:25. https://www.france24.com/en/20180319- france-evangelical-churches-christians-popularity-expansion-technology-religion.

France Mission. 2019. "Church Planting." http://france-mission.com/fmtrust/web/page/3- Church-planting.html.

French Constitution. 1958. "Constitution of 4 October 1958." https://www.conseil- constitutionnel.fr/en/constitution-of-4-october-1958.

Godin, Henri, and Yvan Daniel. 1943. *La France: Pays de Mission?* Paris: Editions du Cerf.

Hervieu-Léger, Danièle. 1999. *Le Pèlerin et le Converti; la Religion en Movement*. Paris: Flammarion.

————. 2003. *Catholicisme, la fin d'un monde*. Paris: Bayard.

Institut Biblique de Nogent. "Building for the Future." https://www.ibnogent.org/building-for-the-future/.

Knecht, Robert J. 2002. *The French Religious Wars 1562–98*. Oxford: Osprey.

Lausanne Occasional Papers No. 2. 1978. "The Willowbank Report: Consultation on Gospel and Culture." Charlotte: Lausanne Committee for World Evangelization.

Lhaik, Corinne. 2018. "Macron, Dieu et La Politique," *L'Express*, 23 Janvier, 2018.

M4 Europe. "Ce qui nous définit et nous guide." http://m4europe.com/fr.

Maclure, Jocelyn, and Charles Taylor. 2010. *Laïcité & Liberté de Conscience*. Paris: La Découverte.

Makolkin, Anna, 2015. "Aristotle's Views on Religion and His Idea of Secularism." E-LOGOS—*Electronic Journal for Philosophy* 22 (2): 71–79. https://nb.vse.cz/kfil/elogos/history/22_16_makolkin.pdf.

Maurot, Élodie. 2012. "Jean Baubérot: 'N'utilisons pas la laïcité contre l'islam.'" *La Croix*, October 2. https://www.la-croix.com/Debats/Opinions/Debats/Jean-Bauberot-N-utilisons-pas-la-laicite-contre-l-islam-_NP_-2012–02–10–767265.

Mills, C. Wright. 1959. *The Sociological Imagination*. Oxford: Oxford University Press.

Newbigin, Lesslie. 1989. *The Gospel in a Pluralist Society*. Grand Rapids: Eerdmans.

——. 1991. "An Informal Backyard Interview with Lesslie Newbigin ca. 1991." Interviewed by Chad Crouch. Video, 28:46. https://www.youtube.com/watch?v=b5BO40CUYXs.

Norris, Pippa. 2003. "The Secularization Debate." Chap. 1 in *Sacred and Secular: Religion and Politics Worldwide*. New York: Cambridge University Press. https://sites.hks.harvard.edu/fs/pnorris/Acrobat/Sacred_and_Secular/Chapter%201.pdf.

Norris, Pippa, and Ronald Inglehart. 2011. *Sacred and Secular: Religion and Politics Worldwide*. 2nd ed. New York: Cambridge University Press.

Obispo, Pascal. 2017. *La Fresque Musicale Jésus—De Nazareth à Jérusalem*. http://www.nrj.fr/artistes/pascal-obispo/albums/la-fresque-musicale-jesus-de-nazareth-a-jerusalem.

Redeemer City to City. "Europe." https://www.redeemercitytocity.com/europe.

Religious Literacy Project. 2019. "Historical Legacies." Country Profiles, Religious Literacy Project, Harvard Divinity School, https://rlp.hds.harvard.edu/for-educators/country-profiles/france/historical-legacies.

Sherwood, Harriet. 2018. "'Christianity as Default Is Gone': The Rise of a Non-Christian Europe." The Guardian, 21 March 20, https://www.theguardian.com/world/2018/mar/21/christianity-non-christian-europe-young-people-survey-religion.

Smith, James K. A. 2014. *How (Not) to Be Secular: Reading Charles Taylor*. Grand Rapids: Eerdmans.

St-Pier, Natasha. 2018. Thérèse de Lisieux—Aimer C'est Tout Donner. http://www.nrj.fr/artistes/natasha-st-pier/albums/therese-de-lisieux-aimer-c-est-tout-donner.

Stark, Rodney, and Roger Finke. 2000. *Acts of Faith: Explaining the Human Side of Religion*. Berkeley, CA: University of California.

Taylor, Charles. 2007. *A Secular Age*. Cambridge, MA: Belknap Press of Harvard University.

————. 2015. "Interview with Charles Taylor." Interviewed by Glenn Smith. August. Video, 16:30. https://vimeo.com/143608489.

Thrall, Steve. 2009. "Engaging in Art with Missional Intent in Paris." Lausanne World Pulse Archives issue 2 (2009). http://www.lausanneworldpulse.com/urban-php/1082/02–2009.

Thuswaldner, Gregor. 2014. "A Conversation with Peter L. Berger: 'How My Views Have Changed.'" The Cresset 77 (3): 16–21. http://thecresset.org/2014/Lent/Thuswaldner_L14.html.

United Nations Report. 2014. World Urbanization Prospects, 2014 Revision. https://esa.un.org/unpd/wup/Publications/Files/WUP2014-Highlights.pdf.

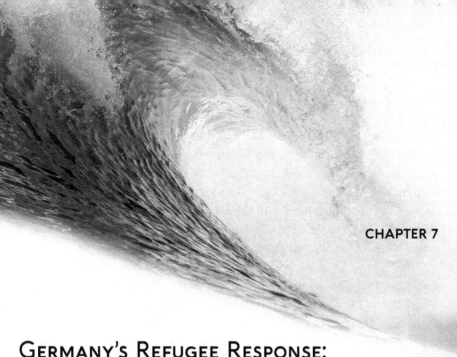

CHAPTER 7

Germany's Refugee Response: Implications for Ministry in a Secularized World

Steven B. Kern

Five hundred years ago, it would have been difficult to imagine Germany in its current spiritual state. After all, spiritual life was at the core of personal life and even national identity. Catholicism was widespread. Even though the beginning of the Reformation seemed to polarize people, it also resulted in a galvanizing of faith convictions. Spiritual orientation and influence were pervasive.

Fast forward to today. With the five hundredth anniversary of the publication of Luther's theses now in the recent past, one can appropriately ask, "What has changed over the centuries?" As with other nations, Germany has certainly felt the secularizing influences of the Enlightenment, industrial revolution, and scientific age. These have moved the attention of Germans from the intangible to the tangible, from spiritual to material, and from the less quantifiable to that which can be measured.

Evidence of Germany's Secularization

In addition, Germany has also felt the secularizing impact of the Weimar Constitution of 1919 and the German Basic Law (constitution) of 1949. On the one hand, these guiding documents grant the individual German states the right and responsibility to rule in areas of church-state relationships, even making provision for religious instruction in public schools. Still, they make clear "that there is no state church and that religious societies regulate and administer their affairs independently, thereby generally establishing a separation between church and state" (Gesley 2017).

But is the "Land of Luther" really all that secular? At first glance, it may seem as if spiritual influence continues to play a critical role in German life. Church membership statistics seem to point to a vital spiritual life. After all, 2016 reports indicate that roughly 23.6 million Germans are members of the Catholic Church. Meanwhile, some 21.9 million are members of the Protestant Church (Katholische Kirche in Deutschland 2017, 7). Together, these numbers total church membership of more than 55 percent of the German population of 82 million. Note that while other denominations and faiths are represented in Germany, their numbers pale in comparison to these two primary expressions (Forschungsgruppe Weltanschauungen in Deutschland 2018).

Church membership, however, has seen a steady decline over the last twenty-five years. In contrast, some 72 percent of Germans claimed church membership in 1991, just two years after the time of East/West reunification (Wolf 2008, 114). This represents, then, a 17 percent drop in church membership between 1991 and 2016.

Still, even the more recent 55 percent figure seems to represent an impressive statistic. Can such a land be considered "secular"? After all, the majority of Germans are still members of one of the two main churches (Catholic or Protestant). Membership, however, does not tell the full story of these faith adherents. As Wolf pointed out more than ten years ago, "This process [of declining church membership] could have been seen as positive if the remaining members had become more committed" (ibid.). Have they become more committed? Not if church attendance is any indication. The Catholic Church reports that only 10.2 percent of Catholics were in church on one of two Sundays in 2016 when numbers were tallied (Katholische Kirche in Deutschland 2017, 46). That is less than half of the 21.9 percent who attended in 1990 (Secretary of the German Bishop's Conference 2011). Meanwhile, the

Lutheran Church describes more stable attendance percentages over the same time period, but also more discouraging statistics, with an average of about 766,000 church attenders on a given Sunday, totaling roughly 3.4 percent of their total membership (Evangelische Kirche in Deutschland 2017, 20).

As a whole, then, only 3.9 percent of the German population is in church on a given Sunday. Based on these statistics, Wolf's decade-old comments are even more appropriate today: "Taken together, these findings [of declining membership and church attendance] clearly demonstrate a tremendous decline of traditional church-based religiosity in Germany" (Wolf 2008, 114). While other declining statistics could be explored, as Warner states in a similar evaluation of Great Britain, "This statistical decline is symptomatic of the fact that the Christian religion has been suffering from a profound decline in social and religious significance" (Warner 2010, 13).

The progressive erosion of church membership, attendance, and the spiritual influence in how a person acts and thinks is indicative of a larger problem—the secularization of Germany. Bryan Wilson describes secularization as "the declining social significance of religion" (Wilson 1966, 14), while Steve Bruce defines it as "the displacement of religion from the center of life" (Bruce 2011, 1).

The presence of secularization and the degree of its influence may also be measured by tools like surveyed assessments of spiritual beliefs. Still, even faith convictions do not tell the full story. While secularization can be related to convictions, it is not equivalent to the absence of faith conviction. A secular culture may still have faith convictions, but the growing pluralization of their beliefs may make them more difficult to assess. At the same time, the increasing privatization of and/or the perceived irrelevance of faith issues have moved them from Bruce's "center of life." Germany's secularization, then, includes both instances of the discarding of faith altogether and also those of its relegation to a position that is removed from the mainstream of daily living.

Signs of Spiritual Vestiges: German Refugee Response

On the surface, it would seem that secularism has doused the flames of Germany's past spiritual passion and priority. But in a 2017 presentation to the synod of the Protestant Church in Germany, Lucian Hölscher, professor at the Ruhr-Universität Bochum, took comfort in the idea that "many, who are no longer church members, still stand on the side of the church in its battle against hunger and war, against the destruction of the environment, and for a humane community"[1] (Hölscher 2017). The nation's response to the recent refugee crisis is evidence of Hölscher's statement. This reality points to embers of faith that are still glowing and perhaps even to tender kindling ready to be lit. Before exploring these, however, it is important to note how generous Germany has been in the reception of refugees.

Germany's willingness to offer protection and provision to more than 1.75 million asylum applicants from 2011 to 2017 (Bundesamt *für* Migration und *Flüchtlinge* 2017)[2] places it among the most hospitable countries in the world (Busso and Czuczka 2017). Syrians, for example, have been among the greatest beneficiaries of Germany's open doors. Within Syria itself, more than half of the population fled from their homes during that time frame due to civil war (United Nations Office for the Coordination of Humanitarian Affairs 2017). Of those migrants, an estimated 5 million refugees left the country in search of a new start in a safer environment (United Nations Human Rights Council 2018). Germany has been one of the most responsive to these migrants and others like them. Under Chancellor Angela Merkel's leadership, roughly 266,000 Syrians were among the more than 720,000 non-EU citizens who filed as first-time applicants for asylum in 2016 alone (Eurostat 2017).

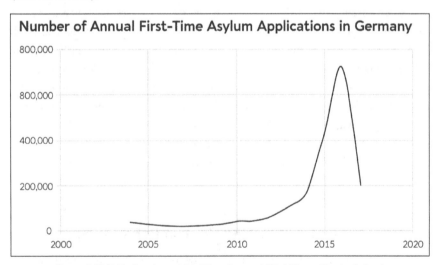

Figure 2: "BAMF—Bundesamt für Migration und Flüchtlinge—Startseite" n.d.

---

1 Unless otherwise specified, all translations are my own.

2 This is a compilation of figures gathered from the annual reports of the Bundesamt für Migration und Flüchtlinge, available at http://www.bamf.de/DE/Startseite/startseite-node.htm.

Germany's generous reception of refugees over these years has no single driving force. Though the influences leading to the nation's receptivity will be addressed separately, the reality is that the factors contributing to Germany's willkommen attitude are complicated and intertwined. Oliver Schmidtke is a native of Germany, an expert on migration, and director of the Centre for Global Studies at the University of Victoria. In a 2015 interview with Canadian Broadcasting Corporation (CBC) News, Schmidtke was asked, "Germany had emerged as the [European] leader in accepting these refugees. Why so generous?" Schmidtke summarized with these thoughts:

> Domestically there has been a growing consensus that Germany cannot sit idle watching the humanitarian catastrophe unfold. Germans welcomed refugees with compassion and an outpouring of generosity. There's been a lot of discussion by German opposition parties and media outlets about moral imperatives resulting from the Holocaust and Germans' own experience with massive post-war migration.
>
> It's also a reaction against the xenophobic backlash in recent months.
>
> Added to that is Germany's controversial role in the Greek debt crisis and the negative portrayal of Merkel because of austerity measures imposed on Southern Europe.
>
> So, Germany's decision to accept up to 800,000 refugees this year was seen as an opportunity to demonstrate that it can lead by example. (Clibbon 2015)
>
> Indeed, there are many factors contributing to Germany's welcoming attitude.

Merkel's influence

The author of Proverbs 21:1 describes a reality that is certainly true of German chancellor Angela Merkel: "The king's heart is like channels of water in the hand of the LORD; He turns it wherever He wishes" (NASB). In spite of strong public criticism, Merkel has been outspokenly supportive of and influential in her country's response to the refugee crisis. Her words, *Wir schaffen das!* ("We can do it!"), spoken originally on August 31, 2015, expressed her confidence that Germany could overcome any obstacles created by the country's admission of refugees by the tens of thousands (Bannas 2015). In the months that followed, those same words became the rally cry for many—Germans and refugees alike. For others, they have given reason for opposition.

Indeed, Merkel has personally been one of the strongest advocates for refugees. Her support seems to stem, at least in part, from her own experience. She was born in 1954 in Hamburg, Germany (Qvortrup 2016, 27). At eight weeks old, in a day when people were fleeing by the tens of thousands from East Germany to West Germany, she moved with her family to the East. Her father, a Lutheran pastor, had accepted a post in a church there (ibid., 24). Merkel remained in East Germany until after the fall of the Berlin Wall in 1989. Along with millions of others, she experienced the warmth of former West Germany as they embraced their new fellow countrymen (LeBor 2015, 14). The compassionate embrace she experienced has influenced the empathetic understanding she has extended to others, and it has also come to influence the policies of the nation as a whole.

Moral responsibility

As mentioned above, Merkel grew up in the home of a Lutheran pastor. Todd Statham suggests that the influence of her spiritual and moral moorings should not be underestimated (Statham 2016, 28). Reverend Rainer Eppelmann, Merkel's friend and former political colleague, told reporters at the magazine *Der Spiegel*, "Every day, Jesus and God were discussed in the Kasner [Merkel's maiden name] household.... The daily message was: 'Love thy neighbor as yourself. Not just German people. God loves everybody'" (Feldenkirchen and Pfister 2016). Bastian Friborg (2016, 8–10) argues that Merkel, inspired by the story of the good Samaritan (Luke 10:30–37), has influenced the nation. Even in the face of strong opposition in 2015, she sought to remind people that every refugee is deserving of humane treatment (Springer 2015). In fact, Merkel has gone on record as saying, "Germany is doing what is morally and legally necessary—no more and no less" (Heneghan and Bryant 2015, 16).

To be sure, not every German child grew up in the home of clergy. However, Merkel's moral compass influenced by a spiritual component is not unique to her. Germany is a land with a strong Christian heritage. Roughly 58 percent of all Germans self-identify as Christian (Forschungsgruppe Weltanschauungen in Deutschland 2018). Even though it is known as the "land of the Reformation," the reality is that slightly more people in Germany self-identify as Catholic than as Protestant (Statista 2017). This self-identification should not be misunderstood. As pointed out earlier, the Christian label worn by many does not, however, bring with it broadscale church involvement. In reality, "... most people rarely darken the church door between their baptism and funeral" (Statham 2016, 29). Self-identifying Christians, however, should not be equated with the total number of evangelicals, estimated at roughly 2 percent (Heitmüller 2017). Still, Merkel's spiritual and moral influence has fallen on largely receptive hearts, allowing for doors relatively wide open to the refugee.

That principled sense of moral responsibility is indeed strong. Still, reality is, at times, different. It is true that many Germans may have originally opened their doors out of a sense of idealistic moral or even spiritual responsibility. Today, the challenges and sheer scope of the work are impacting the way that some feel about the reality of such a flood of refugees.

Economic necessity

The reasons for German hospitality offered to refugees reach beyond Merkel's influence or a heartfelt (even spiritual) sense of obligation. There is also a financial dimension to the national response. Eurostat, the statistical office of the European Union, projects that the German population will decline in the decades to come due to low birth rates (Eurostat 2015). In the face of this downturn, Adam LeBor, in a 2015 *Newsweek* article, summarizes that "the German economic machine needs new workers" (LeBor 2015, 14).

For a country faced with a future marked by more jobs than potential employees, refugees, then, represent more than just people in need of humanitarian aid. They are seen as ones who could offer strength to a diminishing workforce. While commenting on the challenges of receiving refugees by the hundreds of thousands, Dieter Detsche, head of Mercedes-Benz, stated, "In the best case, it [the refugee challenge] can be a foundation for an economic miracle." After acknowledging the refugee's personal drive necessary to leave the familiar behind and make his/her way to a new land and culture, Detsche went on to say, "That is exactly the kind of person we are looking for at Mercedes and everywhere in our country" (Frankfurter Allgemeine Zeitung 2015).

Unfortunately, the initial optimism about the economic strength that may arise from the reception of so many refugees is waning. For many, that optimism is being replaced by the sobering reality that such gains will not be visible in the near future. In a 2017 interview with the global business publication, *Financial Times*, Aydan Oezoguz, Commissioner for Immigration, Refugees, and Integration, projected that only a quarter to a third of refugees would find work in the next five years, and "for many, we will need up to 10 [years]" (Chazan 2017).

Still, German economic experts like Marcel Fratzscher and Simon Junker are very optimistic. Although they recognize the short-term challenges, they conclude that "over the long term, the net contribution of refugee migration to the overall economic performance will be positive" (Fratzscher and Junker 2015, 616). The welcoming of men and women from other cultures and countries in anticipation of their eventual assimilation as productive contributors to the German economy is certainly a long-term investment. Nevertheless, the economic necessity has been a strong driving force that has caused Germany to be so welcoming to people fleeing their homeland.

Repentant reputational recovery

Germany's Nazi past will likely never be forgotten. Under the leadership of the infamous Adolf Hitler, the lives of an estimated six million people, primarily supposed Jews, were taken. In addition, hundreds of thousands of others were persecuted because of their racial inferiority. While nothing can be done to erase those facts from German history, Germany has done much to demonstrate its remorse for such a tainted past. A 2015 cover story in *Time* magazine described it like this:

> There are many ways that Germany has made payments on its Nazi past—like its emphatic support for Israel (flights from which are met at Germany's airports by armed guards), its reluctance to use its military and the intensely felt, almost constant reminders of collective guilt embedded in school curricula and every other facet of public life that make up what Germans call, after taking a deep breath, Vergangenheitsbewältigung—roughly translated as "wrestling the past into submission." (Vick, Shuster, and Calabresi 2015, 85)

An agreement signed on September 10, 1952, in Luxembourg was one of the first significant, tangible payments. There, Germany agreed to pay more than $800 million in compensation (Schorr 1952). In addition, it has not only used money as a means of changing its global reputation. Statham writes, "Politicians, church leaders and others urging a generous refugee policy make their case by reminding Germans that their bitter past should soften their hearts for present kindness" (Statham 2016, 29).

Since World War II, Germany's generous immigration and refugee policies have helped people from diverse nationalities find a home within their borders. Just after the war, displaced Germans were welcomed back. Turkish guest workers came in the following decades. Next were Spanish,

Portuguese, Greeks, and Italians in search of work (Vick, Shuster, and Calabresi 2015, 86). After the fall of the Wall in 1989 until 2002, Germany also welcomed 2.72 million people from Eastern Europe. Of these, 2.18 million later left (Dietz 2004). In retrospect, the influx of these people was like a trickle priming the pump for the more recent reception of the flood of refugees by the hundreds of thousands in a narrow window of time.

A final word on German hospitality

As the graph above illustrated, the number of first-time applicants has declined. So has some of the initial welcoming spirit. Even at the peak of the wave of immigrants, Statham indicated, "Most like the idea of welcoming refugees to my country, but to my neighborhood?" (Statham 2016, 28). This idealistic, but arm's-length hospitality, has transformed into concerned reticence for many. In a January 2017 article, *Die Welt* magazine reported, "Germany is no longer what it was on New Year's Eve 2015/2016" (Sturm et al. 2017). In that night more than 1,200 women in Köln, Hamburg, Stuttgart, and other cities were victims of sexual offenses. Among the many suspects was a large percentage of male asylum applicants from North Africa.

Die Welt describes the outcome of experiences like this one with these words:

> Opinion pollsters from Allensbach [Germany] report that Germans are insecure. Five years ago [2011], only 29% feared that they could be the victim of a crime. This percentage has climbed over the years to more than 60%. In the last year, this long-time trend has combined itself to fear associated with the migration crisis. (ibid.)

More recently, a fourteen-year-old girl was reported missing on May 22, 2018. On June 7, 2018, her body was discovered. She was reportedly raped and murdered by two refugees (Springer 2018). News of such crimes has certainly played a role in a growing sense of fear and uncertainty that Germans feel as refugees live in their land.

Added to these growing tensions within Germany created by insecurity is the challenge of seeing integration realized. Indeed, Angela Merkel's words, *Wir schaffen das!* ("We can do it!"), have inspired many. But now, months later, many are seeing that the goal is not achieved as simply as originally thought. In June of 2016, Bavarian Minister President Horst Seehofer responded to Merkel's statement by saying, "Even with the best of intentions, I cannot embrace this sentence" (Die Presse 2016). Since then, the tension associated with refugee politics has increased. The influence of the political party Alternative for Germany is increasing. Known, at least in part, for its anti-refugee stance, the Alternative for Germany party became the third strongest in the German parliament (Bundestag) in the 2017 elections (tagesschau.de 2017).

Recommendations for Ministry in a Secularized Germany... and a Secularized World

Germany certainly has its own unique story. No other country has experienced the same spiritual pilgrimage. Similarly, no other country can point to the same factors that have contributed to its specific response to refugees. Meanwhile, other aspects of Germany's story parallel that of many countries and cultures today. Other people groups have seen similar signs of secularization, while still offering potential touchpoints for the ministry and message of the gospel. Thus, this last section focuses attention on how Germany's recent refugee response points to four practical and transferrable implications for effective ministry in the context of an increasingly secularized world.

Identify spiritual vestiges in the target culture

Chancellor Merkel's response to refugees, and the response of Germany as a whole, was rooted, at least in part, in a common familiarity with and appreciation for spiritual truths and moral responsibility. Whether supportive Germans identify their motivations to help refugees as somehow spiritual or not, it seems that their spiritual underpinnings as Catholics, Protestants, or simply as people made in the image of God have resulted in a welcoming response. Recognizing these remnants can open the door to holistic ministry opportunities and gospel dialogue among both Germans and refugees seeking asylum in Germany.

Germany is not unique, however, in possessing underlying signs of spiritual life. Evidences of spiritual vestiges can be observed in Germany, as well as in other secular cultures, in one of three ways. The first is found in a parallel with the apostle Paul's first-century address to those in the synagogue in Pisidian Antioch (Acts 13:16–41). In Pisidian Antioch, Paul spoke to people who shared some of his own spiritual background. They were people with some familiarity with the teachings of the Old Testament. Paul recognized that and tailored his teaching with that reality in mind. Similarly, as God's people represent his Son in an increasingly secular culture, they must identify those spiritual vestiges and utilize them for the sake of the gospel. Christ followers, then, do well to look for those spiritual vestiges as evidenced in a residual knowledge of and sensitivity to the special revelation of the Bible.

A second evidence of spiritual vestiges in secular culture is not quite so obvious. It does not necessarily manifest itself in a familiarity with biblical teaching. Instead, it may be a more general, moral awareness of what is right. Certainly not every advocate of a generous German refugee policy knew the story of the good Samaritan or would cite that story as the reason for generous refugee response. Nevertheless, many others simply understand it as the morally right thing to do. That, in itself, is the outworking of general revelation as evidenced in the conscience of man given by God.

Paul points out that even those void of a knowledge of the Old Testament law possess an innate awareness of right and wrong through their conscience (Rom 2:14–16). Conscience is not a fail-proof system assuring that individuals or culture as a whole will always make the right moral choice. People can ignore their conscience or even have their conscience "seared" (1 Tim 4:2) into insensitivity. Still, the impulses of conscience can prod even Germans who seemingly lack a spiritual awareness to recognize injustices in the world such as the current refugee crisis. This shared sense of conscience provides Christ's ambassadors opportunity to join hands with secular people as they address a common area of compassion. It also allows God's people to join the conversation with secular people as they speak out on areas of common conviction.

Thirdly, spiritual vestiges may even be observed in things that seem initially profane or idolatrous. That was certainly the case in Paul's encounter with the Athenians in Acts 17. There, he was distressed as he observed a "city full of idols" (Acts 17:16 NASB). Clearly, idol worship is contrary to God's desire (Ex 20:3–5) and to reality (1 Cor 8:4). Paul's contextualized presentation to those gathered in the Areopagus reflected their ignorance of biblical truth. Their unfamiliarity did not imply, however, that they were void of spirituality. In fact, Paul began his address on Mars Hill with the recognition that they were "very religious" (Acts 17:22 NASB).

As image-bearers of God (Gen 1:26), who is spirit (John 4:24), all people have a spiritual component. John described our attempts to fill this aspect of life apart from Christ in terms of water that does not truly satisfy (John 4:7–15). Jeremiah illustrated it similarly, as the people of Israel had forsaken

God and attempted to hew out their own cisterns that could not hold water (Jer 2:13).

Blaise Pascal echoed those thoughts with these lines:

> What else does this craving, and this helplessness, proclaim but that there was once in man a true happiness, of which all that now remains is the empty print and trace?
>
> This he tries in vain to fill with everything around him, seeking in things that are not there the help he cannot find in those that are, though none can help, since this infinite abyss can be filled only with an infinite and immutable object; in other words by God himself. (Pascal, translated 1995, Section 425)

Even though spirituality may not be obvious or central to life in secular cultures, its influence is likely still there under the surface. Whether evidenced by familiarity with special revelation, reflections of moral conscience, or even misguided devotion, secular cultures show evidence of God's thumbprint. Believers who identify these spiritual vestiges will discover opportunity for ministry.

Discover causal on-ramps

Recognizing these influences, God's children are positioned to serve and engage the culture in ways that even the secular identify as relevant and critical. As illustrated with refugees, believers are able to join hands with secular people passionate about a righteous cause. By finding these causal on-ramps, they are not only able to address important issues but also to make an eternal difference. In Matthew 5:16, Jesus points out that such good works can cause others to take notice and give praise to God.[3] This principle of good works resulting in divine praise was experienced by the Jerusalem church as they experienced "favor with all the people" (Acts 2:47a NASB). This favor was a contributing factor to the Lord "adding to their number day by day those who were being saved" (Acts 2:47b NASB).

At times, this causal on-ramp may revolve around a pressing crisis. The refugee crisis has been the example used here. It has not just been evangelical Christians who have sought to compassionately help asylum seekers. Countless Germans have also been moved by the desperate needs and have offered time and resources to help.

---

3 "Let your light shine before men in such a way that they may see your good works, and glorify your Father who is in heaven" (NASB).

One finds similar responses in the face of all crises. Whether the crisis is the result of an earthquake, tsunami, hurricane, flood, or the outcome of war, the needs evoke a heart response in many—both believers and unbelievers. God's people can find welcome access to those suffering and to compassionate, secular people as they identify personal and cultural crises.

Born-again believers do not merely do good, however, as a means of attracting the attention of the surrounding secular world in the hope of sharing the gospel. Paul has clearly instructed Christ followers: "While we have opportunity, let us do good to all people, and especially to those who are of the household of the faith" (Gal 6:10 NASB). Discovering causal on-ramps for doing good is always the right thing to do, independent of an anticipated response. It is interesting to note, however, that even Paul's instruction to do good to all people is couched in terms of reaping a spiritual harvest (Gal. 6:7–10).

One final caveat to the recognition of these causal on-ramps merits noting. The windows of opportunity can open and close suddenly. While Christian workers will have opportunity to minister to refugees in the days to come, the tide is turning. The doors of hospitality are not as widely open as they once were. Opportunities to serve alongside of unbelieving Germans with a similar passion are diminishing. The number of asylum applicants is decreasing. In like manner, Christians in an increasingly secularized world must be prepared to access those causal on-ramps as the opportunities are available. As Jesus said, "We must work the works of Him who sent Me as long as it is day; night is coming when no one can work" (John 9:4 NASB).

Emphasize relational approaches

The Spirit-empowered influence of the corporate body of Christ doing good in the secular world should not be underestimated. Still, the obstacles to overcome in impacting others for eternity are often large. As stated earlier, the secular mind-set has relegated religion and its significance to the periphery of life. Secular thought about religious groups has been tainted by everything from Enlightenment thinking[4] to the media's report about the latest sex or money scandal within the organized church. The perspective of the secular world may, then, range from irrelevant to antagonistic; and it may be based,

---

4 Wienclaw and Baker maintain, "One of the roots of modern thought can be traced back to the attitude of skepticism that arose in Europe during the Enlightenment. This method of reasoning and approaching problems paved the way for today's scientific method. The popularization of skepticism, however, led to a questioning of tradition and the substitution of rational thought for faith" (Wienclaw and Baker 2013).

at least in part, on straw-man stereotypes of religion and religious groups and their deficiencies. There is, then, yet a third principle for spiritual engagement in a secular world that is learned from the German refugee crisis. It is the value of personal relationships.

Changing the perspectives and perhaps even the stereotypes of a secular culture is, on the one hand, part of a spiritual battle beyond the realm of natural human ability to overcome. As the apostle Paul put it, "The god of this world has blinded the minds of the unbelieving so that they might not see the light of the gospel of the glory of Christ" (2 Cor 4:4 NASB). God's servants are dependent upon him to enlighten the understanding of the unbeliever and reliant on the Holy Spirit to "convict the world concerning sin and righteousness and judgment" (John 16:8 NASB). God alone can infuse life into spiritually dead people (Eph 2:1–5). His people, then, find themselves prayerfully dependent upon his work.

Still, while he is the only one who can cause growth, he uses the planting and watering efforts of his servants (1 Cor 3:5–9). This planting and watering may look different than it once did, in spite of the presence of the vestiges of spiritual life. For example, the door-knocking efforts of a complete stranger ready to explain the "Four Spiritual Laws" will likely be met with an eye roll—or worse. In the context of relationships, however, as they engage in holistic, causal ministries, God's people will find themselves in close proximity to spiritually needy people who share that same passion or who benefit from the services being offered.

It is in those proximal relationships that respect grows and the potential for influence is multiplied. By the grace of God, opportunity for interaction about the good news of Jesus Christ may be afforded. Peter describes the potential impact of a righteous, hope-filled life on others who seem apathetic or antagonistic:

> Who is there to harm you if you prove zealous for what is good? But even if you should suffer for the sake of righteousness, you are blessed. AND DO NOT FEAR THEIR INTIMIDATION, AND DO NOT BE TROUBLED, but sanctify Christ as Lord in your hearts, always *being* ready to make a defense to everyone who asks you to give an account for the hope that is in you, yet with gentleness and reverence; and keep a good conscience so that in the thing in which you are slandered, those who revile your good behavior in Christ will be put to shame. (1 Pet 3:13–16 NASB)

In this secular world where spiritual matters are deemed irrelevant to the ebb and flow of life, the value of Christ followers engaging in personal (and redemptive) relationships with those who do not yet know Christ cannot be overstated.

Conclusion

Sam George, Catalyst for the Diasporas with the Lausanne Movement, refers to the current refugee realities as "the greatest humanitarian crisis of our times" (George 2017). As tragic as the crisis is, it has, nevertheless, surfaced the spiritual vestiges in what is otherwise deemed "secular Germany." Germany's openness to receiving many asylum seekers is largely rooted in its spiritual roots and God-given moral conscience. More than a mere point of interest, Germany's response has exposed opportunities for Christ's church to engage in meaningful mission. This mission is certainly to those seeking asylum, but it is also to secular Germans who share the passion. George continues, "Only God could have turned such a desperate situation into such a mission opportunity" (ibid.). This is true not only for the refugees but also for the hosts.

As argued in this chapter, Germany's experiences and opportunities, though unique in their own right, illustrate missional practices that can be implemented in any secular culture. As Christ followers identify spiritual vestiges, discover causal on-ramps, and emphasize relational approaches, they will find themselves next to people who have moved religion to the periphery of life. There they can engage in meaningful conversation that begins with a shared passion and can lead into the gospel.

George's opinion about the potential of ministry to and through the refugees in secular Europe provides a fitting close. In his 2017 article, he wrote, "In the year of the 500th anniversary of the Protestant Reformation, God is once again reviving the church in Europe, this time through refugees from the Middle East" (ibid.). This may happen through the reawakening of a God-given moral conscience and biblical ethic among secularized persons in a largely post-Christian society. Is it possible that every culture has its own spiritual vestiges and causal prospects that open doors to fruitful ministry for those who will choose to engage them through personal relationships?

References

"BAMF—Bundesamt für Migration und Flüchtlinge—Startseite." n.d. 2018. http://www. bamf.de/DE/Startseite/startseite-node.html.

Bannas, Guenter. 2015. "Flüchtlingsfrage: Merkel: „Wir schaffen das"." *FAZ.NET*, Politik, August 31. http://www.faz.net/1.3778484.

Bruce, Steve. 2011. *Secularization: In Defence of an Unfashionable Theory*. Oxford: Oxford University Press. http://ezproxy.ciu.edu:2079/eds/ebookviewer/ebook/bmxlYm tfXzQ3NTg1Nl9fQU41?sid=3fa26dd6-e58e-4e27–9edf-e8fbebcf8684@sessionmgr 4008&vid=3&format=EB&rid=16.

Bundesamt fuer Migration und Fluechtlinge. 2017. "BAMF—Bundesamt für Migration und Flüchtlinge—Aktuelle Zahlen zu Asyl—(03/2017)." http://www.bamf.de/ SharedDocs/Anlagen/DE/Downloads/Infothek/Statistik/Asyl/aktuelle-zahlen-zu-asyl-maerz-2017.html?nn=7952222.

Busso, MaryAnn, and Tony Czuczka. 2017. "Turkey, Pakistan, Lebanon Host the Highest Number of Refugees." *Bloomberg.com*, July 6. https://www.bloomberg.com/ graphics/2017-countries-of-asylum-for-migrants/.

Chazan, Guy. 2017. "Most Refugees to be Jobless for Years, German Minister Warns." *Financial Times*, June 22. https://www.ft.com/content/022de0a4–54f4–11e7–9fed-c19e2700005f.

Clibbon, Jennifer. 2015. "Why Germany Is Taking in So Many Refugees—the Benefits and Risks." *CBC News*. September 14. http://www.cbc.ca/news/world/ why-germany-is-taking-in-so-many-refugees-the-benefits-and-risks-1.3226962.

Die Presse. 2016. "Seehofer distanziert sich von Merkels 'Wir schaffen das.'" *Die Presse*. July 30. https://diepresse.com/home/politik/aussenpolitik/5060273/ Seehofer-distanziert-sich-von-Merkels-Wir-schaffen-das.

Dietz, Barbara. 2004. "Ost-West-Migration nach Deutschland im Kontext der EU-Erweiterung | Bpb." Bundeszentrale für Politische Bildung. January 30. http://www.bpb.de/apuz/28543/ ost-west-migration-nach-deutschland-im-kontext-der-eu-erweiterung?p=all.

Eurostat. 2015. "Population Projections." 2015. http://ec.europa.eu/eurostat/tgm/table. do?tab=table&init=1&language=en&pcode=tps00002&plugin=1.

———. 2017. "Five Main Citizenships of (Non-EU) Asylum Applicants, 2016 (Number of First Time Applicants, Rounded Figures) YB17.png." Statistics Explained. March 15. http://ec.europa.eu/eurostat/statistics-explained/index.php/File:Five_main_ citizenships_of_(non-EU)_asylum_applicants,_2016_(number_of_first_time _applicants,_rounded_figures)_YB17.png.

Evangelische Kirche in Deutschland. 2017. "Die Äuserungen des kirchlichen Lebens im Jahr 2015."

Feldenkirchen, Markus, and René Pfister. 2016. "The Isolated Chancellor: What is Driving Angela Merkel?" *Spiegel Online*, International, January 25. http://www. spiegel.de/international/germany/why-has-angela-merkel-staked-her-legacy-on-the-refugees-a-1073705.html.

Forschungsgruppe Weltanschauungen in Deutschland. 2018. "Religionszugehörigkeiten in Deutschland 2017." August 10. https://fowid.de/meldung/ religionszugehoerigkeiten-deutschland-2017.

Frankfurter Allgemeine Zeitung. 2015. "Daimler-Chef Zetsche: Flüchtlinge könnten Wirtschaftswunder bringen." *FAZ.NET*, September 15. http://www.faznet/1.3803671.

Fratzscher, Marcel, and Simon Junker. 2015. "Integrating Refugees: A Long-Term Worthwhile Investment." *DIW Economic Bulletin* 5, (45/46): 612–16.

Friborg, Bastian L. 2016. "The Influence of Christianity on German Migration Policy during the Refugee Crisis from June 2015 till January 2016." http://ezproxy.ciu.edu:2293/docview/1830802939/B3C6D06FEC74D0EPQ/5?accountid=27682.

George, Sam. 2017. "Is God Reviving Europe through Refugees?" *Lausanne Movement* 6, no. 3 (May). https://www.lausanne.org/content/lga/2017–05/god-reviving-europe-refugees.

Gesley, Jenny. 2017. "The Relationship Between Church and State in Germany" Custodia Legis: Law Librarians of Congress." Webpage. May 3. https://blogs.loc.gov/law/2017/12/the-relationship-between-church-and-state-in-germany///blogs.loc.gov/law/2017/12/the-relationship-between-church-and-state-in-germany/.

Heitmüller, Ulrike. 2017. "Deutsche Evangelikale." *Telepolis*, October 1. https://www.heise.de/tp/features/Deutsche-Evangelikale-3835606.html.

Heneghan, Tom, and Elizabeth Bryant. 2015. "Churches Vary in Response to Refugees." *Christian Century* 132 (21): 16–17.

Hölscher, Lucian. 2017. "Orientierung für eine Kirche im Säkularen." https://www.ekd.de/s17–4-prof-dr-lucian-hoelscher-bochum-30348.htm.

Katholische Kirche in Deutschland. 2017. "Katholische Kirche in Deutschland Zahlen und Fakten 2016/17." Annual Report. Bonn, Germany: Catholic Church.

LeBor, Adam. 2015. "Angela Merkel: Europe's Conscience in the Face of a Refugee Crisis. *Newsweek*, September 5. https://www.newsweek.com/2015/09/18/angela-merkel-europe-refugee-crisis-conscience-369053.html.

Pascal, Blaise. 1995. *Pensees*. Translated by A. J. Krailsheimer. Rev. ed. London and New York: Penguin Classics.

Qvortrup, Matthew. 2016. *Angela Merkel: Europe's Most Influential Leader*. New York and London: The Overlook Press.

Schorr, Daniel. 1952. "Bonn Signs Pact With Israel For $822,000,000 Payment; 24 World Jewish Groups Are Represented in Stiff Ceremony—Goods and Services Will Be Given for Crimes of Nazis BONN, ISRAEL SIGN RESTITUTION PACT." *The New York Times*, Archives, September 11. https://www.nytimes.com/1952/09/11/archives/bonn-signs-pact-with-israel-for-822000000-payment-24-world-jewish.html.

Secretary of the German Bishop's Conference. 2011. "Eckdaten des Kirchlichen Lebens in den Bistuemern Deutschlands—1990 Und 2010."

Springer, Axel. 2015. "„Wir Sind Das Pack": Merkel wird ausgebuht." *Die Welt*, August 26. https://www.welt.de/politik/deutschland/article145659437/Wir-sind-das-Pack-Merkel-wird-ausgebuht.html.

———. 2018. "Vermisste 14-jährige Susanna aus Mainz ist tot: Polizei veröffentlicht Fahndungsfoto." *Die Welt*, Panorama, June 7. https://www.welt.de/vermischtes/article177125702/Vermisste-14-jaehrige-Susanna-aus-Mainz-ist-tot-Polizei-veroeffentlicht-Fahndungsfoto.html.

Statham, Todd. 2016. "Deutsche Post: Do-Gooders, Christians and Refugees in Germany." *Presbyterian Record* 140 (8): 27–30.

Statista. 2017. Dieser Text stellt eine Basisinformation dar Eine Gewähr für die Richtigkeit und Vollständigkeit der Angaben kann nicht übernommen werden Aufgrund unterschiedlicher Aktualisierungsrhythmen können Statistiken einen aktuelleren. "Statistiken Zu Religionen in Deutschland." De.statista.com. https://de.statista.com/themen/125/religion/.

Sturm, Daniel Friedrich, Manuel Bewarder, Florian Flade, Matthias Kamann, and Marcel Leubecher. 2017. "Flüchtlinge und Terror: So sehr hat sich Deutschland in einem Jahr verändert." *Die Welt*, Politik, October 1. https://www.welt.de/politik/deutschland/article160961730/So-sehr-hat-sich-Deutschland-in-einem-Jahr-veraendert.html.

Tagesschau.de. 2017. "Bundestag Wahl 2017 Deutschland." Tagesschau.de. September 24. https://wahl.tagesschau.de/wahlen/2017–09–24-BT-DE/index.shtml.

United Nations Human Rights Council. 2018. "UNHCR Syria Regional Refugee Response." February 22. http://data.unhcr.org/syrianrefugees/regional.php.

United Nations Office for the Coordination of Humanitarian Affairs. 2017. "About the Crisis | OCHA." September. https://www.unocha.org/syrian-arab-republic/syria-country-profile/about-crisis.

Vick, Karl, Simon Shuster, and Massimo Calabresi. 2015. "Chancellor of the Free World." Cover story, *Time* 186 (25/26): 52–99.

Warner, Rob. 2010. *Secularization and Its Discontents*. London: Continuum. http://ezproxy.ciu.edu:2079/eds/ebookviewer/ebook/bmxlYmtfXzM1MDI3NF9fQU41?sid=4702070d-a16e-498a-9639-aa6b29239639@sessionmgr4008&vid=0&format=EB&rid=8.

Wienclaw, Ruth A., and Jeremy Baker. 2013. "Secularization." *Research Starters—Sociology* (online edition).

Wilson, Bryan. 1966. *Religion in Secular Society*. Harmondsworth, UK: Pelican.

Wolf, Christof. 2008. "How Secularized Is Germany? Cohort and Comparative Perspectives." *Social Compass* 55 (2): 111–26.

CHAPTER 8

Mission and Evangelism in the Desecularizing World of the Russian Federation

Marc T. Canner

The process of secularization may be broadly defined as a modification over time of the patterns of religious expression and influence on human society. Much of the literature on secularization links it to the phenomenon of modernization in an increasingly globalized world, although the exact relationship between these forces has been much debated (see Berger 2014; Netland, this volume). Besides the dynamic relationship between secularization, modernization, and globalization, the process of secularization can also be attributed to a number of historical causes. The phenomenon tends to be most prevalent in those nations and among those peoples that have been influenced either directly or indirectly by a number of key developments in Western European history. Among these are the European Enlightenment and the rationalism it spawned, the rise of scientism, and the doctrine of a "separation of church and state" that resulted from a confluence of the philosophies of the Western Enlightenment and aspects of the Protestant Reformation. The nations of the Western world (Europe and the Western hemisphere) have long been the locus of the trend toward secularization, from where it has spread to many other contexts today, including Eastern Europe.

Among European countries, however, the trend toward secularization has one notable exception: the peoples and nations dominated by East Slavs, and especially the Russian Federation. In the modern East Slavic context of the Russian Federation, the growth of state secularism thus far has not gained much traction in society (Blitt 2010). In many respects, this is due to a number of developmental issues following the demise of the Soviet Union. Among the three East Slavic nations of Belarus, Russia, and Ukraine, the Russian Federation (RF) stands out as a context where the austere type of secularism that existed under the Soviet system has not only ceased but has seen a dramatic reversal since the late 1990s. This is directly observable in the Russian Orthodox Church's favored status over other religious expressions today in Russian government policies, a status that even contradicts provisions of the Russian constitution of 1993 (ibid.). Since Putin's rise to power in 2000, Russia has experienced a growing desecularization, which is characterized by a number of developments that have catapulted the Russian Orthodox Church (ROC) to a position of hegemony over religious expression and a growing political influence (ibid.). The Russian Church[1] now has a privileged status and has experienced an attendant growing influence on public discourse, education, domestic politics, and even foreign policy and military affairs. This transformation has had a direct impact on Western missionaries and their effectiveness in cross-cultural ministry in this part of the world.

This chapter discusses the historical and cultural causes of desecularization in the Russian Federation (RF), with an emphasis on its impact on Western missionary efforts and their effectiveness. The Russian Orthodox Church has experienced a dramatic renaissance since the 1990s, and its influence on modern Russian government and society has had a tremendous negative effect on Western evangelistic and church-planting efforts in the RF (Kravtsev 2016). Much of the Western missionary literature on the subject cites the influence of the ROC on new government legislation as the direct cause of such difficulties (see Kravtsev 2016, 39). However, this conclusion is an oversimplification of the issue. The failure of most Western efforts there is rather due to a confluence of issues related to these modern trends, Russia's cultural past, and Western models of ministry and tendencies inherent in

---

1 The terms "Russian Orthodox Church" (ROC) and "Russian Church" are used synonymously

Western culture, which make Western-prepared missionaries ill-suited for the Russian context. The common Western (and especially American) tendency to dichotomize life and ministry can greatly hinder accurate perceptions of Russian life and spirituality. One could conclude that perhaps the ultimate expression of this tendency is the Western value placed on a separation of secular and religious spheres of life itself. These cultural values can have a significant impact on the Westerner's overall perceptions of Russian expressions of Christian faith, politics, and the role of the Russian Orthodox Church in government and society. The post-Soviet desecularization evident in the RF only serves to complicate the difficulties Western missionaries already experience in ministry to Russian nationals.

A Modern Renaissance

The fall of the Soviet Union and its system represented a period of extreme confusion for the various peoples of that ethnically diverse empire. Central Asians, Baltic peoples, the peoples of Siberia, the peoples of Transcaucasia, and the East Slavs—all literally awoke one morning and were told that the country they lived in no longer existed. In the aftermath of their country's implosion, the Russian people experienced an identity crisis. Along with the other fourteen Soviet "republics," Russia began searching for herself. The result of this search was that the people of this vast nation found their identity in the past; many Russians, including the nation's leaders today, see themselves and their nation as a Christian beacon to the rest of the world (Szporluk 2000). The journey the nation would take to arrive at that point, however, was a rocky one that began with Western-style economic reforms designed to develop a free-market economy without Soviet-style price controls, and attempts at social and political reforms. Likely due to the complexities related to quickly transforming a controlled economy to a more capitalist system, these attempts at reform backfired, and the Russian ruble crashed in 1997 (Freeland 2000).[2]

In 1997, the Russian parliament passed the new Law on Freedom of Conscience and Religious Associations. The law intensified the friction between two factions in Russian society: the conservative nationalists, who desired to ensure the protection of the Russian Orthodox Church, and the liberal Democrats, whose goal was to guarantee religious freedom

---

2 During the crash of 1997, the currency was devalued to such an extent that what cost 10 rubles in 1996 cost between 7,000 and 10,000 rubles a year later. Citizens' savings accounts were literally wiped out overnight.

for adherents of all faiths (Knox 2005, 1). Western-leaning President Boris Yeltsin was, at the time, opposed to the law based on the idea that it violated international human rights conventions (ibid.). With the passage of the 1997 law, the pro-Orthodox nationalists gained greater influence, since the law created certain restrictions on non-Orthodox expressions of the Christian faith. The law acted as a catalyst for the rebirth of the Russian Orthodox Church's spiritual hegemony over the nation.

Shortly after Putin's inauguration as president in January 2000, the rebirth of Russian Orthodoxy as a powerful political ally of the state was symbolized: Putin's first act as president was to receive the blessings of the Russian patriarch (Wines 2000). The authoritarian nationalist and liberal factions would jostle with each other for influence over the government for the next several years. By December 2003, the nationalists, organized under the banner of Putin's "Rodina" party, secured their dominance over Russian politics, sealing a resurgence of the power and influence of the official Russian Orthodox Church and its patron, Putin's new political machine (Knox 2005, 2). The Russian people's search for identity took a new turn.

In his seminal work, *Russia in Search of Itself*, James Billington concluded, "The Russian peoples' current search for identity is, in many ways, a renewal of the interrupted creative fervent of the Russian Silver Age under the last tsar" (Billington 2004, 148). One of the core themes of Russia's Silver Age was the concept of *sobornost*, a term that can be used to describe various councils, especially in the church. It represents the "togetherness" found in church congregations, the family, and the nation (ibid., 149). While few Orthodox Christians in Russia regularly attend church, this identity as a Christian nation in a context of *sobornost* is incredibly important to the country's new identity. As Putin stated while standing at the site of the first Gulag labor camp of Lenin's Russia, "Without Christianity, Russia could hardly exist" (Radio Free Europe 2001).

In her search for identity, the Russian people returned to their pre-Soviet past, a trajectory that was decidedly different from than the Western experience of the same period. To many historians, Soviet Communism was merely a temporary detour, albeit one that "destroyed civil society—social bonds and institutions" (Young 2017). The destruction of Russian society and identity was virtually complete. According to Andrej Zubov, a former history professor at the Moscow Institute of International Relations, Russian Communism was "worse than Nazism since it left nothing untouched; art, literature, education, the whole of civil society was sacrificed to the goal of creating *Homo Sovieticus*" (Owen 2011).

For most Westerners, the nature of Christian life under the Soviet system is extremely difficult to imagine. The "registered" Baptist church our missionary team worked with in the early 1990s had nine pastors who served the church prior to our arrival. All nine of them had served prison sentences for expressing their faith publicly, while seven of them had died for their faith in prison. The anti-religious laws of the Soviet Union were extreme. Those Russian Orthodox, Catholic, and Protestant church leaders or laypeople who refused to adhere to state regulations on proselytism or other outlawed Christian activities were persecuted greatly. Incredibly, the government was especially hard on the Orthodox Church.[3] It is estimated that between 1918 and 1940, 40,000 Orthodox priests were put to death and the government closed or destroyed perhaps as many as 76,000 churches and other religious buildings (von der Heydt 1993, 47).

The form of secularism in the Soviet Union was clearly of the extreme anti-religious type, a type still seen today in countries such as North Korea. How did such a radical shift from that form of secularism to the renaissance of the Russian Orthodox Church that now wields such influence occur? The answer to that question is found in Russia's rich history and in the unusual nature of its culture.

To Be Russian Is to Be Orthodox

Though some believe it was LeoTolstoy, it was perhaps Fyodor Dostoevsky, one of the most beloved Russian authors, who first said that "to be Russian is to be Orthodox" (Szporluk 2000, 169). This frequently repeated saying encapsulates the common sentiment among many Russians today of their true, but almost lost, identity as a people. Westerners often misinterpret the statement, however. It is not so much a pronouncement that the nation is Orthodox, which to Russians is a given fact. Instead, it relates to the people's awareness of the attributes or character of "Russianness," which stems from the core cultural characteristics expressed in Russian Orthodoxy. The "Orthodox" nature of Russian styles of worship, with their tendency toward high liturgy and the many visual representations of beauty and the sound of

---

3 While they endured much persecution, Russian evangelicals were not targeted for execution to the degree the Orthodox were. This was due to their perceived high productivity in agriculture (see von der Heydt 1993).

bells and voices, are readily apparent during any visit to a Russian Baptist, Pentecostal, or other type of Christian worship service.

Throughout the country's history, the Russian national experience served to reinforce a holistic Orthodox identity: the Russian people perceived any attack on the Russian nation as an attack on the Russian Church. Any attack on the church was immediately understood as an attack on the people or the nation. The Russian people have retained this sense of Orthodox Russianness as the core of their identity far longer than Western expressions of Christianity have held a center stage in the "enlightened" West (Billington 2004, 147).

For a number of important reasons, the cultural, political, religious, and twentieth-century economic history of Russia is what separated the country from the West. That history and the nature of Russian culture prevented some of the most significant aspects of the Western experience from influencing Russia. These factors ensured that Russians would never develop the Western tendency to value a separation between the church and the state.[4] To most Russians, the church is the nation. The church, nation, and state, are one. This frame of mind is the antithesis of the Western phenomenon of secularization.

Where the East Does Not Meet the West

The phenomenon of secularization in the Western context is the result of a multitude of historical factors and modern trends. Some of the most salient historical factors include the modern acceptance of science as the chief explanation for our existence, the historical experience of Western peoples in the context of a state-controlled church, the Protestant reaction to the same, and the broad influence of the French Enlightenment and the rationalism it inspired. While the influence of science and scientism cannot be underestimated, for the purpose of this brief overview the emphasis will be on the Reformation and the thinking derived from the Enlightenment— perhaps the two most important developments in Western civilization that contributed to modern secularism.

The Protestant Reformation was partly a reaction to the abuses of the age of Christendom and the theocratic tendencies of European monarchies and their state-run churches, as was the case with the Church of England, from

---

4 The rejection of such separation is seen in the theocratic form of government Russia adopted after the Byzantine model, based on her "Doctrine of the Third Rome." The Russian Church has historically had a great influence on government; the czars (a word derived from the Latin "Caesar") were seen as "in authority like unto God Himself," a statement made at the Russian Church Council of 1504 (see Kochan 1997; Riasanovsky 1984).

which so many fled for religious freedom to the New World. The Protestant Reformation provided an early articulation of the concept of a "separation of church and state," seen in Luther's "Doctrine of the Two Kingdoms" (Hart 2014). The idea of such a separation was strengthened by the philosophy of the European Enlightenment. The principle of this separation of the secular from the spiritual is directly reflected in the First Amendment to the US Constitution. Although there are differences between the European and American expressions of this separation of the two spheres, Western peoples typically see the principle as a necessary aspect of any just and democratic government that would preserve its citizens' religious freedoms.

The US founding fathers understood the need for a political secularism that separates church and state, a practical principle that would enable the new nation to avoid the pitfalls of a single state-sanctioned religion (McClay 2007). Political secularism allows the free public expression of religion and has contributed in the West to a greater degree of pluralism It differs from philosophical secularism, which attempts to eliminate such public expression from the government sphere (ibid.). While one impact of secularism, especially in its political form, has certainly been the development of a greater degree of pluralism, adherents of philosophical secularism, many of whom are atheists, are behind the modern push for eliminating any public expression of faith in the West. As such, the more philosophical brand of secularism in the United States represents one of the chief sources of anguish among many adherents of evangelical Christianity, as seen in the many titles recently devoted to the subject—e.g., *The Unintended Reformation: How a Religious Revolution Secularized Society*, by Brad Gregory; *Globequake: Living in the Unshakeable Kingdom While the World Falls Apart*, by Wallace Henley; or Ravi Zacharias' popular CD series, *Secularization: Its Control and Power*.

It has been argued that the form of secularization in the United States and Western Europe is a natural outcome of the Western Enlightenment's humanistic tendencies and the philosophy of rationalism it inspired (Sheehan 2003, 1064). A major historical factor influencing the rise of modern secularization, the Western Enlightenment ushered in the age of humanism, rationalism, and the modern Western concept of human rights. The Enlightenment had a number of key themes, including a) an emphasis on democratic principles that would ensure the creation of government structures that represent the peoples governed; b) a preoccupation with human reason, rationality, and empiricism and a rejection of prior patterns of thought that do not adhere to these principles; and c) a search for the knowledge that would allow humankind to control nature and its own destiny (Perry 2014, 60). The last two themes of the Enlightenment listed above, a preoccupation with human reason and the search for the means for humankind (and not God) to control human destiny and the natural world, have characterized the process of secularization both in the West and throughout those nations and cultures that fell under Western influence—a trend that continues today. The Western forms of secularization that are spreading around the world have secular governments that either do not favor any religion or favor one religion (see the second and third columns in Table 4).

Table 4 Types of State-Religion Regimes				
	Religious State	*State with an Established Religion*	*Secular State*	*Anti-religious State*
Legislation and judiciary	religion-based	secular	secular	secular
State's attitude toward religions	officially favors one	officially favors one	officially favors none	officially hostile to all or many
Examples	Vatican Iran Saudi Arabia	Greece Denmark England	US France Turkey	China North Korea Cuba
Number in the world	10	100	95	22

Kuru 2007

This is especially true of contemporary Eastern Europe, where most countries are adopting Western-style rationalism, concepts of human rights, and specifically Western expressions of government, an emphasis on pluralism, and the principle of a separation of church and state (Lazin 2014). An interesting example is the Czech Republic, where Western reforms have combined with a dominant intellectual atheism in society and a nonreligious secular state in a post-Communist society, which creates a challenging environment for the expression of Christian faith.[5]

---

5 During the Communist years the Czechoslovak state enforced Marxist atheism as the de facto state religion and exercised control over all religious denominations. The Czech Republic today takes a neutral stance on religion. While it can be inferred from the Czech Charter of Fundamental Rights and Liberties, the Czech constitution does not state specifically any principle of religious equality. For further discussion, see Horak 2010.

Of all the regions of Europe, however, the Russian-dominated East Slavic context was destined to reject major aspects of these characteristics of the Enlightenment. The ROC and Russian government today reject Western-style democracy, political and social reforms, human rights, and, interestingly, modern notions of secularization (Orthodox Declaration of Human Rights 2006). In some respects, the Russian state today also rejects, at least domestically, the kind of Western free-market system that is a hallmark trait of globalization. Russia has returned to a Soviet-style controlled economic system, and since 2000, major sectors of the economy have fallen once again under state control under Putin's leadership, creating a hostile environment for multinational corporations. This rejection of the hallmarks of Western civilization stems from an entrenched fear of the West. For centuries, Russia has feared what is called "Western guile," a fear in the Russian psyche borne out of a long history of attempts by Western nations to control or influence Russia, which never benefited the Russian people (Kochan 1997, 54). The Russian historical experience is characterized by a series of invasions and protracted struggles, mostly with Western powers and Western philosophical movements.[6]

Most historians consider the Protestant Reformation and the Enlightenment to be the two most powerful defining periods of modern Western civilization. Apart from these two forces, the modern trend toward secularization in the West is difficult to imagine. A key observation is that Russia experienced neither a religious reformation nor any type of cultural or rationalistic enlightenment. Instead, attempts to bring the Enlightenment to Russia during the late eighteenth century were met with a severe reaction from the Russian Church and the Russian people, a powerful movement known as the Russian "anti-enlightenment" (Billington 1970, 270).[7] The Eastern Orthodox emphasis on anti-rationalism found in its theology, its perceived messianic mission, and the Russian nation's people's "fear of Western

---

6 Russia endured invasions in the seventeenth century from the Polish Empire, the Grand Dutchy of Lithuania, and Sweden; in the eighteenth century again from Sweden; on a devastating scale in 1812 by Napoleon; and the massive invasion by Nazi Germany in the twentieth century. This general xenophobia was only reinforced by the perception that the nation was encircled by NATO during the Cold War. The ROC also viewed the influx of eighteenth-century ideas of the Western Enlightenment as an "invasion" of another kind.

7 During the late seventeenth century, Catherine II fancied herself "an enlightened soul" and toyed with the main ideas of the Western Enlightenment. A twist of irony was that the influence of the Russian Church on her was so great that she in fact moved Russia in the opposite direction. She is often referred to by historians as the "Enlightened Despot."

guile" appear to have worked together to cause a rejection of these aspects of Western culture. Russia's conservative cultural and theological forces produced the opposite effect of what resulted from the forces of the Enlightenment.

The Russian people have no historical context from which they can relate to what Westerners consider their own treasured values: freedom from a government-controlled church or a church-influenced government, individual rights and freedom of expression, and the varied ways they are extended in the Western context. Interestingly, the historical conservative tendencies preventing Russia's transformation were reinforced by the nature of the culture itself. It appears that a combination of these two forces very well may prevent Russia from ever adopting specifically Western notions of secularization. In many of the dimensions of a standard cultural continuum, the Russian people are on the opposite extreme from Western Europeans, and especially Americans (see Table 5).

Table 5: Cultural Continuum for "Self-Concept" and "Task Based"

Erin Meyer, *The Culture Map: Breaking through the Boundaries of Global Business* (2014)

A People More Eastern Than Western

In his short story "The Man Who Was," Rudyard Kipling described the common Western difficulty in "handling" Russians when he wrote: "As an Oriental he [the Russian] is charming. It is only when he insists upon being treated as the most easterly of Western peoples, instead of the most westerly of Easterners, that he becomes a racial anomaly extremely difficult to handle" (Kipling 2017, 1). An observation often repeated by both Western and Russian authors, the Russian people are a curious mixture. An old Russian saying states, "If you scratch a Russian, you'll find a Tatar (Mongol)." From Dostoevksy's statement that Russians are "half saint and half savage" to Churchill's description of Russia as "a riddle wrapped in mystery inside an enigma," the Russian people have baffled generations of Western observers, diplomats, and missionaries (Smith 1976, 105).

A former American student who studied in one of my Russian Civilization classes was adamant while he was with our institute that "Russians are just like us." About a year later, he wrote a letter from Russia in which he expressed his utter bafflement at their behavior and inability to accept and appropriate the message of the gospel he and his team had come to teach! The initial confusion he experienced stems perhaps in part from the remarkable historical similarities between Westerners, and especially Americans, and Russians. Similarities in physical appearance, traditional national interests such as "Manifest Destiny," and a similar vision of a messianic role in the world: American exceptionalism as the "city on a hill" and Russia's "transcendent mission—to bring the world to the God-Man Christ" (Dostoevsky 1869). Despite the few similarities, Western workers in the RF have extreme difficulties bridging the cultural divide they soon discover.

The Russian people are collectivists (Meyer 2014; Storti 1999). This is readily observed in the way communities take collective responsibility for raising children or enforce conformity of their members. School-age children are pressured to conform in terms of their dress, behavior, and especially their studies, a phenomenon not unlike what is observed in Japanese or Chinese culture. All one needs to do is observe how Russian classrooms are typically run to learn that the culture is also clearly based on the principles of honor-shame. Teachers publicly use shame to motivate students to work harder and call them out for being different (De Vries 1998, 22). Students are not motivated so much by an individual sense of guilt as they are by being conformist and not bringing shame upon the group. My own experience adapting to this system first as a student, and then when conducting discipleship groups and teaching Russians English, was a very challenging and frustrating aspect of my own cross-cultural ministry.

The Russian people also fall heavily on the holistic side of the cultural continuum (Heretz 2008, 48). For Russians, any key aspect of life will invariably intersect with and impact other spheres of life. If the characteristic is patriotism for the fatherland, then such patriotism will typically affect all of life, expressing itself in virtually all activities. The same holds true for matters of faith. Russian believers who passionately follow a major doctrine of belief tend to bring it into all aspects of life (ibid., 49). These tendencies combine with a polychronic and relational orientation (relationships are far more important than goals) and a past orientation (any change or new ways of doing things are shunned) to create considerable differences for Westerners (see Meyer 2014; Storti 1999). One would think that Western missionaries would readily recognize the differences and adapt their strategies to fit the context. Yet these cultural attributes are often either missed or entirely overlooked even by major mission agencies that are not new to work in Russia.

As Churchill said, Russia is indeed an "enigma" and difficult for Westerners to understand. Russian culture can be mystifying even for "experts" on culture. An informational brochure created by a large mission organization that has worked there since the late 1990s stated that Russian culture falls in the guilt-innocence category, just like Western Europe and North America. Remarkably, a well-known tome on intercultural communication identifies Russian culture as "future oriented," much like European culture (Smith 1992, 157).[8] Reasons for such failure may relate to the confusion Russian people cause Westerners by their exterior, "European-like" shell or the superficial aspects of culture we share. The curious mixture of Western dress and traditional ways, a penchant for hierarchical authority and yet a love of freedom from such authority,[9] and the Russian government's emphasis on production and making Russia "great" can all easily motivate false interpretations.

Another major issue is the continued absence of good-quality East Slavic missiological literature, which would help inform Western missionary efforts so that such misperceptions might be avoided (Cherenkov 2009). The only journals that are somewhat accessible to East Slavs (though not indigenous) are several international missiological journals that are translated into Russian, such as the *International Bulletin of Missionary Research* and the *International Journal of Frontier Missions*. It is also likely that the type of failure discussed above is due in large part to the nature of Western culture and the cultural "baggage" that Western missionaries bring wherever they go. A few examples from recent history demonstrate this unfortunate tendency.

---

8 This misinterpretation is likely due to the past Soviet emphasis on industrialization and modernization that was so prevalent during the twentieth century. Russians do value technological progress, although they look to past experiences, history, and traditions to inform the present (see Billington's *The Icon and the Axe*).

9 The common Russian translation of the English word "freedom," *svoboda*, is accurately defined as a "loosening of restrictions" rather than the sense of self-determination without interference associated with the English word.

Lessons Learned

In late 1992, I received a phone call from a representative of a large collaborative project, led by a prominent evangelical mission agency, that was designed to bring Christian ethics training to Russian public schools. The Russian Ministry of Education had asked Western Christian leaders to embark on a five-year initial collaboration. This was an extraordinary invitation. After an explanation of the goals and mission of bringing ethics curriculum to Russian schools, I was asked if the missionary-training organization we were forming, Russian Language Ministries (RLM), would be interested in participating in the new project. I therefore asked to review a copy of the curriculum they were planning to use.

In reading the Russian curriculum, my Russian colleagues and I were immediately struck by its Western flavor, including many points that would either not be understood or could potentially be misconstrued by Russian readers. The extreme goal-oriented tendency and dichotomist aspects of American thinking were readily apparent. It was obvious that Americans had written the curriculum in English, which they then had translated into Russian. We also noted that the stated goals associated with the project's promotion in the West evangelization and church planting—did not fit the project's original purpose statement, which was to "develop morals and ethics programs and curricula for Russian public schools, to distribute education materials, and to conduct educational conferences and consultations" (Glanzer 2000). This violated the Russian cherished notion of "keeping one's word."

I immediately called the organization to ask questions and give them some input, as they had invited me to do. When I offered the above observations and expressed concern as to American intentions when compared with Russian expectations, I was told that the curriculum was finalized. No revisions of this curriculum were possible since the organization had already set its goals and deadlines. Begun in 1992, the project was suspended by the Russian Ministry of Education in early 1995, almost three years short of the five-year agreement (ibid.).

The failure of the project was interpreted by many in the West to be a natural result of the controlling influence of the ROC, which has issued statements designed to limit Western forms of religious expression. Father Vladimir Yashchenko, who was assistant to the chief ROC representative involved in the project, was quoted as stating, "We can't do as Americans do, because we can't have such sects [*sekty*—defined as "cults"] equal to our traditional Orthodox Church. We need legal laws to prevent them from their activity" (ibid.). The American response of placing the blame for the project's demise on the ROC is understandable. Yet in light of the ROC's tentative state at the time and the common problems in intercultural communication between Americans and Russians, Yashchenko's statement makes sense. The Russian Church was struggling to overcome years of disintegration and persecution. More importantly, the lack of American introspection over the obvious cross-cultural missteps discussed above is disturbing.

The experience of the aforementioned project demonstrates how easy it is for Westerners to project their own cultural values and assumptions on a sensitive cross-cultural endeavor. It was only natural for Westerners, who have been "programmed" to think of democracy as promoting freedom of religious expression without favoring any particular confession (pluralism), to conclude at the time that the new glasnost (cultural openness) meant a new future for mission work in Russia. This was clearly a misunderstanding of the Russian search for stability at the time, in the context of a holistic national identity that would inevitably include their historic faith, which has resulted in a growing desecularization. In light of the drastic political change afoot in Russia after the Soviet breakup and sudden attempts to democratize the nation, many Westerners believed that a more favorable "open door" to religious expression had been created.

The case above also demonstrates the American goal orientation in spreading the gospel (a noble goal) along with a complete disregard for (or ignorance of) the values and interests of the other culture. A pertinent question that arises out of such observations relates to the extent that Western values and cultural expectations play a role in interpreting other contexts. Is it possible, for example, that one of the difficulties Western, and especially American, missionaries have in adopting strategies that might work in the Russian context stems from the tendency to interpret life through a dichotomist lens that hinders an accurate view of the holistic aspects of Russian culture that have led to Russia's desecularization? Though they may have difficulty labeling it as such, a number of Russian evangelical Christians have noted that this dichotomist nature of Americans is indeed a major issue (Canner 2000).

In 2000, the nonprofit organization I lead (now called LCTI) began a research project designed to discover Russian (and Ukrainian) Christians' attitudes on American evangelistic and discipleship programs within the Russian Federation and Ukraine. One hundred and five individuals participated in the survey we had designed for the project (ibid., 5). Various questions were included related to their experiences with American missionaries, including questions about the effectiveness of American mission efforts, how Russians and Ukrainians perceive American intentions, etc. The difficulty associated with conducting a survey of this kind relates to the East Slavic tendency to "save face." We were forced to discard or rewrite some of the questions early on due to skewed results shown in the face-to-face post-survey interviews we conducted. We noticed that it was important to build a strong rapport with respondents and convince them that their responses would not be shared with their "American friends." Saving face in that culture extends to your friends and family.

The results of the survey were telling and somewhat difficult to swallow. Of the 105 responses, 64 percent included comments that were critical of American efforts (ibid., 11). Of the forty-two participants within the Russian Federation, the percentage of responses that portrayed American efforts negatively was 79 percent (ibid.). Common critiques included statements to the effect that "Americans are phony"; "Americans only come here to do their projects so that they can impress their friends in the US"; "Americans do not really care about us or our culture" (ibid., 9). Several of the more extensive interviews with Russian Baptist church leaders and pastors illuminated the issue of American misperceptions of Christian life in Russia and confusion related to the dichotomist nature of Western strategies for discipling new believers.

In the words of a church pastor who lives in a village outside of Vladimir, Russia, "Americans only talk about projects. They talk about what we need to know.[10] They simply do not know how to help our people actually live the Christian life. That is why so many people return to the Orthodox Church, because at least in the Orthodox Church they will learn something about how to live the Christian life" (ibid.).

This response demonstrates perhaps one of the most difficult aspects of ministry in the RF for American missionaries: Americans tend to bring various educational systems or programs, but they just do not seem to understand the nature of the Russians' holistic world. A natural result of their holistic orientation is either an unwillingness or, more likely, an inability to separate

---

10 This sentiment is indicative of a general Western tendency to emphasize knowledge at the expense of practical application. Some studies indicate that indigenous workers trained under the Western model are ill-equipped to serve effectively. See Shamgunov 2009 for an interesting treatment of this topic.

or secularize life into different spheres. This explains much of the common disconnect between Western programs and Russian expectations. One such expectation is their inclination toward hierarchical decisions that are made for the collective. Westerners naturally dichotomize church life, education, projects, and work, whereas Russians expect different aspects of life to flow into others. Having the church hierarchy make decisions and issue edicts is perceived to be a form of security in the Russian psyche.[11] Such security is provided in part by a desecularized system of government that has the official church playing a direct role, a holistic orientation expressed nationally in the form of a state-sponsored church.

Such a hierarchical view of authority explains some of the common misinterpretations that can easily occur in evangelism and discipleship in that context. For example, during one large evangelistic crusade held in Moscow in the early 1990s, a fellow missionary conducted some informal survey work through the response cards they had distributed to those who came forward when invited to receive Christ. When asked why they had decided to come forward, a majority of respondents gave reasons other than "To receive Christ." One common response was "Because I was asked to come forward by the leader," or an equivalent statement.

There are many examples of similar types of cultural dissonance. In one Russian church plant in St. Petersburg, Russia, that was initially successful (in terms of the number of attendees), the Western organization involved decided that it was time to prepare the church for indigenous leadership through a "discipleship training program," with congregational input in the process. As a Russian friend relayed to me, over the next several months members became increasingly disinterested and alarmed at the "lack of stability" or "insecurity" of such a structure. The church's membership dropped from about 1,200 to less than 200 attendees shortly thereafter. That particular church eventually failed altogether.

The most common statements on the part of American missionary organizations about the difficulties faced in cross-cultural ministry in Russia, including the reasons agencies provide for having to close down work there, relate to "troublesome Orthodox priests," "new restrictive laws against Protestants," etc. While these observations are true, very few people in the West are thinking through the underlying causes of these developments,

---

11 This tendency stems from the development in their history of a fear of anarchy, each experience of which reinforced such fear, which began during a terribly tumultuous period in the early seventeenth century known as the "Time of Troubles."

an observation further discussed below. Few American organizations are reflective enough to entertain the possibility that perhaps one reason for the difficulties and restrictions missionaries experience today is found in past activities and programs that were conducted without first taking the time necessary to understand their potential impact and ensure effective communication of the intentions behind such programs in advance.

The inability to critically assess a context prior to conducting ministry, as seen in the large collaborative project mentioned earlier, may be a major cause of the very difficulties now faced by missionaries in that part of the world. Part of the difficulty in making such assessments is related to American dichotomist and goal-related cultural tendencies, which act to filter received information. For example, Russian state policies are designed to protect an Orthodox faith (part of the Russian identity) that was nearly destroyed by Soviet secularism. In such a context, the success of alternative expressions of faith, aided by the wealth and power of the West, is naturally seen as a threat to the church's existence—thus the ROC's favored status. It is only natural for goal-oriented and dichotomist individuals to interpret policies meant to protect a national church in a desecularized (and not pluralist) environment as policies designed to prohibit evangelical faith.

A similar situation stems from a Western purpose or goal orientation. A focus on goals causes a failure to devote energy to building bridges of understanding and mutual respect; a preoccupation with results hinders much-needed efforts to contextualize Western mission efforts in this holistic context. Russians have long felt a deep distrust of Western motives. It appears that many of our past high-powered efforts may have inadvertently fed this distrust. Such missteps only serve to reinforce the desire to enact laws that further restrict missionary activities in Russia.

In July of 2016, amendments to the Law on Religious Organizations were signed by President Putin. Article 8 of Law No. 374 states (Library of Congress 2016):

1. Missionary activities cannot be conducted on behalf of a representative office of a foreign religious organization (Law No. 374, art. 8, § 1.).

2. Literature and printed, audio, and video materials issued by a religious organization and distributed within the framework of its missionary work must be marked by the issuing religious organization and bear its name (*Id.* § 2.).

3. Religious organizations have the exclusive right to invite foreign nationals for the purposes of conducting professional religious activities, including missionary work, under labor or civil law contracts concluded with these organizations (*Id.* § 3.).

"Missionary activities" are defined in the new law as work "aimed at distributing information about [the organization's] own religious beliefs among people who are not followers of this religious association, with the purpose of involving these people in the membership of the religious association" (ibid.).

Prior to this new law, the RF approved a "foreign agent" law in 2012 that was designed to restrict foreign NGOs from operating in the country. These developments have impacted the ability of many Western-led mission efforts to operate in the Russian Federation. The law of 2012 requires foreign groups to file detailed paperwork and be subject to government audits and at times "enforcement visits" of NGO offices, resulting in government statistics that show that since its enactment, the number of foreign NGOs has decreased by a third (Shellnutt 2016). Sergej Rakhuba, the president of Mission Eurasia, has said that in the building that housed their mission in Moscow, not one foreign expatriate agency has remained (ibid.).

The combination of these two laws severely restricts the registration or operation of foreign missions. It is also clear, however, that because of other challenges the reduction in the number of mission organizations operating in Russia began long before these new laws were enacted. One large organization, which has been considered very effective, began reducing its activity in the RF before 2008, when there were approximately half a dozen cities where Americans could serve long-term. There are only two today: Moscow and St. Petersburg (Cru 2019). While most of the Western mission agencies that were once active in Russia have since discontinued their ministries there, evangelical church denominations in the RF have also not experienced any significant growth. The number of Russian Baptists, for example, has remained at .05 percent of the general population, which is approximately the same as it was prior to the fall of the USSR (Kravtsev 2016, 37).

Conclusion

According to Peter Berger, secularization is perhaps best discussed in the context of pluralism or pluralistic societies (Berger 2014). This fact perhaps helps to explain the enigmatic desecularization occurring in the Russian Federation.

While the Russian Church's recent revival and growing influence on government and society following the fall of the Soviet Union has occurred despite extreme efforts to secularize the country and destroy Christian expression during the Soviet period, one crucially missing element to life in the Russian context is pluralism. As part of the Western formulation of a just and equitable form of government, pluralistic societies were a natural result of the Enlightenment philosophy Russia rejected in the eighteenth century. Russian society is characterized by strong, conservative forces that have resisted Western-style democratic principles and the open society pluralism affords.

In the aftermath of the destruction of Russian civil society and pre-Soviet values, the Russian nation began a search for her historical identity, a search that brought her to seek aid from the West. Western solutions of economic "shock therapy" and the expectation that Russia would readily adopt Western principles of human rights and democracy were apparently destined to fail due to an absence of the historical groundwork necessary for such a transformation. Most importantly, the destruction of traditional Russian culture and faith caused by atheistic, socialist doctrine created a crisis of ethics and morality on such a scale that it was only natural for the Russian people to look elsewhere for potential solutions. The inability of the Western church to provide adequate answers to this dilemma is perhaps one of the greatest failures of recent missionary practice. The lack of success is likely due to a number of issues, including insufficient training in Russian history, culture, and the nature of Russian Orthodoxy, resulting in an absence of proper contextualization to the Russian context. In light of the perplexing nature of Russian culture and Western cultural tendencies, such failure is understandable.

The desecularization in Russia witnessed today makes sense in light of the Russian people's post-Soviet search for identity, their history and cultural tendencies, and, in particular, holistic aspects of what it means to be Russian. The holistic role of the Russian Orthodox Church in both society and government is an integral part of the nation's historical identity. A type of desecularized symbiosis between state and church appears to be the current modus operandi of the Russian state. An unfortunate consequence of this development, however, is the growing influence of the ROC on government policies, which has created greater barriers to Western mission efforts there.

Since the late 1990s, what was once an "open door to ministry" in Russia has degraded to a context that should be characterized today as "creative access." Many Western agencies' attempts at evangelism and discipleship have failed, and a great number of ministries have closed down their work entirely and left for regions that are more hospitable. Much of Russia is undoubtedly a challenging destination, but such failure is not only due to the increasingly anti-Western policies that hinder missionary efforts there. Such policies are merely the symptom of a far more complex cause: a deep-seated distrust caused by various historical forces and developments that have served to alienate Russians from the West. This distrust of Westerners has only been exacerbated by Western ministry projects that failed to take into account Russia's history, cultural worldview, the nature of Russian spirituality, and/or the Orthodox faith.

The general failure of many Western strategies in the RF can be attributed in part to a Western misunderstanding and, consequently, mishandling of the Russian context. The dichotomist tendencies among Westerners serve to create confusion for nationals, who require a far more holistic and practical approach to spirituality rather than the standard Western knowledge-oriented strategies. This holistic approach is apparently better served by the increased influence of the Russian Church over society in a context of desecularization. The result of Western efforts is often a cultural dissonance that complicates ministry there.

While there are some examples of effective ministry on the part of Western workers in Russia, they tend to be rare. During my travels throughout the Russian Federation over the past twenty-five years with scores of visits among Western missionaries working there, I have rarely witnessed the kind of contextualized mission efforts that are necessary for Christlike transformation. Much of this failure is due to the nature of Western culture as compared to Russian cultural tendencies on a traditional cultural continuum. Western, and especially American, programs with names like "2000 Churches by the Year 2000," or the translation into Russian of Western books with the term "purpose-driven" in the title demonstrate the depth of our lack of cultural understanding. In essence, the Western context and historical experience, key aspects of Western culture, Western models of cross-cultural ministry, and the type of training typically provided to missionary candidates have combined to hinder many Western missionaries from creating the fertile ground necessary for effective evangelism, discipleship, or church planting in an increasingly desecularizing Russian Federation. Most of the effective ministries I have observed tend to be led by Ukrainians rather than Westerners (which has recently become more problematic due to the current animosity between the two countries). Based on what I have written here, one might conclude that the situation is hopeless and that we Westerners should give up on Russia entirely. However, there is hope and promise for the future.

The nature of most recent Western mission efforts in Russia notwithstanding, there are some encouraging exceptions to this situation as well as some encouraging signs of change. First, not all Westerners or even Americans fit the typical Western cultural profile. Some of my past students, especially those who are more holistic in their thinking, have moved into ministry roles in Russia that have seen some excellent progress. Those who serve holistically never allow their goals or programs to interfere with their relationships. The missionaries who are most loved are those who are willing to drop what they're doing for the sake of their Russian friends. Similarly, there are others, who I would say have the "cross-cultural gift". Several of my former students do not only have that gift; they have truly fulfilled the Pauline mandate to "become all things to all men" (1 Cor. 9). These individuals love the Russian people they serve so deeply and have acculturated and contextualized their work so thoroughly, that their ministry there has thrived. For some of them, their work has found support even with the governing authorities and/or the Orthodox church. One encouraging sign is that since the turn of the century a number of mission agencies have perceived the need to equip their candidates more thoroughly with the specific training (Russian culture, history and language) they need for long-term success in that context.

While I cannot be too specific due to security concerns, examples of Western-led success in the Russian Federation include some excellent life-changing work among former orphans and street children, and contextualized teaching, discipleship and new churches that look and feel genuinely Russian or even Orthodox. Many of these more successful works have become indigenized, the baton passing to nationals who share the vision and passion of Christ-led transformation. These positive examples serve as reminders that when approached correctly and with the right people involved, cross-cultural ministry can be effective even under the most difficult circumstances.

The Russian Federation is an incredibly diverse nation. Of the hundreds of ethnic groups found there, the majority are characterized as having little or no viable Christian witness. The spiritual void in many regions remains acute, and the nation is still in desperate need of qualified cross-cultural workers. This environment has combined in the modern day with a revival of Russia's nineteenth-century Silver-Age formulation of an Orthodox Christendom that has great sway over government policies and the public expression of faith—a move toward a possibly entrenched form of desecularization. This state of affairs poses a great dilemma and challenge for twenty-first-century missions.

One way forward in solving this modern missiological dilemma is to provide more than the standard training typically available to those preparing for life and ministry in the Russian Federation. Many missionary candidates fail to acquire proper cross-cultural preparation for that part of the world. It will be important for future workers to have the background, experience and training necessary to adequately adapt to Russian culture and build bridges of understanding with the Orthodox. Prior ministry experience in a similar region, such as Ukraine or Kazakhstan, or even an enclave of Russian people in the West, could help provide the necessary experience. Western workers should acquire quality training in Russian history, Russian Orthodoxy, the language, cultural traditions, and a firm understanding of the Russian cultural worldview prior to serving there.

It will be important to adopt missional approaches that are relevant to the Russian people, approaches that reflect a deeper understanding of Russian spirituality and expression. Those efforts that will stand the test of time in that region will need to adopt more holistic and relational ways to serve, and then develop the kind of ministries that reflect indigenous expressions of genuine Christian faith—expressions that will solve real issues of what it means to be genuine followers of Jesus in the desecularized context of the Russian Federation.

References

Berger, Peter. 2014. *The Many Altars of Modernity: Toward a Paradigm for Religion in a Pluralist Age*. Boston: Walter de Gruyter.

Billington, James. 1970. *The Icon and the Axe: An Interpretive History of Russian Culture*. New York: Random House.

———. 2004. *Russia in Search of Itself*. Washington DC: Johns Hopkins University Press.

Blitt, Robert C. 2010. "One New President, One New Patriarch, and a Generous Disregard for the Constitution: A Recipe for the Continuing Decline of Secular Russia." *Vanderbilt Journal of Transnational Law* 43: 1337–67.

Canner, Marc. 2000. "Russian and Ukrainian Attitudes and Perspectives on American Religious Workers: A Field Study." *RLM Publications*, 7–12.

Cherenkov, Mikhail. 2009. "Toward Appropriate Missiology for Post-Soviet Evangelicals." *Cherenkoff Online*, July 7. http://cherenkoff.blogspot.com/2009/07/toward-appropriate-missiology-for-post.html.

Cline, Austin. 2017. "Secularism as a Humanistic and Atheistic Philosophy." *ThoughtCo*, March 24. https://www.thoughtco.com/secularism-as-a-humanistic-atheistic-philosophy-250856.

Cru. 2019. "Locations–International: Central/Eastern Europe and Russia." https://www.cru.org/us/en/opportunities/internships/international/locations/eeur.html.

De Vries, M. F. R. Kets. 1998. "The Anarchist Within: Clinical Reflections on Russian Character, Leadership Style, and Organizational Practices." Fountainebleau, France: Insead Working Paper.

Dostoevsky, Fyodor. 1869. "Letter to Strakhov," no. 325. In "Dostoevsky on Russia's Mission." Mark Hackard, *The Soul of the East Blog*, February 27, 2015. https://souloftheeast.org/2015/02/27/dostoevsky-russias-mission/.

Freeland, Chrystia. 2000. *Russia's Wild Ride from Communism to Capitalism*. New York: Crown.

Glanzer, Perry. 2000. "A Troubled Troika: The CoMission", the Russian Ministry of Education, x.

Hart, Daryl. 2014. "The Two-Kingdoms Theology and Christians Today." *Ecclesial Calvinist*, March 4. http://theecclesialcalvinist.wordpress.com/2014/03/04/the-two-kingdoms-theology-and-christians-today/.

Heretz, Leonid. 2008. *Russia on the Eve of Modernity: Popular Religion and Traditional Culture under the Last Tsars*. New York: Cambridge University.

Horak, Zaboj. 2010. "Religion and the Secular State in the Czech Republic." In Religion and the Secular State: National Reports, Interim National Reports, edited by J. Martinez-Torrón and W. C. Durham Jr., 251–60. XVIIIth International Congress of Comparative Law, Washington, DC, July 2010.

Kipling, Rudyard. 2017. "The Man Who Was." Musaicum Books: Kindle ed.

Knox, Zoe. 2005. *Russian Society and the Orthodox Church: Religion in Russia after Communism*. New York: Routledge.

Kochan, Lionel. 1997. *The Making of Modern Russia: From Kiev Rus' to the Collapse of the Soviet Union*. Middlesex, England: Penguin Books.

Kravtsev, Andrej. 2016. "Missionary Sending Structures in the Russian Baptist Union: The Past, Present and Future," *Theological Reflections* 16: 29–48.

Kuru, Ahmet T. 2007. "Passive and Assertive Secularism: Historical Conditions, Ideological Struggles, and State Policies toward Religion." *World Politics* 4 (4): 568–94.

Lazin, Fred. 2014. "Local Government Reforms in Eastern Europe after the Collapse of the Soviet Union: Some Observations." *Hrvatska i komparativna javna uprava : časopis za teoriju i praksu javne uprave* 14 (1): 59–84.

Library of Congress. 2016. "Russia: New Law Regulates Missionary Work." *Global Legal Monitor*, July 14. https://www.loc.gov/law/foreign-news/article/russia-new-law-regulates-missionary-work/.

McClay, Wilfred. 2007. "Religion and Secularism: The American Experience." Pew Forum Faith Angle Conference. *Pew Research Center, Religion and Public Life*, December 3. http://www.pewforum.org/2007/12/03/religion-and-secularism-the-american-experience/.

Meyer, Erin. 2014. *The Culture Map: Breaking through the Boundaries of Global Business*. New York: Public Affairs.

"Orthodox Declaration of Human Rights." 2006. The Tenth World Russian People's Council, April 6. http://www.pravoslavieto.com/docs/human_rights/declaration_ru_en.htm.

Owen, Geoffrey. 2011. "Communist Hangover." *Standpoint*, September. https://standpointmag.co.uk/open-season-september-11-communist-hangover-geoffrey-owen-russia-lenin-stalin-andrei-zubov-communism.

Perry, Marvin. 2014. *Sources of the Western Tradition. Volume 2 of From the Renaissance to the Present*. New York: Wadsworth.

Radio Free Europe. 2001. "Putin Says All Peoples 'Equal Before God.'" *Newsline*, August 21. https://www.rferl.org/a/1142467.html.

Riasanovsky, Nicholas Valentin. 1984. *A History of Russia*. New York: Oxford University Press.

Shamgunov, Insur. 2009. "Listening to the Voice of the Graduate: An Analysis of Professional Practice and Training for Ministry in Central Asia." PhD thesis, Oxford University, UK.

Sheehan, Jonathan. 2003. "Enlightenment, Religion, and the Enigma of Secularization: A Review Essay." *The American Historical Review* 108 (4): 1061–80.

Shellnutt, Kate. 2016. "Russia's Newest Law: No Evangelizing Outside of Church." *Christianity Today*, July 8. http://www.christianitytoday.com/gleanings/2016/june/no-evangelizing-outside-of-church-russia-proposes.html.

Smith, Donald K. 1992. *Creating Understanding: A Handbook of Christian Communication across Cultural Landscapes*. Grand Rapids: Zondervan.

Smith, Hedrick. 1976. *The Russians*. New York: Quadrangle/New York Times Book Co.

Storti, Craig. 1999. *Figuring Foreigners Out: A Practical Guide*. Boston: Intercultural Press.

Szporluk, Roman. 2000. *Russia, Ukraine, and the Breakup of the Soviet Union*. Stanford: Hoover Institution Press.

von der Heydt, Barbara. 1993. *Candles behind the Wall*. Grand Rapids: Eerdmans.

Wines, Michael. 2000. "Putin Is Made Russia's President in First Free Transfer of Power." *New York Times*, May 8. https://www.nytimes.com/2000/05/08/world/putin-is-made-russia-s-president-in-first-free-transfer-of-power.html.

Young, Cathy. 2017. "Is Communism Worse than Nazism?" *Forward*, October 3. https://forward.com/opinion/world/384097/is-communism-worse-than-nazism/.

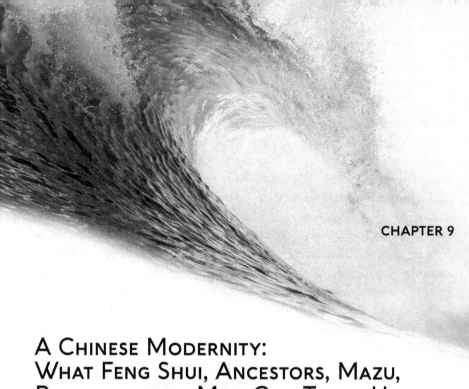

CHAPTER 9

A Chinese Modernity: What Feng Shui, Ancestors, Mazu, Buddhism, and Mao Can Teach Us about a Different Kind of Secularization 莊智超

Tony Chih-Chao Chuang

In his influential book, *The Sacred Canopy*, Peter Berger (1967, 107) defines secularization as "the process by which sectors of society and culture are removed from the domination of religious institutions and symbols." Berger, along with numerous other authors, proposed the secularization thesis that essentially argues that increasing modernity will decrease religious influence on society. Many scholars have since nuanced and modified this secularization thesis, including Rodney Stark, José Casanova, and even Berger (1999) himself. Berger (2014) now thinks that pluralism, not secularization, is the end result of modernization. Nevertheless, most scholars still contend that religiosity at least changes, if not decreases, as secularization increases.

How does this fit with the sociological realities of Chinese societies? Growing up in Taipei City, I experienced the visible signs of modernization. When Taipei 101 was built, we all celebrated it being the tallest building in the world. As portable computing took off, we took pride in Taiwan Semiconductor Manufacturing Company, still a leader in the field. Along with the technological advancements, I also saw the constant erection of new temples dedicated to various local deities. At home, our ancestors and certain deities sat on the shrine by the central wall of the living room. Smaller shrines are visible in many local restaurants and corporate offices of Taiwanese companies. At least in my circle of relatives and friends, traditional religious beliefs and practices remain a staple of daily living. In broader society, religious symbols did not seem either to increase or decrease as modernization continued. This leads to the question: What is it about the way Chinese people treat religion that creates such staying power for these sacred symbols? As time progresses, are current models based on European and American modernization sufficient to predict the place of religion in Chinese societies? Do the Chinese even have the same definitions for fundamental concepts like religion, modernity, and tradition?

To begin to answer these questions, this chapter will analyze one central aspect of the secularization thesis, the concept of modernity, according to a Chinese[1] frame of thinking. Specifically, I will address how two aspects of modernity—namely, religion and tradition—are affected by the increasing modernization in the two spheres. I offer a comparative analysis of the two countries' different approaches to modernizing a society and explore their thinking behind what modernity entails. My contention is that this Chinese modernity is different enough from popular Western[2] concepts of modernity that it warrants further study and different approaches to missiological thinking.

Defining Measurements for Modernization

To begin, it is useful to look at what measurements one uses for defining modernization. Do these measurements focus on certain aspects of what we call modernization today and therefore privilege certain localities? If so, does the definition itself spur a certain kind of modernization globally? Even if the measurement is unbiased, does it apply to each context with little to no adjustment?

---

1 The Chinese diaspora makes an all-encompassing "Chinese mind-set" impossible to summarize. For the purposes of this chapter, we limit ourselves to Taiwan and China.

2 Defining terms like "Western" is always difficult. For my purposes, I will consider the United States, Canada, much of Western Europe, and Australia as part of the "West." Despite its problematic aspects, I have decided to still use the term "Western" to draw attention to the global power structure in academia and beyond.

Berger helps with these questions by at least providing a baseline from which we can start working. He draws a distinction between *development* as "economic growth processes" and *modernization* as "various socio-cultural processes concomitant with them" (1974, 6). Nevertheless, he stresses a close relationship between them, ultimately defining modernization as "the institutional concomitants of technologically induced economic growth" (ibid., 9). Among other things, Berger (ibid., 23–96) examines the institutional carriers of this "modern consciousness," including technological production, bureaucracy, and pluralization of social life. Moreover, he sees every culture as being on a different place on a continuum of modernity, with no culture being completely *modern* nor *non-modern* (ibid., 9).

Defining tradition

My usage of *non-modern* indicates a slight departure from some definitions of modernity. The typical antonyms of *modern* are *old-fashioned* or *traditional*. Anthony Giddens uses the terms *premodern*, *modern*, and *postmodern* to define locations on this continuum. He uses *premodern* and *traditional* almost synonymously throughout his work (Giddens 1991, 6). Giddens' biggest contribution is in his explanation of how modernity is defined by the "separation of time and space," the "development of disembedding mechanisms," and the "reflexive appropriation of knowledge" (53).

In light of these ideas, Giddens defines tradition as "a mode of integrating the reflexive monitoring of action with the time-space organisation of the community" (37). Viewed in this way, any cultural artifact can become "traditional' with enough reflexivity. Tradition is then simply a way of doing things that is justified, gains meaning, and receives identity "only from the reflexivity of the modern" (38). Modern reflexivity then brings "emancipation from the dogma of tradition" (48). In essence, modernity undercuts tradition, including but not limited to religion itself.

Giddens offers an insightful and progressive look at the formation of tradition. For him, tradition is something to be judged by the modern, with the unworthy parts discarded and new parts created in the emancipating tool called reflexivity. However, to what extent is tradition validated by modern reflexivity, and to what extent does tradition shape processes of reflexivity? Moreover, in defining the modern as oppositional to tradition, Giddens may be describing a phenomenon in a certain geographical context that does not ring true in all parts of the world.

To be fair, Giddens' concern was with the lack of morality that he saw modernity bringing and how tradition can survive in that context. He was not undermining tradition so much as analyzing its demise. My point is that even though globalization has led to broader acceptance of Giddens' ideas of modernity, his theory is by no means universally applicable. Tradition does not always lose its place in society with the influx of modernity. China and Taiwan provide a localized glimpse into how tradition factors into modernization differently in certain cultures.

Defining religion

We have seen that part of the definition of modernization treats tradition as something to be updated by modern reflexivity. Religion is another factor that plays into the definition of modernization significantly in current debates. Anthropologist Clifford Geertz, cited by scholars in many disciplines, can shed some light on the role and use of religion in societies. In *The Interpretation of Cultures*, Geertz (2017, 97) defines religion in five points. He spends a whole chapter unpacking these five points. Point one pertains most to our discussion, even though all the points provide an important backdrop to later discussions. Like Max Weber, Geertz sees religion as "a system of symbols" that helps people provide meaning in an otherwise chaotic life. These religious symbols serve as both models *of* reality as well as models *for* reality. Geertz's definition is useful to our discussion in that he provides a framework for the explanation of certain socioreligious behaviors in postwar China and Taiwan.

Harold Netland summarizes a less anthropological and sociological but more philosophical definition of religion. He leans on Roger Schmidt's definition of religions as "systems of meaning... that articulates a view of the sacred" (Netland 2001, 193) Netland also points to Fenggang Yang (2011, 36), who stresses a communal aspect, highlighting not just the sacred or the supernatural but also that religion must "unite the believers or followers into a social organization of moral community." While Geertz allows us to explain individual behaviors, Schmidt and Yang allow us to understand the importance of the supernatural, as well as the behavioral conditioning done by the community itself. This framework for understanding religion thus gives a useful lens through which we can view religion in Taiwan and China.

Why a Chinese Modernity Is Different

The above understanding of modernization, specifically with its relationship to tradition, stems mostly from Western scholars. Giddens' view of the oppositional nature between modernization and tradition needs more nuancing for it to completely fit in the contexts of Taiwan and China.[3] For example, on the surface China may be a modernized country, with a formal governmental structure that is officially secularized (i.e., government officials must publicly hold to atheism). But the Chinese government claims to be able to determine the true reincarnation of the Pancheon Lama, distinguish true religions from evil cults, and support the spirit of Confucianism, Daoism, and Buddhism. In this way, Richard Madsen (2011, 250) explains that the secularization that comes with modernization may be accurate on the formal, structural level, but "it doesn't adequately describe the interior spirit" of countries like China.

Religion in modernized Taiwan and China

One example of the "interior spirit" unnoticed on a formal level is popular/folk religion, sometimes referred to as diffused religion (in contrast to institutional religion; see C. K. Yang 1961). Jeaneane and Merv Fowler (2008, 224) describe popular religion as based on "local customs, myths, legends" and lying "outside the realms of institutional, established beliefs and practices." Popular religion "could thrive alongside a state structure" due to its inherent fluidity and particular expressions (ibid., 225). In fact, it is not just the religion of the common folk but of many elite families as well (ibid., 226).

The deities of Chinese popular religion can be quite varied, especially in Taiwan, including the likes of local heroes, robbers, virgins, and even dogs (Weller 1996). 媽祖 (*Mazu*) is one of the well-known deities in Taiwan, with many people praying to her and elaborate yearly ceremonies that welcome her presence to the island. These ceremonies are part of Taiwanese identity and advertised as such by the board of tourism.

---

3 I am speaking in generalizations, as theoretical works necessarily must. Just as modernity may look different from country to country, there will be many cases in which this analysis is inaccurate. Even within Taiwan there are vast differences between various cities, not to mention the rural to urban differences. Nevertheless, for the majority of cases in the population of 1.4 billion people, this should hold true.

Burning paper money as part of ancestor rites in Taiwan.
Photo courtesy of Ethan Christofferson.

Ancestor rites in South East Asia. Photo courtesy of Scott Beveridge.

The temples serving popular religion (and to a certain extent, Daoism as well) are largely run by the local laity, usually by a lay committee that handles the administration, funding, and services provided by any one temple (ibid., 242). Anyone can enter the temple at any time, burn incense, offer prayers to certain deities, toss special artifacts, and leave without a trace. The lack of ministers and sometimes even the lack of any staff presence (usually at smaller temples) make tracking visitors difficult, if not impossible.

The popular religion described above typifies much of Taiwan, but China is a different story. China and Taiwan share thousands of years of history; however, when Chairman Mao Zedong successfully overthrew the nationalist government in 1949, the histories split. The nationalist government retreated to the island of Taiwan, while the Communist government took over the rest of the land of China. Both governments continued the path of rapid modernization that started decades earlier. However, the divergent histories led to different strategies on how to deal with the issue of religion.

As the modern governments of China and Taiwan sought to "create national unity, maintain social control, and mobilize large and diverse populations," two strategies were utilized: 1) "Suppress religious practice—destroy temples, ban public religious rituals, eliminate religious leaders"; 2) "Co-opt religious leaders" (Madsen 2011, 253). China utilized the first strategy, while Taiwan utilized a mix of the two (with a focus on the latter). Taiwan took leaders of various religious groups and made them leaders in state-sponsored commissions. In this way, religion was not portrayed as the enemy (which was the strategy in China), but rather used to support the agendas of the state.

The Cultural Revolution of 1966–76 in China saw the destruction of many religious as well as traditional objects, including temples, altars in home, and even ancient artifacts. A bit ironically, Chairman Mao essentially deified himself as a way to consolidate power and modernize. Even after dying, Mao is still venerated in many places in China through prayer and by offering cigarettes[4] to idols of him in folk religious temples (F. Yang 2016, 18). The point is that Chinese religiosity, as the result of all these efforts, did not seem to suffer. In fact, certain religions saw tremendous growth in the eras of religious oppression. By some counts, Christians rose from two million to sixty million within a span of fifty years (Hirsch 2006, 18–19).

Taiwan, on the other hand, has seen similar levels of strong religiosity amid modernization. A difference was that Taiwan (post-1949) did not destroy temples so much as suppress the spreading of major religions, limiting most to local expressions (Madsen 2011, 263–64). Buddhism itself was limited through the establishing of state control. However, the presence of many Christian missionaries (the strong political arm of the Presbyterians,

---

4 People would literally put cigarettes into the hands of these idols. Normally, incense sticks are used. But Mao was supposedly a heavy smoker, which led to the use of cigarettes instead of incense. It could also be that cigarettes (used by everyone) are somehow less religious than incense (used only for religious rites), but that is only conjecture.

especially) led to the establishment of many Christian schools, hospitals, and churches. Peter Wang (2001, 323) calculated only 51,000 Protestants and 13,000 Catholics in Taiwan in 1948. However, there were about 540,000 Christians by 1960 (ibid., 325), a 744 percent increase.

Thus, we see that both China and Taiwan have seen tremendous growth in the number of Christians. By some official counts, China now has close to 70 million Christians while Taiwan has about 917,000 (Central Intelligence Agency 2019. A closer look reveals that the growth of Christianity in Taiwan slowed down a bit since the mid-1960s to a "mere" 70 percent increase. China, however, has seen a constant rapid growth until now. Explanations abound in recent scholarship.

Looking strictly at the secularization thesis, one could perhaps say that Taiwan was faster at modernizing and China's Christian growth will plateau at some point as well, once it is fully modernized. Aside from the fact that the secularization thesis has been largely debunked, this explanation does not adequately explain the intentional and also rapid modernization that China underwent. Another explanation is that many of the earlier Western missionaries did not allow the laity and indigenous leadership to assume responsibility (Wang 2001, 326).

Instead of looking at how Taiwan's church growth paled in comparison to China's, another explanation is to look at the circumstances that allowed China's Christianity to soar. Rodney Stark and Wang Xiuhua (2015, 72) explain how persecution in China "served as a potent selection mechanism" and that "a high level of member intensity is always what it takes to achieve rapid growth." Furthermore, unlike Taiwan, the expulsion of all foreign missionaries in China meant that indigenous leaders had no choice but to take over. These last two explanations then serve as probable causes for the different rates of the growth of Christianity in two similar modernizing countries.

Looking just at Christianity, then, it is clear that religiosity does not decrease with modernization, at least not with China. With Taiwan, though it might initially seem like religiosity has declined, our discussion of popular religion earlier shows that Taiwan is simply showing a different, noninstitutional form of religiosity, one that China is no doubt displaying as well. If Fowler and Fowler's study is any indication, religiosity has neither declined nor increased in conjunction with modernization. Certain religions might have gained adherents (i.e., Christianity in China)—which is already one proof against the secularization thesis—but there is little indication that religiosity as a whole has decreased. The problem is that overall religiosity of any culture is difficult to measure outside of institutional measurements. The next section explains why, for Chinese religiosity, it is ever harder.

Problems with Western definitions of religion and modernity

Madsen astutely points out the problem with the study of religion in Asia. "When Western scholars have looked for religion in Asian societies, they have often looked for it in the form of private faith. But in most Asian societies, much of religion is neither private nor faith" (Madsen 2011, 251). Religion in places like China and Taiwan is defined by neither formal creed nor private beliefs, but more by adherence to ritual practices that signify the possibility of the supernatural. Citing people like Zhixin Wang (王治心) and ancient sage Yi Zhou (周易), Lizhu Fan (2011, 90) argues for defining a Chinese concept of religion as "moralization by sacred ways" in order to not study Chinese religions with Western mind-sets.

Madsen and Fan explain a needed change in the mentality needed to understand Chinese religiosity, which in turn explains what Chinese modernization may look like. A Chinese modernity does not require strict secularization, nor does it require a decline in religiosity. The secular is instituted in the public, formal, or even governmental structures (i.e., China). Religiosity is built into the very fabric of the Chinese cultural milieu. For many Chinese, religion is as separable from life as culture is separable from society. Now the form of said religion might change (i.e., from Buddhism to Mao-venerating nationalism), but the society's religiosity remains. Looking at intellectual consent to creeds or membership counts in religious organizations may be an accepted[5] way to gauge the religiosity of the West, but it does not accurately reflect the religiosity of the East. For Chinese religiosity, one must measure *faithfulness* in adherence a lot more than *faith* in doctrines (reminiscent of πιστη in Greek).

Although the classic secularization thesis has been contested in this case study, the thesis is not entirely irrelevant in the Asian context. Ian Reader (2012) provides a good argument supporting the secularization thesis by showing how in Japan both institutional and popular religion are on the decline in levels of faith, adherence, and practice. But Reader is still only noting the surface displays of religiosity instead of the underlying religious mind-set of the people, something that Fan and Madsen warn against and

---

5 I use the word *accepted* instead of *good* or *accurate* on purpose. My contention is that this the method mentioned is not accurate at all even in the West. But arguing that is beyond the scope of this chapter.

that Yao and Badham (2007) try to do (to be discussed below). Nevertheless, what Reader rightly reminds us is that we should not be so quick to consign the secularization thesis to the grave, something that Stark and others are too quick to do (according to Reader). However one views the secularization thesis, it seems that as China and Taiwan continue to modernize, the importance of tradition and religion are not waning in the way that Charles Taylor (2007) described Europe's own religious decline for the past five hundred years.

Mixing tradition with religion

Besides the differing definition of religion for the Chinese, another reason for the difference in the modernization process for China and Taiwan is the conflation of religion and tradition in the Eastern mind. Take Buddhism, for example. For Eastern Buddhists, Buddhism was something passed down by masters and somewhat adhered to at home. In fact, "Before the modern era, and even in many areas in Asia today, the written text was regarded as ancillary to oral tradition" (Netland 2015, 85). A person was Buddhist because she practiced Buddhism and perhaps would buy a talisman that contained sutras read a certain number of times by monks so that she could hang them at home. The practice of Buddhism, in this way, is considered more traditional than religious. In some senses, a Chinese who does those things is not so much religious as traditional, being more syncretistic and involving more traditional beliefs and practices than strict Theravada Buddhism. Even highly modernized Taipei sees such practices often, as evidenced by the high number of talismans available for sale on many street corners.

Analyzing data from a four-year study of religion in China, Xinzhong Yao and Paul Badham (2007, 153–64) found not only great syncretism in the beliefs of the religious but great inconsistency in the beliefs of the nonreligious too. They discovered that only 8.7 percent of Chinese claim to be religious, while 52.3 percent claim to be nonreligious. Looking at only the nonreligious sample, only 6.8 percent believe in reincarnation, but 50.8 percent believe that familial relationships result from actions in a previous life. Likewise, 49.5 percent see great value in choosing auspicious dates for events. Additionally, good feng shui is upheld by 34.6 percent, and 28.9 percent believe in rewards from offering proper sacrifices to ancestors. Also, 77.2 percent believe that one's fortune can be changed through the accumulation of virtues (with the reverse being true as well). Lastly, there is no significant difference between the responses of the nonreligious versus the whole sample.

Yao and Badham's quantitative study has shown that so-called nonreligious people are in fact quite religious when it comes to belief in the supernatural and also traditional behaviors associated with such beliefs (i.e., ancestral worship). If only 8.7 percent claim to be religious, there is no explanation for the survey data except for the different way that the Chinese view religiosity.

Another thing that this data shows is the mixing of religion with tradition. Feng shui could be perceived as popular religion, tradition, or even good interior design. Ancestral worship is something that falls under the category of both popular religion and tradition. Even though popular/folk religion has never been officially mainstream, Gao Shining (2010, 171) argues that its impact is "much greater and stronger" than Christianity, Buddhism, and Taoism. Since the 1980s, the speed and scale with which popular religion has grown is even greater than Buddhism and Christianity (ibid.). Many people and scholars, including Gao (ibid., 175), see, according to lived reality, that popular religion (especially ancestral worship) is so central to the thinking of Chinese people that it has not left China throughout the whole process of modernization.

The plausibility structure of the sacred in Chinese modernity did not diminish, but was rather shifted and sometimes conflated with the secular. For example, the word 孝 (*xiao*—filial piety, or the honoring of and caring for one's ancestors) is said to originate as early as the beginning of the Zhou dynasty (1047–772 BC) and is popularized by sages like Confucius. One primary way to do *xiao* is to obey what one's ancestors say and to consult them about things like career, romantic relationships, politics, and even religion. For parents who have passed on, one must bury them and commemorate them according to the tradition that they wish (which often has elements of many religions). One example is the burning of silver paper money (not gold), which allows the deceased to live well in the afterlife. In this way, *xiao*, along with tradition, pushes people to continue with at least one aspect of popular religion.

One can see that, unlike Giddens' view, Chinese tradition shapes modern reflexivity more than it is justified by it. For many, ancestral worship is more about virtue and adhering to certain traditions than about religiosity. Nevertheless, the religious element is not lost but rather conflated with tradition. Understanding the intertwined relationship of the two is essential to understanding Chinese modernity.

Implications for Missiology

One notable scholar who understands this intertwined relationship and has published extensively in English is 杜明 (Tu Wei Ming), especially with his work on Confucian religiosity. Non-Chinese scholars have also contributed to this understanding, an example being Philip Clart (2003), whose analysis of 善書 (*sanshu*–moral/religious books) shows not only that morality and religion are closely related but also that much of tradition follows from this mode of thinking. Clart (95) concludes by explaining that the unique circumstances of the modernization that happened in postwar Taiwan "has produced a form of religious traditionalism that reinterprets tradition in a highly flexible manner and constructs new identities, not against, but within and for a modern Taiwanese society." Clart's idea of tradition is reminiscent of Gidden's view, except while Giddens believes in the undercutting of tradition and religion in modernity,[6] Clart sees how Taiwan builds on it in fresh, new ways.

For the Taiwanese church, modernity is not a force that undermines religiosity but an opportunity for conversion, to give meaning to the younger generation disillusioned with popular religion. Fredrik Fällman (2008, 103) explains how intellectuals in China are actively pursuing modernity and perceives its achievement as closely linked with "salvation," which has "personal, national, or cultural" connotations. He argues that in their desire to save China, some have turned to Christianity as the answer. In both Taiwan and China, then, modernity is (or at least can be) an agent that actively draws people to Christianity.

For the churches and Christian organizations that are aware of this and capitalizing on it, numbers have grown tremendously. The fastest-growing church group in Taiwan, 靈糧堂 (Bread of Life Church), is one example of a church taking the religiosity that its members once directed toward popular religion and turning it toward charismatic expressions toward God. In fact, the Chinese word used for the God of the Bible (上帝—*Shangti*) is a "strange name of God" (Kim 2005) that originates from the traditional high god of the heavens in popular religion. This is an example of a Western missionary (Matteo Ricci) using tradition and religion to his advantage. In some ways, it could be seen as both cultural appropriation and contextualization. As Taiwan and China continue to modernize, one could learn from Ricci in

---

6 It is worth reiterating that Giddens does not seem to have a negative view of tradition. It is just his conclusion after analyzing his context, which may well be valid for his context.

the usage of Chinese tradition and religion to strengthen Chinese Christianity instead of to detract from it.

If Chinese religiosity is in fact as diffused as I contend, then perhaps a diffused ecclesiology and missiology is better. Perhaps this is why the Chinese house churches are growing at such a remarkable rate. Perhaps in a globalizing world, a more diffused mission-sending structure (from everywhere to everywhere) is a better model. Instead of a concept merely talked about by scholars it should be a strategy actively implemented by more mission organizations (Escobar 2003).

Likewise, as the gospel travels from everywhere to everywhere, it is important to bear in mind that perhaps the Chinese idea of tradition (which is conflated in many ways with religion) is not merely a Chinese mentality. Many religious rituals and symbols that missionaries carry to foreign cultures may be more tied to Western tradition than to Christian religion. Ecclesiology (especially church polity) may be one religious tradition that is more Western than it is religious.

Modernization may have many similarities across the globe (i.e., industrialization and urbanization), but it is important to know where the similarities end (i.e., in relation to religion and tradition). The idea of multiple modernities is not new (Preyer and Sussmann 2015; Eisenstadt 2017), but it seems yet to be reflected in mission praxis. In order to do so, we need to do more global theologizing instead of just theologizing for the globe. The former understands that modernity takes various forms, but the latter prescribes forms of modernity for others to follow. While the former utilizes sociocultural realities of various localities, the latter at best takes into account—and at worst exports—Western ideas of religiosity to many geographies. This chapter is a starting attempt to draw attention to the latter in order to strengthen efforts for the former.

References

Berger, Peter L. 1967. *The Sacred Canopy*. Garden City, NY: Doubleday.

———. 1974. *The Homeless Mind*. New York: Vintage Books.

———, ed. 1999. *The Desecularization of the World: Resurgent Religion and World Politics*. Grand Rapids: Eerdmans.

———. 2014. *The Many Altars of Modernity: Toward a Paradigm for Religion in a Pluralist Age*. Boston: Walter de Gruyter.

Central Intelligence Agency. 2017. "The World Factbook." https://www.cia.gov/library/publications/the-world-factbook/geos/xx.html.

Clart, Philip A. 2003. "Chinese Tradition and Taiwanese Modernity." In *Religion in Modern Taiwan: Tradition and Innovation in a Changing Society*, edited by Philip A. Clart and Charles B. Jones, 84–97. Honolulu: University of Hawaii.

Eisenstadt, Shmuel N., ed. 2017. *Multiple Modernities*. Abingdon, UK: Routledge.

Escobar, Samuel. 2003. *The New Global Mission: The Gospel from Everywhere to Everyone*. Downers Grove, IL: IVP Academic.

Fällman, Fredrik. 2008. *Salvation and Modernity: Intellectuals and Faith in Contemporary China*. Rev. ed. Lanham, MD: University Press of America.

Fan, Lizhu. 2011. "The Dilemma of Pursuing Chinese Religious Studies." In *Social Scientific Studies of Religion in China: Methodologies, Theories, and Findings*, edited by Fenggang Yang and Graeme Lang, 87–107. Leiden, Netherlands: Brill.

Fowler, Jeaneane, and Merv Fowler. 2008. *Chinese Religions: Beliefs and Practices*. Eastbourne, UK: Sussex Academic Press.

Gao, Shining. 2010. "The Impact of Contemporary Chinese Folk Religions on Christianity." In *Christianity and Chinese Culture*, edited by Mikka Ruokanen and Paulos Huang, 170–81. Grand Rapids: Eerdmans.

Geertz, Clifford. 2017. *The Interpretation of Cultures*. 3rd ed. New York: Basic Books.

Giddens, Anthony. 1990. *The Consequences of Modernity*. Stanford, CA: Stanford University.

Hirsch, Alan. 2006. *The Forgotten Ways: Reactivating the Missional Church*. Grand Rapids: Brazos.

Kim, Sangkeun. 2005. *Strange Names of God: The Missionary Translation of the Divine Name and the Chinese Responses to Matteo Ricci's Shangti in Late Ming China, 1583–1644*. New York: Peter Lang Inc., International Academic Publishers.

Madsen, Richard. 2011. "Secularism, Religious Change, and Social Conflict in Asia." In *Rethinking Secularism*, edited by Craig Calhoun, Mark Juergensmeyer, and Jonathan VanAntwerpen, 248–69. Oxford: Oxford University.

Netland, Harold A. 2001. *Encountering Religious Pluralism: The Challenge to Christian Faith Mission*. Downers Grove, IL: IVP Academic

———. 2015. *Christianity and Religious Diversity: Clarifying Christian Commitments in a Globalizing Age*. Grand Rapids: Baker Academic.

Preyer, Gerhard, and Michael Sussmann, eds. 2015. *Varieties of Multiple Modernities: New Research Design*. Leiden, Netherlands: Brill Academic.

Reader, Ian. 2012. "Secularisation, R.I.P.? Nonsense! The 'Rush Hour Away from the Gods' and the Decline of Religion in Contemporary Japan." *Journal of Religion in Japan* 1 (1): 7–36. doi.org/10.1163/221183412X628370.

Stark, Rodney, and Xiuhua Wang. 2015. *A Star in the East: The Rise of Christianity in China.* West Conshohocken, PA: Templeton.

Taylor, Charles. 2007. *A Secular Age.* Cambridge, MA: The Belknap Press of Harvard University.

Wang, Peter Chen-Main. 2001. "Christianity in Modern Taiwan—Struggling Over the Path of Contextualization." In *China and Christianity: Burdened Past, Hopeful Future,* edited by Stephen Uhalley and Xiaoxin Wu, 321–43. Armonk, NY: M.E. Sharpe.

Weller, Robert P. 1996. "Matricidal Magistrates and Gambling Gods: Weak States and Strong Spirits in China." In *Unruly Gods: Divinity and Society in China,* edited by Meir Shahar and Robert P. Weller, 250–68. Honolulu: University of Hawaii.

Yang, C. K. 1961. *Religion in Chinese Society: A Study of Contemporary Social Functions of Religion and Some of Their Historical Factors.* Oakland: University of California.

Yang, Fenggang. 2011. *Religion in China: Survival and Revival under Communist Rule.* Oxford: Oxford University Press.

———. 2016. "Exceptionalism or Chinamerica: Measuring Religious Change in the Globalizing World Today." *Journal for the Scientific Study of Religion* 55 (1): 7–22.

Yao, Xinzhong, and Paul Badham. 2007. *Religious Experience in Contemporary China.* Cardiff, UK: University of Wales.

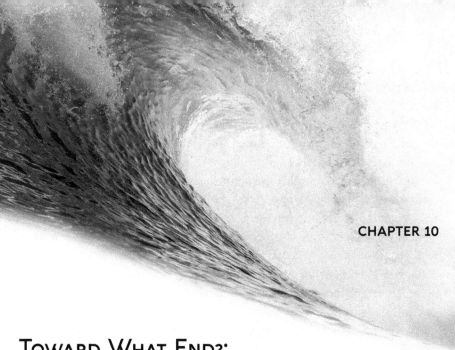

CHAPTER 10

Toward What End?: An Evaluation of Religion in Liberia's Public Sphere and Its Implications for Evangelism and Discipleship

Boye-Nelson Kiamu

Among the strategic social forces that significantly affect the West African landscape are religion and politics. The relationship between these two forces has become very problematic. Religions in Africa, especially Islam and Christianity, have experienced much growth, but alongside this growth is an ever-constant transformation of political governance toward secularization. Jon Abbink (2014, 84) writes, "While we see continued strong religious adherence among people in Africa, most are living in secular states." This inherent paradox becomes clearer in Abbink's crucial question, "How do these two phenomena coalesce, and will the secular model last?" (ibid.).

Given the trajectories in Europe and the Americas, it seems fair to also wonder, "Will religion last?" It is not difficult to concur with Abbink (ibid.) that the question of the relation of religion and the secular model animates much of the political debate within Africa. For example, Liberia's population is about 85 percent Christian, yet the country is constitutionally secular. Several questions arise from this situation: What exactly is the role of religion in the public sphere when a nation is constitutionally considered a secular state? How does religion influence public discourse amid the rise of more religious fervor on the one hand and the rise of democracy and adoption of the secular-state model on the other? To what extent should religion affect reasoning, policy, and decision making within the public sphere?

In this chapter, I seek to explore these questions while arguing that secularization provides an opportunity for the church to reclaim and practice its prophetic role in true humility. I reject the view that secularization is generally bad for religion. Rather, it I will argue that the church's tendency to advocate for a religious nation and Christian legislation as a response to secularization is inadequate. A religious state undermines the very principle of religious tolerance for which proponents of a religious state argue. Instead of seeing secularization as anti-religion, the church can see secularization as providing a means to reevaluate its mission and reconstruct effective methods of evangelism and discipleship in the secular public sphere. In this chapter, I will engage with a combination of John Rawls' theory of the liberal state and Jurgen Habermas' theory of the public sphere. I will also employ a case study of Liberia to envision the role that religion can play in the public sphere.

Between Religion and the Public Sphere: John Rawls and Jurgen Habermas

The relationship between religion and the public sphere has been somewhat problematic because the nature of religion is fluid. Furthermore, to argue for a public sphere that is religiously exclusive raises questions about the potential of religions to affect every sphere of the lives of its adherents. With the danger of being overly simplistic, there are three major ideas about the role of religion in the public sphere:

1. Religious beliefs should be banned entirely from public political discourse (Richard Rorty).[1]
2. Religious beliefs are valid arguments in political discussions without any restriction (Nicholas Wolterstorff and Stanley Hauerwas).

---

1 In 2003 Rorty provided a more nuanced view about his stance on religion in the public sphere. In his article, "Religion in the Public Square: A Reconsideration," he notes that it is mainly formal religion and arguments based upon religious authority that he opposes.

3. Religious beliefs can enter political discourse if they are restricted to claims that are intelligible to reason, independent of faith (Rawls, Audi, and Habermas. See Irlenborn 2012, 433).

These three forms have at one point or another dominated the public debate. Into the sixteenth century, religious presence within the public sphere and in public reason was highly accepted. The concept of a state implied that a region had a religious identity and affiliation. Religion and state remained intertwined until the age of the Enlightenment and the onset of secularization.

Secularization argued for a separation of church and state and the exclusion of religious reasoning from the public sphere. There is general agreement among scholars that the modern state must be "secular" (Taylor 2011, 34). However, Charles Taylor notes that there is a problem with this term. For him, the classical forms of secularism required a kind of separation of church and state in the sense that the state is not officially linked to some religious confession" (ibid.). The state needs a principled distance from religion, but this does not mean that other forms of secularism do not recognize the role of religious factors in the state. More scholars are now leaning heavily toward a mode of secularization that focuses more on providing religious freedom for all rather than obstructing religion.

With the acceptance of secularization, the role of religion in the public sphere of the secular state became debatable and reduced to the sphere of the private. The publication of John Rawls' *Political Liberalism* (1996) prompted an extensive debate about the role of religion in politics and public political discussion among citizens. Rawls and Audi have argued that citizens in liberal democracies should exercise restraint in the use of religious reason in public political discussions (Hugh 2011, 193). On the other hand, Nicholas Wolterstorff (1984) and Paul Weithman (2002) argue for the admittance of religious reasoning within the public sphere.

Another interesting figure in this debate is Jurgen Habermas (2002). Participants in the debate have criticized Habermas for his "neglect of religion" and "anti-religious assumptions" in his early writings (Mendieta and VanAntwerpen 2011). These critics usually refer to Habermas' *Theory of Communicative Action* (1984) to support their claims that Habermas was an advocate of secularization theory. But looking at his writings after 2000, Habermas changed his views and speaks of a post-secular society in which religion and the secular coexist. He recognized that religion will not disappear as a significant influence, neither in the lives of individuals nor within the cultural and political arena. He wrote several works regarding a positive engagement with religion (Habermas 2006a).

Christina Lafont (2007) and Austin Harrington (2007) amply document Habermas' "switch" from a "neglect" of religion to a "focus" on religion. Therefore, based on his post-secular categorization of society, he provides a middle ground and argues that religious reasons can only be admitted within the formal public sphere if they are presented in the form of public reason. For Habermas, this middle ground works on the *institutional translation proviso* that argues thus:

> All citizens should be free to decide whether they want to use religious language in the public sphere. Were they to do so, they would, however, have to accept that the potential truth contents of religious utterances must be translated into a generally accessible language before they can find their way onto the agendas of parliaments, courts, or administrative bodies and influence their decisions. (Habermas 2011, 25–26)

Citizens can introduce religious reasons into the debate in the informal public sphere provided that, in the course of the debate, these religious reasons are adequately translated into secular reasons equally accessible to all (Habermas 2011). Therefore, this proviso stands as a filter.

The views of John Rawls and Habermas have some similarities and major differences on the topic of religion in the public sphere. Rawls (1971) writes on the background of how a society can be just and how such a just society can work. For Rawls, the principles of social justice are those that people will choose under a certain kind of ideal condition. The problem with Rawls' ideas is the practicality of his concept of an "ideal circumstance of choice." Nevertheless, Rawls' view is helpful because it recognizes the tension of diversity.

Rawls (2005, Lecture 1)[2] observes that his key question is "How is it possible for there to exist over time a just and stable society of free and equal citizens, who remain profoundly divided by reasonable religious, philosophical, and moral doctrines?" In response to this question, Rawls offers his concept of a neutral and fair liberal state, an overlapping consensus, and a state that is committed to the democratic process (ibid.). In *Political Liberalism* ([1971] 2005), Rawls argues that the liberal state must

---

2 *Political Liberalism* was first published in 1971 and has seen several revisions of its parts.

be neutral—giving no privilege to one conception of good over another. Also, it must be committed to democratic values that supersede religious, political, and moral convictions when there is no choice but to legislate an issue (Lecture 4). So, like Habermas' proviso, Rawls presents his *overlapping consensus* (ibid.). This consensus allows a diverse community of people to agree on principles of justice even as they disagree on the deeper reason for those principles.

Rawls sees public reason as the only tool for making amendments to a constitution in the framework of a liberal state. For John Rawls, public reason "in a democratic society is the reason of equal citizens who, as a collective body, exercise final political and coercive power over one another in enacting laws and in amending their constitution" (Rawls 1996, 214). Like Habermas, Rawls emphasizes that political decisions are legitimate only to the extent that they are based on a reasonable agreement between citizens.

Public sphere

Jurgen Habermas pioneered research in the public sphere with his work *The Structural Transformation of the Public Sphere*. In this book Habermas traces how the public sphere evolves. He identifies a political public sphere (equal to a public sphere in a political realm), a literary public sphere (present in the world of letters), and a representative publicness as evolutionary stages of the concept of the public sphere (Habermas 1989, 14–26). Just like religion, there is hardly any water-tight definition of the public sphere mainly because the concept of a public sphere is always evolving.

In offering a definition of public sphere, Habermas (1991, 398) writes, "By 'Public Sphere' we mean first of all a domain of our social life in which such a thing as public opinion can be formed." Habermas goes on to describe the evolution of several public spheres until we get to the political public sphere. The political public sphere is the focus of my chapter here. According to Habermas, the political public sphere exists "when the public discussions concern objects connected with the practice of the state" (ibid.). But in a democratic state the political public sphere is not powerful on its own. The public sphere only becomes powerful when "public authority has actually been subordinated to the requirement of democratic publicness" in such instance the political public sphere "acquires an institutionalized influence on the government, by way of the legislative body" (399). From Habermas' discussion, one can conclude that the political public sphere is made of private persons who operate as a public and not based on personal statuses.

Second, the public sphere can form public opinions and have authority in a democratic society by legislative decisions alone.[3] Habermas' public sphere must be free from the influence of individual statuses in the marketplace, or state, or family background. The basis for this distinction, in my opinion, is to ensure equality—a key factor for the operation of the public sphere.[4] In *The Structural Transformation of the Public Sphere*, Habermas all but ignores the role of religion in the forming of the bourgeoisie public sphere.

Third, the public sphere is a place where citizens can exchange opinions regarding public issues and form public opinion.

Fourth, the public sphere is a link between public life and civil society. A concern, however, arises as to what role religion should play in the public sphere.

Religion in Liberia's public sphere

On November 17, 2016, the Liberian legislature approved seven of twenty-five propositions as items for a referendum. But the controversial Proposition 24, which argued that Liberia should be declared a Christian nation, was put on hold (Sonpon, 2016). Proposition 24 in the post–civil war era is arguably the most discussed and debated proposition among the Liberian public. This journey of Proposition 24 defines a new and unfolding historical epoch for Liberia and presents many questions about the role that religion, particularly Christianity, has played and will play within the Liberian public sphere. Liberia was formed by the American Colonization Society (ACS). One of the main purposes of Liberia's formation was to be a place to solve the American problem of freed black slaves. But the ACS was also a very religious association that saw its efforts to resettle freed slaves as both a social, religious, and moral effort (Boley 1983, 12).

From the onset, religion, especially Christianity, has had a place in Liberia's public sphere. Lamin Sanneh (1983, 102) writes of Liberia, "The religious life of the settlers was closely interwoven with their public life." He further notes:

---

3 Public opinion "refers to the functions of criticism and control of organized state authority that the public exercises informally, as well as formally during periodic elections" (Habermas 1991, 399).

4 A problem remains, as was noted by Dr. Bruce Reichenbach during a discussion and review of this chapter. "Is it possible to compartmentalize our life in such a way that marketplace, state, or family background does not affect our actions? We cannot compartmentalize our lives as it were, but we can make propositions in a manner that relegates the influence of state, family, and economical disposition." A strong critique of compartmentalization and the need in the public sphere can be explored in *Habermas and the Public Sphere*, edited by Craig Calhoun (1992).

A point to be made in conclusion is the significance of Church-state relations in Liberia. Political leaders acted as patrons of churches and missions, and the state became a sponsor of religious life in the country; the president and other high-ranking officials of the state were also church officials. The organizing of Christian mission became an important element of foreign policy decision. The Church not only became the focus of political power but assumed an ethnic identity. (Sanneh 1983, 105)

Sanneh is correct in his assertion. Every president of Liberia has identified with the Christian religion. Most notable was President William R. Tolbert Jr. (1971–80), who, in 1965, became the first African to serve as president of the Baptist World Alliance. Tolbert freely appealed to "Almighty God" and considered religion indispensable to Liberia's development (Tolbert 1984, 158). However, it is significant to realize that these settlers never called Liberia a Christian nation or a secular state. They adopted a form of the American constitution that allowed religious fervor to shape morality and value systems, but never saw a need to label Liberia a "Christian nation." Nevertheless, it is beyond doubt that the settlers expected religion, in this case Christianity, to be a part of who they were as a people and hence influence decision making.

In Liberia, the church and religion, particularly Christianity, play the role of moral conscience, political patron, social actor, state-identity creator, and an ethnic indicator. These roles of religion in the public sphere played a part in all three republics and is still occurring today, even under a constitution that calls Liberia secular. Religion has always existed in the Liberian public sphere. The secularization occurring in Liberia is very different from secularization occurring in the West. For Liberia, secularization does not mean the absence of religion in the public sphere; this is so because the majority of Liberians cannot contemplate any aspect of their life that lacks a religious persuasion. Secularization in Liberia is directed to the question of taking Christianity, not just religion, out of the public sphere.

I am convinced that taking religion, in this case Christianity, out of the public sphere provides the only foundation for the realization of a truly tolerant state. Such a state allows the voices of each religious group to be heard and provides a common ground for interaction, in direct opposition to the arguments of the proponents of Proposition 24. Secularization redefines the role of religion in the public sphere and provides opportunities for discovering new methods of evangelism and missions. In my opinion, John Rawls' proposition of a liberal state provides an efficient template for a tolerant state.

Finding common ground is difficult, because the proponents of Proposition 24 want one extreme: not to restrict religious voices in the public sphere. They even go beyond this and advocate that Christianity should be given a privileged status and its values should have a privileged position in public policy making. On the other end, those against Proposition 24 argue against allowing religion in the public sphere. Trying to find common ground is difficult unless one can find a claim that both the proponents and the opponents of Proposition 24 agree on, and that has to do with the issue of a religious-tolerant state.

Proponents of Proposition 24 petitioned the legislature to state in the constitution that "Liberia is a Christian nation with religious tolerance." President Ellen Johnson Sirleaf also noted, "The Liberian people wanted more than what the 1986 constitution contained. They wanted to ensure that certain equity and participation of the people were pronounced" (United Nations Development Programme 2015). The claim to be a religious state automatically means that the state cannot be a tolerant state. As history has shown us, a religious and tolerant state is an oxymoron. A religious state, by virtue of what it is, cannot be completely tolerant. Declaring Liberia, or any other nation, to be a Christian nation subjects other religions to an inferior role in the public sphere, leading toward a religious hegemony that shuts out people who are of the non-majority religion.

Therefore, we can see that bringing religion into the public sphere without any control cannot support a tolerant state, and neither would the exclusion of religion provide a tolerant state. This leaves us with a third option—introducing religion into the public sphere but in such a manner that religious tolerance is not abused. I suggest that a Rawlsian view provides the best way for religion to interact in the public sphere and still gives voice to every religious view.

My argument opts for a Rawlsian view because it is mainly in his understanding of state and religion that equality is achieved. It is also because the proponents of Proposition 24 believe that the 1986 constitution favors a Rawlsian understanding of religion and state that they are advocating for an amendment to the constitution. I will now proceed to propose what religion's role should be within the limits of this Rawlsian concept.

The Arguments for a Christian Nation

Amid this current debate surrounding the controversial Proposition 24 in Liberia, the goal in this section is to look at the reasons for this appeal via

Rawls' idea of public reason and the liberal state. Public reason is the reason of its citizens and those sharing the status of equal citizenship (John Rawls, cited in Quong Jonathan 2013). Public reason is public when it represents the public and it serves the good of the public. It is also public if it is constructed on the ideals and principles allowed for within the concept of political justice (Rawls 2005, 213).

Considering the role religion has played in Liberia, we will proceed to look at the reason for Proposition 24 based on the petition itself. To begin with, the petition to make Liberia a Christian nation argues that the 1847 clause, "…in granting to us the blessings of the Christian religion," which was removed from the 1986 constitution, should be returned (Kiamu 2016a). On this point, the petitioners have a case. Christian history is a part of Liberia's multifaceted and complex national history, and it is only fair that this history, no matter how bad, should be honored and reflected. But the petition gets into some challenges further down the road.

The first hint of a problem with this petition is that all its signatories are Christian religious leaders. There is not a single non-Christian on the petition committee. To be fair, seven hundred thousand Liberians affixed their signatures to the petition, but there is no evidence that any of these seven hundred thousand were non-Christian or irreligious. Indeed, if one factor is the fact that 85 percent of Liberians are Christians, the probability of non-Christians or irreligious people supporting this becomes even slimmer.[5] This is evidence that the merits of the petition are not interpreted by other than religious reasons.

John Rawls (2008) notes that the constitutional freedom of conscience and religion is the appropriate political response to the challengers of religious pluralism, and these cannot be exercised in a non-secular state. Liberia has more than one religious affinity. Rawls raises an important issue: he notes that the parties themselves must come to an agreement on the "precarious demarcations between the positive liberty to practice a religion of one's own and the negative liberty to remain unencumbered by the religious practices of others" (as summarized by Habermas 2008, 120). If this legislation passes, it will need to demarcate the positive and negative liberties of minority religious groups and the majority Christian group in Liberia. This actually

---

5 This statistic was reported by Liberia's 2008 census. This statistic is also supported by the U.S Department of State (https://www.state.gov/j/drl/rls/irf/2010/148698.htm). Joshua Project disagrees with this statistic, placing ethnic religion (42.6 percent) as the dominant religion in Liberia (https://joshuaproject.net/countries/LI).

begins to raise the question about what "tolerance" means. Does it give equal rights to all? Or is inequality embodied in the very proposition?

Second, for these petitioners, faith by itself is knowledge and reason that is able to uphold itself. Rawls and Habermas argue otherwise. Habermas' view can be summarized in this way, "...in order for the 'vital semantic potentials from religious traditions" to be made available for wider political culture (and, in particular, within democratic institutions), they must be translated into a secular idiom and a 'universally accessible language,' a task that falls not only to religious citizens but to all citizens—both religious and secular—engaged in the public use of reason" (Mendieta and Anantwerpen 2011, 5). One might ask why the opposition should concede to Rawls and Habermas' point. If faith is simple knowledge, then one can also claim that faithless people do not have knowledge; therefore, all faithless (secular) people (secular) should be excluded from the public discourse. Again, one can see how the goal of equality is not achieved. In seeking to have a religious state, one is preferring one group over another; "tolerance" is then just another cover for discrimination.

Another point where this petition falls short is on the grounds of its reasoning. The petition lists six reasons, but only two (1 and 6) can strongly appeal to the general public.[6] Reasons four through five—and especially five—are clearly religious and biased to religion. Based on their religious reasoning, the arguments fail to meet Rawls's proviso, which states:

> Reasonable comprehensive *doctrines*, religious and non-religious, may be introduced in public political discussion at any time, provided that in due course proper political reasons—and not reasons given solely by comprehensive doctrines—are presented that are sufficient to support whatever the comprehensive doctrines are said to support. (Rawls 1999, 152)

An appeal that argues along the lines of a stolen national identity better suits Rawls' provisio. The Association of Evangelicals of Liberia (AEL) approach follows this kind of reasoning. The AEL observed:

---

6 The reasons are as follows: Why are we here? 1) We honor the political and religious will of more than seven hundred thousand Liberians. 2) The grace of God that brings morality, peaceful coexistence, tolerance, and prosperity will rule over us again. 3) According to President Joseph J. Roberts, we will be blessed if we return to status quo—Christian heritage ("Blessed is the nation whose God is the Lord"–Psalm 33:12). 4) We will build a national filter against all the junk of modernization. 5) We will foster love in our communities. 6) We will cultivate the spirit of nationalism (Kiamu 2016c).

The debate [declaring Liberia as a Christian nation] is simply this, that the current *Liberian Constitution* has altered a significant foundation landmark of the nation-state Liberia that unless we take active, conscious and concrete steps to seek redress, Liberia will stand to lose much, suffer and gain very little if anything of significance at all. (Kiamu, 2016b)

The AEL rejected Proposition 24 insofar as it called for providing Christian privileges and faith-forming benefits within the public sphere for Christians. But on the other hand, the AEL acknowledges that Liberia's historical Christian foundation should be historically recognized. The AEL's response thus makes its argument along the lines of historicity, not religion. This kind of reasoning makes sense to citizens irrespective of their religious affiliation, but it fails to say exactly what will be lost or what will be gained as a result of adopting this proposition. Is this one thing equality? For Proposition 24 to be successful, it will have to discriminate, and in so doing it will lose much and gain little. Furthermore, not only the AEL but also the Liberia Council of Churches (LCC) opposed Proposition 24. "According to the President of the LCC, Bishop Jonathan B. B. Hart, the Council believes that the mission of the church is to teach all nations and make disciples and not to 'legitimize' the word of God" (Brooks, 2016).

Implications of Secularization for Evangelism and Discipleship

Until a constitutional amendment can take place, Liberian Christianity will have to function under a secular state, as in many other nations in the world. The question, then, is how this affects the church. Working in the age of secularism is profitable to the church in several ways. First, a secularist society forces and provides an atmosphere for the church to be prophetic. Often when church and state are bound, the church becomes complicit in matters of state. The church also often becomes dependent upon the favors of the state. In this way, the church loses the ability to be a public prophetic voice in opposition to state policies that are inconsistent with human rights or biblical values. By being prophetic, the church constantly remembers the reality that it is in this world but not of this world, and therefore functions in a manner that is consistent with being in but not of the world. The church, being prophetic, discovers a prophetic perspective and has a prophetic proclamation for the world. In its prophetic role, the church embodies that role of being the social conscience of society, unbought by the state and free to proclaim God's word.

One will realize that in biblical times the role of the prophet was absent when the kingdom was in right standing with God, but whenever the kingdom of Israel needed confrontation, the ministry of the prophet came to the forefront (1 Kgs 18:16–19; Jer 23:21–22; see also Acts 13:6–12). This is the same for Christianity in Liberia. In this age of secularism, when the gospel is taken out of the public sphere but yet needed by society, the church can clearly and distinctly remain the conscience of the state and God's prophets to the nation in a manner that supersedes political legislation.

Second, with secularism (the status quo) the impetus of the church to be witnesses increases rather than decreases. The task for world evangelization will remain at the forefront of the message because Christian leaders will clearly be able to identify the fact that the world is in dire need of a Savior. This by itself will force the church to remake itself and become more innovative. For instance, open-air crusades, even if effective, will not be allowed in many places due to secularization. Therefore, the church now has an opportunity to pursue methods such as social media and other technologies in order to share the Christian message.

For the Liberian church, once a person accepts Christ it seems like all is done. Many churches do not have a well-devised plan for discipleship. The secularization of the state has caused the church to begin to look for ways to influence policies and society long-term. Hopefully, this will lead to a revision of discipleship programs. Well-tailored programs will be helpful for subtly influencing the state with Christian principles, so that Christian principles become so intertwined with society that it is hard to argue that people's political reason is simply a religious reason and not a public opinion. Secularism is now forcing the church to revert to God's method of evangelism, which is friendship evangelism and building community with individuals rather than necessarily changing a nation into a Christian state. The church in the secular age cannot make disciples of Christ if they have not made friends with prospective converts. The secularization of society allows the church to reinvestigate the potential for friendship evangelism and a commitment to form strong faith relationships in our societies.

The opportunity to focus on strategic youth programs in churches is another opportunity created by secularization. Several churches in Liberia have a restricted approach to instructing youths and young adults about their Christian formation. But as churches become more aware of the nature of secularization, they have become acutely concerned about the lack of biblical knowledge among their members. Consequently, there is a renewed interest in having structured programs for youth and young adults that allow them to interact with the Bible. For instance, evangelical churches are developing a program for their youth that will deal with issues of homosexual marriages, polygamy, and teaching of the doctrines and principles of the church.

Prior to the realization that Liberia will continue to operate as a secular state, many Christians felt that by virtue of declaring Liberia a Christian state, the state would impose laws that would guide religious fervor. Therefore, active Bible literacy and trainings were not encouraged. But with secularism establishing its strength, the Liberian church now needs to effectively ensure that it has programs that train its children, youth, and adult members in such a way that, hopefully, these people go into the society with a clear understanding of what they believe.

Secularization allows the church to fulfill its role of being a blessing to the nations. In the context of the church and secularization, the church becomes the particular group through which God can bless the world. Chris Wright, in his book *The Mission of God*, shows how the identity of Israel as a nation is "redefined and refined" so that Israel begins to be a demonstration of the blessing of God to the nations (2006, 236). But God desires to not only bless his people, but to also bless others through this people. During this age of secularization, the church can provide a way for people living in a secularizing world to be blessed and become a blessing to their world. The church can enjoy the privilege of existing in a secular world, because then it also gets the exceptional blessing of becoming partners with God in blessing the world and the nations.

Sadly, secularism is not all good news for evangelism and discipleship. The church under a secular government will be subjected to laws that might oppose its religious beliefs and ideology (hopefully as it also restricts other religious views). It would be difficult for Christians to share Christ as they wish in a fully secular society; however, under such a state, the church can also trust that other religions are not given a privileged position. The church is not to rule the world before Christ comes, but rather the church is to gradually influence society daily by being salt and light until the return of Christ. There will be pain and suffering, and Jesus Christ himself tells us to expect it; but even in such circumstances, the church has an opportunity to reinvent itself and remain relevant. The secularization of society keeps the church daily cognizant of its transformative role in society.

What historical precedents are there for the positive influence of secularization regarding the vitality of Christianity? Has secularization in America and Europe led to stronger and more influential and vibrant Christianity in these areas? Secularization has certainly helped to reduce the number of nominal Christians in the West, but it has also provided the West with a new type of Christianity. While there is a decline in the number of churchgoers in Europe and America, secularism has pushed the church in the US and in Europe to reinvent itself and critically explore its methods, theology, and practice.

A notable example is Stefan Paas's *Church Planting in the Secular West* (2016). Paas deals with the issue of church planting in a thorough and well-researched manner, clearly showing that there are more factors responsible for the decline in church membership than just secularism, and that there is still a need and hope for church planting in Europe in spite of secularism. While there has been a decline in church membership, some of these nations still have a high number of formal members (ibid., Introduction). Secularization of society has forced the church to depend more on God's Spirit and to continuously look for innovative ways to actively participate in God's mission. If nothing else, secularization has refined and continues to refine the church in the West.

Conclusion

Religion historically has had a deep grounding within Liberia's political realm. Religion has been a social and moral influencer, a developer, and political patron to the state. Christianity has been the religion de facto. But it seems this might not continue to be, especially if the nation wants equality for all its citizens. We have also seen that, via Rawls' theory, the reasons for making Liberia a secular state fall under a religious category and will need reshaping if they are to meet Rawls' proviso. However, to respect the pluralistic nature of the Liberian state, it is better to have the nation as a secular state. As a secular nation, every religious identity can be sure that policies are made in a way that does not promote discrimination. The constitution should be balanced in such a way that every Liberian can relate to it.

The principle of separation of church and state obliges politicians and officials within political institutions to formulate and justify laws, court rulings, decrees, and measures exclusively in a language that is equally accessible to all citizens. Calling Liberia a Christian nation would be inconsistent with this principle. Barney Pityana of the Cape Town Research Institute on Christianity stated this well:

> In order to live together in a community, we must respect one another in our differences and our similarities. We need to recognize that we need one another, we are interdependent. Unless we work together and try to build up a new moral community together, we will soon have no community at all. The African moral principle of "Ubuntu" will have to become something more than a mere catch-phrase. (cited in Hofmeyr 2007, 317)

A good way to show this respect is by providing a system that allows people to come to salvation in Christ through an encounter with Christ rather than by political legislation, fear, or abuse. Religion's role in the public sphere is actually an embodied role, not through political legislature but through an incarnational lifestyle that changes individuals, who in turn change systems in an equal and tolerant manner. Secularization allows the church to embrace its prophetic role, reinvent itself, innovate, and continue in the task of being witnesses of God.

References

Abbink, Jon. 2014. "Religion and Politics in Africa: The Future of 'the Secular.'" *Afrika Spectrum* 49 (3): 83–106.

Boley, G. E. Saigbe. 1983. *Liberia: The Rise and Fall of the First Republic.* New York: St. Martin's.

Brooks, Cholo. 2016. "Council of Churches Rejects Christian State Proposition." *GNN Liberia*, May 2. http://gnnliberia.com/2016/05/02/council-churches-rejects-christian-state-proposition/.

Bush, Stephen S. 2014. *Visions of Religion: Experience, Meaning, and Power.* Oxford: Oxford University Press.

Habermas, Jürgen. 1984. *The Theory of Communicative Action.* Boston: Beacon Press.

———. 1989. *The Structural Transformation of the Public Sphere: An Inquiry into a Category of Bourgeois Society.* Cambridge, MA: MIT Press.

———. 1991. "The Public Sphere." In *Rethinking Popular Culture: Contemporary Perspectives in Cultural Studies*, edited by Chandra Mukerii and Michael Schudson, 398–404. Los Angeles: University of California Press.

———. 2002. *Religion and Rationality: Essays on Reason, God, and Modernity.* Edited by Eduardo Mendieta. Studies in Contemporary German Social Thought, vol. 1. Cambridge, MA: MIT Press.

———. 2006a. *The Future of Human Nature.* Cambridge: Polity.

———. 2006b. "Religion in the Public Sphere." *European Journal of Philosophy* 14 (1): 1–25.

———. 2008. *Between Naturalism and Religion: Philosophical Essays.* Malden, MA: Polity.

———. 2011. "'The Political': The Rational Meaning of a Questionable Inheritance of Political Theology" In *The Power of Religion in the Public Sphere* edited by Judith Butler, Jürgen Habermas, Charles Taylor, Cornel West, 15–33 New York: Columbia University.

Habermas, Jurgen, and Ciaran Cronin. 2008. *Between Naturalism and Religion: Philosophical Essays.* Cambridge: Polity.

Harrington, Austin. 2007. "Habermas and the 'Post-Secular Society.'" *European Journal of Social Theory* 10 (4): 543–60.

Hofmeyr, J. W. 2007. "Mainline Churches in the Public Space 1975–2000." In *African Christianity: An African Story,* edited by Ogbu U. Kalu, 315–37. Trenton, NJ: Africa World.

Hugh, Baxter. 2011. *The Discourse Theory of Democracy.* Stanford, CA: Stanford University Press.

Irlenborn, Bernd. 2012. "Religion in the Public Sphere: Habermas on the Role of Christian Faith." *The Heythrop Journal* 53 (3): 432–39.

Kiamu, Nuwoe James. 2016a, b, c. Email correspondences with the author.

King, Richard. 2013. *Orientalism and Religion Post-Colonial Theory, India and "The Mystic East."* Florence: Taylor and Francis.

Lafont, Christina. 2007. "Religion in the Public Sphere: Remarks on Habermas's Conception of Public Deliberation in Postsecular Societies." *Constellations* 14 (2): 239–59.

Loobuyck, Patrick, and Stefan Rummens. 2011. "Religious Arguments in the Public Sphere: Comparing Habermas with Rawls." *Ars Disputandi: The Online Journal for Philosophy of Religion.* http://hdl.handle.net/1874/294494.

Manyou MAS Bility, n.d "The Attempt to Make Liberia a Christian State is Bad for the Future of Liberia!' printed in the New Dawn Magazine retrieved from (www.thenewdawnliberia.com/feature-op-ed/special-feature/7099-the-attempt-to-make-liberia-a-christian-state-is-bad-for-the-future-of-liberia.

Mbiti, John S. 1969. African *Religions and Philosophy.* Heinemann: London.

Mendieta, Eduardo, and Jonathan VanAntwerpen. 2011. "Introduction: The Power of Religion in the Public Sphere." In *The Power of Religion in the Public Sphere,* edited by Judith Butler, Jurgen Habermas, Charles Taylor, Cornel West, 1–14. New York: Columbia University.

Nongbri, Brent. 2013. *Before Religion: A History of a Modern Concept.* New Haven: Yale University Press.

Paas, Stefan. 2016. *Church Planting in the Secular West: Learning from the European Experience.* The Gospel and Our Culture Series. Grand Rapids: Eerdmans. EBSCO Ebook.

Parsons, Talcott and Jackson Toby. 1977. *The Evolution of Societies.* Englewood Cliffs, NJ: Prentice Hall.

Quong, Jonathan. 2013. "Public Reason." *Stanford Encyclopedia of Philosophy* (Summer 2013), Edward N. Zalta, ed. https://plato.stanford.edu/archives/sum2013/entries/public-reason/.

Rawls, John. 1971. *A Theory of Justice.* Cambridge, MA: Belknap Press of Harvard University.

———. 1996. *Political Liberalism.* New York: Columbia University.

———. 1999. *The Law of Peoples.* Cambridge: Harvard University.

———. 2005. *Political Liberalism.* Expanded ed. Columbia Classics in Philosophy. New York: Columbia University. EBSCO Ebook.

Rorty, Richard. 2003. "Religion in the Public Square: A Reconsideration." *Journal of Religious Ethics* 31 (1): 141–49.

Sanneh, Lamin. 1983. *West African Christianity: The Religious Impact.* London: George Allen & Unwin.

Sonpon, Leroy M., III. 2016. "Liberia: Seven Propositions Passed for Referendum." *Daily Observer*, November 21, reprinted by *AllAfrica*, November 28. http://allafrica.com/stories/201611210853.html.

Taylor, Charles H. 2011. "Why We Need a Radical Redefinition of Secularism." Chap. 2 in *The Power of Religion in the Public Sphere*, edited by Judith Butler, Jurgen Habermas, Charles Taylor, Cornel West. New York: Columbia University Press. EBSCO Ebook.

Tolbert, William R., Jr. 1984. "An Address to the Nation, President of the Republic of Liberia, Centennial Memorial Pavilion, Sunday, May 5, 1979." In *Liberia: The Rise and Fall of the First Republic*, by G. E. Saigbe Boley. New York: St. Martin's Press.

United Nations Development Programme. 2015. "Constitution Committee Presents Final Report to President Sirleaf," August 18. www.lr.undp.org/content/liberia/en/home/presscenter/articles/2015/08/18/constitution-review-committee-presents-final-report-to-president-sirleaf.html.

Weithman, Paul J. 2002. *Religion and the Obligations of Citizenship.* Cambridge: Cambridge University Press.

Wolterstorff, Nicholas. 1984. *Reason within the Bounds of Religion.* Grand Rapids: Eerdmans.

Wright, Chris. 2006. *The Mission of God: Unlocking the Bible's Grand Narrative.* Downers Grove: IVP Academic.

CONTRIBUTORS

Raphael Anzenberger (DMin, PhD candidate, Columbia International University) was named the Billy Graham Lausanne Scholar for 2018. He is director of RZIM. fr (RZIM for the French-speaking world) and adjunct professor of intercultural studies at CIU. Prior to his current position, he was actively involved in evangelism and church planting in his home country of France. He has authored three books. His forthcoming book, *Is God Dangerous?* (The Good Book Company), deals with current apologetics issues in secular Europe.

Shawn P. Behan (ThM, Fuller Theological Seminary) is a PhD candidate at Asbury Theological Seminary, focusing on the history and theology of mission. His dissertation research is looking at the missionary ecclesiology of Lesslie Newbigin within the Gospel and Our Culture Network's discussion of the missional church. He has published an article on this topic, "A Hermeneutical Congregation," in the *Asbury Journal*.

Marc Canner (PhD, University of South Carolina) is professor of linguistics and dean of the College of Professional Studies at Great Northern University. He previously served in the late 1980s as a military linguist and has had over twenty-five years of cross-cultural experience among Russians and Ukrainians, including church planting and discipleship. He also serves as president of LCTI, a nonprofit agency that equips candidates with linguistic, TEFL, and intercultural skills. He has published two Russian-language textbooks and is currently working on a practical guide for effective cross-cultural discipleship in East Slavic countries.

Tony Chuang (莊智超, MDiv, Moody Bible Institute) is a PhD student at Trinity Evangelical Divinity School, an evangelist with ministry experience on four continents, and director of outreach at First Baptist Church of Park Ridge. He was born in Taiwan, raised in Malaysia, and immigrated to Canada. He grew up in a family that practiced Buddhism/folk religion, converting to Christianity only later in life. His research interests include evangelism, folk religion, modernity, and Second Temple Judaism. He authored the chapter "Process from Neighbor to Disciple-Maker" in *Missional Disciple-Making* (3DM Publishing).

Steven B. Kern (MA, Grace Seminary) is associate pastor at Grace Church in Wooster, Ohio. Prior to his current pastoral position, Steve and his wife served with Encompass World Partners as church-planting missionaries in Germany. His research passions include diaspora missiology. After completion of his PhD, he looks forward to doing more writing and teaching in this and other missiological fields.

Boye-Nelson Kiamu (MATS, Princeton Theological Seminary) is a PhD student at Fuller Theological Seminary. He received an MA in intercultural studies with an emphasis on cross-cultural communication from West Africa Theological Seminary in Nigeria. He has served as a lecturer at ABC University in Liberia and as the CEO of Liberia Renewal Ministries. His research interests have centered on faith and technology, missions in Africa, digital religion, and theology in the public sphere.

W. Jay Moon (PhD, Asbury Theological Seminary) is professor of evangelism and church planting and director of the Office of Faith, Work, and Economics at Asbury Theological Seminary. He formerly served thirteen years as a missionary with SIM, mostly in Ghana, West Africa, among the Builsa people, focusing on church planting and water development. He has authored three books, including *Intercultural Discipleship: Learning from Global Approaches to Spiritual Formation* (Baker Academic). He is also presently a teaching pastor in a local church plant.

Harold A. Netland (PhD, Claremont Graduate University) is professor of philosophy of religion and intercultural studies at Trinity Evangelical Divinity School. He served as a missionary in Japan from 1984–93. He has published extensively on religious pluralism, Buddhism, and theology of religions, including most recently *Christianity and Religious Diversity: Clarifying Christian Commitments in a Globalizing Age* (Baker Academic).

Craig Ott (PhD, Trinity Evangelical Divinity School) is professor of mission and intercultural studies at Trinity Evangelical Divinity School, where he also directs the PhD program in intercultural studies. He previously served for twenty-one years in Germany and has since taught or consulted in over forty countries. He has authored numerous books and articles on theology of mission, contextualization, and church planting, including most recently *The Church on Mission: A Biblical Vision for Transformation* (Baker Academic).

Beth Seversen (PhD, Trinity Evangelical Divinity School) is associate professor of Christian ministries studies and director of the Center for Christian Ministries Studies and Practical Theology at North Park University. She is the former director of evangelism for the Evangelical Covenant Church denomination. She is author of a forthcoming book with IVP on *Reaching Millennials* (working title) based on her research on churches reaching and keeping emerging adults. She has also published several academic articles and is vice president of The Academy for Evangelism and Theological Education.

Steve Thrall (DMin, Bakke Graduate University) has been an urban missionary in Paris, France, since 1988. He has served in a pastoral role in three French churches and for the past ten years has been the director of a multipurpose art space in downtown Paris. He is also an adjunct professor of intercultural studies for Asbury University's Paris semester. Steve and his wife, Miki, are currently launching an artist-in-residence in Normandy, France.